THE LAST TABOO
Money as Symbol and Reality in Psychotherapy and Psychoanalysis

THE LAST TABOO

Money as Symbol and Reality in Psychotherapy and Psychoanalysis

Edited by

David W. Krueger, M.D.

Brunner/Mazel, *Publishers* • New York

Library of Congress Cataloging-in-Publication Data
Main entry under title:

The Last taboo.

   Includes bibliographies and index.
   1. Psychotherapists—Fees—Psychological aspects.
2. Psychoanalysts—Fees—Psychological aspects.
3. Money—Psychological aspects. 4. Insurance, Mental
health—Psychological aspects. 5. Psychotherapist and
patient. I. Krueger, David W.
RC465.5.L37 1986   616.89′14   85-23266
ISBN 0-87630-423-4

Copyright © 1986 by David W. Krueger, M.D.

Published by
BRUNNER/MAZEL, INC.
19 Union Square West
New York, New York 10003

MANUFACTURED IN THE UNITED STATES OF AMERICA

Contents

Preface .... *vii*
Acknowledgments .... *x*
Contributors .... *xi*

I. THEORETICAL AND SYMBOLIC MEANINGS OF MONEY

1. Money, Success, and Success Phobia 3
   David W. Krueger, M.D.
2. Classical Psychoanalytic Views of Money 17
   Paula B. Fuqua, M.D.
3. A Self-Psychological View of Money 24
   David W. Krueger, M.D.
4. The Fee as Focus of Transference and
   Countertransference in Treatment 33
   Rosalea A. Schonbar, Ph.D.
5. Fee Practices of Male and Female Therapists 48
   Mary A. Burnside, Ph.D.
6. Complexities in the Psychology and Psychotherapy
   of the Phenomenally Wealthy 55
   Peter A. Olsson, M.D.
7. A Psychoanalytic View of Personal Bankruptcy 70
   Lawrence M. Ginsburg, J.D., and
   Sybil A. Ginsburg, M.D.

II. MONEY IN THE THERAPIST-PATIENT RELATIONSHIP

8. Fee Policy as an Extension of the Therapist's Style
   and Orientation 79
   Alan B. Tulipan, M.D.
9. The Effect of Fees on the Course and Outcome of
   Psychotherapy and Psychoanalysis 88
   James Raney, M.D.
10. Money Issues That Complicate Treatment 102
    G. A. Williston DiBella, M.D.

11. The Effect of Third-Party Payment on the
Practice of Psychotherapy 111
    Paul Chodoff, M.D.
12. On Negotiating Fees with Psychotherapy and
Psychoanalytic Patients 121
    Daniel H. Jacobs, M.D.
13. The Influence of Fee Assessment on Premature
Therapy Termination 132
    John F. McRae, Ph.D.
14. Psychotherapy Fees and Therapist Training 142
    Stefan A. Pasternack, M.D.
15. Transference, Countertransference, and Other Therapeutic
Issues in a Health Maintenance Organization (HMO) 158
    Sidney S. Goldensohn, M.D.

III. PAYMENT STRUCTURES AND MANAGEMENT ISSUES

16. The Meanings and Effects of Insurance in
Psychotherapy and Psychoanalysis 169
    Eugene Halpert, M.D.
17. Fees in Beginning Private Practice 175
    Thomas G. Gutheil, M.D.
18. The Clinical Management of the Nonpaying Patient 189
    Arthur E. Reider, M.D.
19. The Extension of Credit to Patients in Psychoanalysis
and Psychotherapy 202
    Charles K. Hofling, M.D., and Milton Rosenbaum, M.D.
20. Purchasing a Practice: A Personal Account 218
    Ann E. Carlisle, Ph.D.
21. Money: The Medium and the Message 224
    Daniel V. Voiss, M.D.
22. Cost Effectiveness of Psychotherapy 236
    Seth W. Silverman, M.D.
23. Preferred Provider Organizations and
Psychiatric Treatment 244
    Howard Gurevitz, M.D.
24. Long-Term Psychotherapy and Psychoanalysis
in a Changing Health Care Economy 253
    John J. McGrath, M.D.

Index 257

Preface

A therapist once wrote: "Money questions will be treated by cultured people in the same manner as sexual matters, with the same inconsistency, prudishness, and hypocrisy." The year was 1913. The therapist was Sigmund Freud.

More than 70 years later, most of us have learned to talk more easily about sex, yet remain seclusive, embarrassed, or conflicted about discussing money. Money may be the last emotional taboo in our society.

Americans have been raised in a culture with informal ethical and social strictures concerning the impropriety of candid discussion of money, fees, and personal income. In addition, individual meanings and attributions hitchhike on the issue of money and further complicate our money-associated behaviors.

For most of us, education and training have dealt with a gamut of theoretical and therapeutic issues; for some, personal therapy or analysis has dealt with parts of oneself that have been deleted, omitted, or disregarded, revealing and resolving these powerfully influential aspects of one's development and personal myths. Yet issues involving the real and symbolic meanings of money are typically neglected in even these processes of profound personal understanding, and the very fact of money's isolation uniquely permeates our thoughts and feelings. Even when we come to know ourselves and our personal myths, we may have omitted consideration of how money affects our conscious and unconscious behavior, including the seeming taboo of frank discussion about it.

We can learn a great deal about our patients if we scrutinize how they regard and handle money; the same is true for ourselves as therapists. Such scrutiny seldom occurs, however.

Although the theory and practice of exchanging money are among the least examined of transactions in psychotherapy and psychoanalysis, they are heavily laden with meaning. Like food and sex, money has a strong metaphoric emotional value as well as a readily apparent practical function. The exchange of money for professional service is inherent and immediate in the process of the therapeutic encounter, making it unique. This emotionally significant event is, therefore, more readily available to psychological scrutiny than many traditional human activities.

My own teaching and supervisory experience has been that money issues are frequently omitted in formal training. The omission affects treatment and reflects a multitude of patient and professional concerns: as ubiquitous symbol, as ever-present reality, as an administrative imperative, as a treatment planning concern, as part of the therapeutic structure, as a perceived inconsistency with empathic concern, and in such areas as rehabilitation, medication, and hospital care.

There have been some significant and persistent experiences that led to my interest in compiling this book.

(1) As Director of the Baylor Psychiatry Clinic for five years, I had between 40 and 50 therapists in training each year (psychiatry residents, psychology interns, and clinical social work trainees) who saw patients on a sliding-fee scale. With remarkable regularity, they (as did their patients) wanted to treat money and fees as a separate administrative/institutional issue, apart from psychotherapy. Equally difficult was the discussion of an increase in fee when their patients would get better and earn more money.

(2) There is a striking omission of matters of work and money in evaluation summaries of patients. Although the issues of work and money provide ample windows for significant developmental, adaptational, and psychopathological assessments, they are underutilized regularly.

(3) The impact of reduced-fee and negotiated-fee arrangements on psychoanalysis and psychotherapy is inadequately discussed by therapist, patient, and supervisor. The multiple meanings of low-fee arrangements for control cases came to the rapid attention of myself and my colleagues during our psychoanalytic training. Specifically, the impact became apparent as it affected the analytical framework and the regard of the patient for the analyst, and as it related to both transference material and aspects of gratification of unconscious wishes.

Treatment can be facilitated or sabotaged by the degree of thoroughness with which money matters are dealt. Issues underlying the metaphor of money can be neglected or resolved in treatment. A patient's failure to cooperate with an agreed-upon fee arrangement can be utilized to illuminate unconscious resistances to treatment or can be ignored by the therapist, who thus risks a lost opportunity to explore wider psychic conflicts. Patients entrust themselves to a therapist who is hopefully comfortable in establishing and maintaining the boundaries of the therapeutic relationship. This relationship, in which the handling of money is a necessary and consistent component, comprises a matrix in which frightening, otherwise unacceptable, and taboo material may emerge. The patient and therapist can implicitly collude to maintain the taboo against the discussion of money, fees, collection, and feelings generated by money.

This avoidance has been apparent in the professional literature. This book is intended to remedy the absence of material about the relationship of money to the psychotherapeutic encounter by presenting some systematic inquiries into the matter. There are many aspects of money in our professional work that require comprehensive and extensive exploration. The spectrum of clinical situations in which money is a significant issue has been divided into three sections:

I. Theoretical and symbolic meanings of money
II. Money in the therapist-patient relationship
III. Payment structures and management issues

There has been no attempt in the compilation of the following chapters to present a standardized or ''how-to'' approach to the reality of money and to its symbolism as manifest in therapy or analysis. Rather, the intention of the nationally prominent clinicians and theoreticians writing here has been to examine in detail, from multiple perspectives, the meanings, conflicts, behaviors, and symbolism of money for the patient, the therapist, and the therapeutic context.

We are trained as clinicians, helping professionals, and humanistic scientists while, at the same time, an antithetical pursuit (and image) exists: we make money at it. We must deal daily with issues that may be a repudiated portion of our own ego identity and/or professional identity.

Our own comfort and resolution of the antipodes of altruism and self-interest presage our ability to help our patients resolve and integrate the seeming discrepancies of this same issue. For *some* patients, money has come to be the central focus of emotional conflict; for *all* patients, money is a basic aspect of the framework which we establish and work within, and which becomes internalized by our patients.

David W. Krueger, M.D.
Houston

Acknowledgments

Permission was obtained to reprint all or part of the following journal articles. Along with this acknowledgment, much appreciation is expressed in allowing components of these nodal articles to appear in this book.

McRae, J. F. The influence of fee assessment on premature therapy termination. *Administration in Mental Health* 7(4):282–291, 1980.

Hofling, C. K., and Rosenbaum, M. The extension of credit to patients in psychoanalysis and psychotherapy. *Bulletin of the Menninger Clinic* 44(4):327–344, 1980.

Chodoff, P. The effect of third-party payment on the practice of psychotherapy. *American Journal of Psychiatry* 129:52–57, 1972.

Ginsburg, L. M., and Ginsburg, S. A. A psychoanalytic view of personal bankruptcy. *Journal of Psychiatry and Law* 11:25–27, 1983.

Contributors

Mary A. Burnside, Ph.D. Private practice of clinical psychology, Houston, Texas; Assistant Professor, Clinical Psychology Department of Psychiatry, Baylor College of Medicine, Houston, Texas.

Ann E. Carlisle, Ph.D. Private practice of clinical psychology, Houston, Texas.

Paul Chodoff, M.D. Clinical Professor of Psychiatry, George Washington University; Past President, American Academy of Psychoanalysis.

G. A. Williston DiBella, M.D. Clinical Associate Professor of Psychiatry, New York Medical College; Director of Psychiatric Residency Training and Medical Student Education in Psychiatry, Cabrini Medical Center, New York, New York; private practice of psychiatry, New York, New York.

Paula B. Fuqua, M.D. Attending Physician, Michael Reese Hospital and Medical Center; Candidate, Chicago Institute for Psychoanalysis.

Lawrence M. Ginsburg, J.D. Private practice of law, Syracuse, New York.

Sybil A. Ginsburg, M.D. Clinical Assistant Professor of Psychiatry, Upstate Medical Center, Syracuse, New York; private practice of psychiatry and psychoanalysis, Syracuse, New York.

Sidney S. Goldensohn, M.D. Director, Mental Health Service of the Health Insurance Plan of Greater New York (HIP); Clinical Professor of Psychiatry, Cornell University Medical College, New York.

Howard Gurevitz, M.D. President, California Psychiatric Association; Area VI Representative, American Psychiatric Association; Assistant Clinical Professor, University of California San Francisco, Langley Porter Institute; Lecturer in Psychiatry, Stanford University, Department of Psychiatry.

Thomas G. Gutheil, M.D. Director of Medical Student Training and Associate Professor of Psychiatry at the Massachusetts Mental Health Center, Harvard Medical School.

Eugene Halpert, M.D. Clinical Associate Professor of Psychiatry, New York University Medical Center; Training and Supervising Psychoanalyst, The Psychoanalytic Institute at New York University; Editorial Board of *The Psychoanalytic Quarterly* and *The Glossary of Psychoanalytic Terms and Concepts.*

Charles K. Hofling, M.D. (deceased) Previously: Professor of Psychiatry, St. Louis University School of Medicine, St. Louis, Missouri; Visiting Professor of Psychiatry, University of Cincinnati College of Medicine, Cincinnati, Ohio.

Daniel H. Jacobs, M.D. Assistant Clinical Professor, Harvard Medical School; Faculty, Boston Psychoanalytic Institute.

David W. Krueger, M.D. Clinical Associate Professor of Psychiatry, Baylor College of Medicine; private practice of psychiatry and psychoanalysis, Houston, Texas; Director, Eating Disorders Treatment Program, Spring Shadows Glen Hospital, Houston, Texas; Book Editor of *Psychoanalytic Education.*

John J. McGrath, M.D. Private practice in Washington, D.C.; Member of Board of Trustees, American Psychiatric Association; Teaching Analyst at Baltimore-District of Columbia Institute for Psychoanalysis.

John F. McRae, Ph.D. Psychologist with Spokane Community Mental Health Center, Spokane, Washington.

Peter A. Olsson, M.D. Private practice of psychoanalysis and psychotherapy with The Psychiatric Associates of Houston; Associate Clinical Professor of Psychiatry, Baylor and University of Texas Medical Schools, Houston, Texas.

Stefan A. Pasternack, M.D. Associate Teaching Analyst at the Baltimore-District of Columbia Institute for Psychoanalysis; Associate Clinical Professor of Psychiatry at Georgetown University School of Medicine.

James Raney, M.D. Faculty, Seattle Psychoanalytic Institute and the Lenox Hill Hospital Psychotherapy Program; Clinical Faculty, University of Washington School of Medicine; private practice of psychoanalysis, Seattle, Washington.

Arthur E. Reider, M.D. Assistant Clinical Professor of Psychiatry, Tufts University School of Medicine, Boston; Clinical Instructor in Psychiatry, Harvard Medical School, Boston; Medical Director, The Center for Mental Health and Retardation Services, Inc., Watertown, Massachusetts; Assistant Attending Psychiatrist, McLean Hospital Belmont, Massachusetts.

Milton Rosenbaum, M.D. Distinguished Professor of Psychiatry, Marshall University College of Medicine, Huntington, West Virginia; Visiting Professor of Psychiatry, University of Cincinnati College of Medicine, Cincinnati, Ohio; Professor Emeritus of Psychiatry, Hebrew University School of Medicine, Jerusalem, Israel.

Rosalea A. Schonbar, Ph.D. Professor and Director, Clinical Psychology
Program; Chairman, Department of Clinical Psychology and Psycho-
educational Practice, Teachers College, Columbia University; private
practice of psychotherapy.

Seth W. Silverman, M.D. Private practice of psychiatry, Houston, Texas.

Alan B. Tulipan, M.D. Private practice of psychotherapy and psychoanaly-
analysis, White Plains, New York.

Daniel V. Voiss, M.D. Psychoanalytically trained psychiatrist providing
medicolegal consultation to attorneys, physicians, corporations, and
insurors; past editor of *The Journal of Psychoanalytic Education* (CAPE);
formerly Adjunct Professor of Law, Northwestern School of Law.

I

THEORETICAL AND SYMBOLIC MEANINGS OF MONEY

1

Money, Success, and Success Phobia

David W. Krueger, M.D.

THE SYMBOLIZATION OF MONEY

Money can be understood in several relevant contexts:

1. *Money as a vehicle for exchange of goods and services*. Its value and use can be distinguished from emotional and symbolic attributions.
2. *Attitudes and values regarding money*. Experiences from each individual's emotional past involve money, and these experiences determine one's attitudes, beliefs, and values about what money will and will not do.
3. *Money as a transference object*. Issues of developmental arrest or conflict may be expressed using money as a specific external focus.

Viewing from a position of simplicity, we often come to see how much complexity we attach to things and events. Money is probably the most emotionally meaningful object in contemporary life; only food and sex are its close competitors as common carriers of such strong and diverse feelings, significances, and strivings.

Money is a unit of agreed-upon value exchanged for goods, services, or time. Money is money. From this simplistic view, the meanings that an individual attaches to money can become more evident. Money is imbued by each individual with a number of unconscious equations. Money may come to represent self-esteem and esteem for others, power and impotence, contamination and purity, innocence and worldliness, affection and disdain, fear and security, acceptance and rejection, or virtually any other individually determined meaning. The symbolic representations and perceptions of money are influenced by cultural background, family val-

3

ues, developmental experiences, and emotional needs. Many of these meanings may be outside awareness, as are the early experiences in which they originated.

Unconscious motivations that oppose conscious intents can pose serious threats. Inappropriate use of money, an unrelenting quest to acquire more money, inability to acquire money consistent with one's potential, and inability to enjoy the use of money are some typical consequences of such conflict between conscious and unconscious goals.

Money bears a particularly heavy burden of irrational meaning and can be a potent catalyst or obstacle to one's work and ambitions. Frequently, the underlying meanings are unclear to the individual and often are illuminated only indirectly.

The society in which we live clarifies some equations, such as money as a measure of material value. The pursuit of money may gain ascendancy over the purpose and pursuit of living. Complicating factors include contradictory ethics regarding money. At a social level, a major polarity is the altruistic, selfless, humanistic sacrificing ethic of Judeo-Christianity versus acquisitional, individualistic capitalism. Money is esteemed, yet it is condemned. One who has a great deal of money is viewed as superior, yet the frank desire for money is considered poor taste or worse. Money may not bring happiness, but one may be unhappy without it.

The Puritan ethic emphasizes hard work, thrift, and victory over adversity, but is paradoxical in its proscription of the enjoyment of money earned by hard work, thrift, and victory over adversity. Accordingly, both money and the lack of money produce guilt. Aspirations to wealth may be accompanied by fears of affluence.

We must usually grapple alone with personal attitudes and beliefs about money at social, interpersonal, and intrapsychic levels. Many of our feelings may never have been openly examined or sufficiently resolved. Dealing explicitly with money by consulting a financial advisor does not address the emotional implications of money, which exert powerful influences in making, keeping, spending, saving, investing, or enjoying money.

The magical capacity to alleviate discomfiture and provide limitless pleasure that may be associated with money arises from unconscious needs and perceptions. The fantasy of, or seeking of, limitless wealth may be an attempt to resolve feelings ranging from daily boredom to powerlessness or deprivation experienced in early childhood. Fantasies of social freedom purchased with imagined wealth may compensate for a constricting absence of internal freedom. Envy and acquisitional greed then focus on the particular objects or amount of money one believes necessary to provide happiness. This need can never be satisfied with money or objects, but its boundlessness may remain unrecognized. When perfect contentment remains unachieved despite material gains, one may be led to investigate the integrity of one's personal mythology about money and its actual value. The investigation may create disillusionment, crises of self-esteem, or realization that psychic comfort may come from a different source.

Some individuals seek psychiatric consultation at a time in life when the symbolic meaning of money has been confronted, perhaps after achievement of a long-sought goal, such as becoming a millionaire, receiving a major promotion in social or business status, or purchasing an expensive home in a prestigious neighborhood. When anxieties and inadequacies persist despite attainment of material goals, a mourning reaction for one's failed assumptions can occur. The individual may recognize that what he or she thought would bring happiness hasn't. The confrontation of the fiction of the symbol as illusion can precipitate a review of one's psychic as well as social life, and projection into the future.

DEVELOPMENTAL MODELS AND IDENTIFICATION

Each of us is persistently influenced by the deposits of early important relationships and experiences, especially with parents and siblings. Our emotions, behaviors, and values are personal creations, fashioned from our own ''personal mythology'': the conscious and unconscious autobiographical data formed by an individual's unique personal perception of events, feelings, and reasoning. A perception of reality is full of omissions, distortions, and personal elaboration (1). It is nevertheless the individual's reality, because it is his or her set of experiences as well as an evolving self-definition. The individual's personal myth extends from past history to the present.

Identification with a successful parent increases an individual's expectation that successful work and material acquisition are possible. This model of a parent is observed, imitated, and internalized to become part of a self-definition. Identification with a parent who is, conversely, unsuccessful, limited, or frustrated in the work arena becomes a component in the self-regard of the developing child as well. This negative model can act as an invisible, binding chain as the developing child's self-definition may incorporate this ineptness or incapability.

This identification with parental models should be distinguished from the developmental process and identity formation, such as the *conclusions* of inadequacy or incapability on the basis of significant compromise formation, conflicts, or inadequate parental empathy.

In addition, children of each social class may have different models of money, business, and finance. Children of the more affluent may become comfortable and familiar with thinking and knowing about and handling money. Having money and taking it for granted may become a matrix of daily life, incorporated into the child's identity. An example of parental financial failure, just as an example of poor parental self-esteem, is internalized by the child and must be resolved in order for the child to become a successful adult.

Some individuals attempt to disidentify with early models by rejecting them or rebelling against them. This may create an internal struggle, as the values are still present while requiring active opposition. One source of work compulsion is a need to relentlessly counteract an identification of inadequacy learned from family models. No matter how much someone works and gains financial success, there may still be doubt generated by an unconscious link to an earlier identification with incapability or nonsuccess, and the successful individual may see himself or herself as an impostor who has fooled everyone. These identifications can lead to an underestimation of one's ability and worth, the failure of satisfaction, or an inability to enjoy accomplishments.

Visible, successful models may be actively sought for identification. At times, a mentor is of value in this regard because of the *process* of interaction and modeling as well as the *content* of the information given.

It is difficult for some people to change an internal frame of reference. The son of a factory worker who had followed his own father into the plant had profound difficulty in seeing himself and his options outside the context of the restricting poverty of his youth. He had never seen a family member or contemporary acquaintance pull away from the factory life to change his life and do anything substantially different. He strove to escape from the strictures of his circumstances and background but was inhibited by an internal voice disallowing him to have experiences inconsistent with family customs and the personal belief system these customs had engendered. He had to actively disagree with his internal voice, and to endure the anxiety of a new experience and domain, internally and externally, in order to broaden his ability to succeed on his own terms. In therapy he became better able to objectively view his assumptions and beliefs and to see viable alternatives.

To undergo change is to redefine a certain and secure pathway made known by earlier experiences and incorporate the redefinition into one's identity (2). One may, in neurotic fashion, prefer to maintain a life-style that is unpleasant but predictable rather than risk the uncertainty of change and relief from the problem-laden, but nevertheless accustomed, pattern.

Parents may establish secrecy as a model for matters associated with money. When income, expenses, and other financial issues are not discussed in the family, there is no opportunity for children to integrate a realistic sense of money. The alternative can be fantasies of desperate poverty or, more commonly, of tremendous hidden wealth.

The child sees, hears, and senses the parents' attitudes toward money: their comfort in dealing with it, the importance, regard, and symbolism they bestow upon it, their ease in talking about it, how obtainable and sufficient it seems to be, and the regard in which parents hold those who have more or less money than themselves. The child fashions attitudes and conclusions from these observations. The parents' ability to understand, discuss, and adjust the child's perceptions of money is essential to the development of a well-organized sense of what money and associated issues such as work, acquisition, and security can mean.

A child whose typical curiosity about a parent's salary is consistently thwarted by parental refusal to discuss the matter can well be expected to mature with a sense of money as a deep, dark, adamantly maintained secret, somehow associated with discomfort precluding open discussion.

Money is frequently partitioned from other elements of our experience, and this isolation tends to intensify it as a transference object for many powerful emotional meanings. The separation of money from our daily consciousness may be observed in the methods we use to place it at a distance: credit cards, checks, and charge accounts all serve to alleviate our anxieties about handling, managing, and parting with money.

Children often conclude that things treated secretively and uncomfortably are bad. The concreteness of their logical processes, based in comparatively primitive feelings and limited observation, may create a persistent unconscious equation between money and evil, secrecy, and guilt. Even when children become adults and learn to reason with the powers of a mature intellect and a broad base of experience, that archaic emotional equation may remain rooted in consciousness.

Case Study

Jack had started his own sales company six years ago, marketing computers. He had achieved remarkable success through dedication, hard work, and some very intelligent marketing decisions. However, for the last two years he had been plagued by bouts of anxiety, chest pain, and feeling on several occasions that he was having a heart attack. Several emergency room visits and consultations with cardiologists and gastroenterologists began to suggest to him that his problems were possibly psychological rather than physical in origin, despite their clearly physical painful manifestation.

In psychiatric consultation, he spoke of his work, his success, and the resulting changes in his life. He added that he never believed he would be successful in business because he thought he was stupid. During grade school and high school, he barely passed, earning less than average grades. He was held back in the seventh grade. His father constantly spoke of his underachievement and his stupidity. His father demanded A's: Jack was sent to his room each day after school until bedtime and had to spend a minimum of six hours both Saturday and Sunday studying in his room. He found himself unable to concentrate, feeling angry, and yearning for freedom. He rebelled passively by saying to himself, "He can keep me in here but he can't make me study." His conclusion from these experiences was that he must *really* be stupid or he could make better grades. His self-image and identity came to incorporate a view of himself as lazy, dumb, rebellious, and incompetent in schoolwork.

Now that his success was escalating remarkably, his anxiety increased just as rapidly; he became afraid that he really wasn't smart enough to sustain his new business. He felt like an impostor. He became anxious at each business meeting and afraid of further expansion. His symptoms provided validation that something really was wrong with him.

With treatment, he was able ultimately to deal with multiple levels of his success-related neurosis, including mourning an identity of inadequacy and incompetence in order to fashion a true sense of self.

SUCCESS PHOBIA INVOLVING MONEY

An individual with success phobia or inhibition may work diligently while success or a completed achievement seems to be at a safe distance, but as the goal is approached, he becomes anxious and sabotages efforts at successfully achieving that goal or, just after achieving success, depreciates the achievement or the enjoyment of it.

Success phobia is a specific and definite disturbance of the ability to comfortably complete or accept endeavors of achievement. The phobic avoidance is either of completing the achievement or, when the goal has been reached, to disavow, minimize, or be unable to enjoy the success and what it entails. This inhibition of completing or enjoying successful accomplishment is frequently manifested in the domain of money. I have discussed in a previous work the developmental issues unique to women and the multitude of factors that may deter a woman from pursuing or achieving desired goals (1).

A phobia is a specific defense against anxiety in which a function is inhibited or a perceived dangerous situation is avoided. The danger is symbolically projected or displaced onto an external object or situation, and this object or situation is avoided (3). The phobia is a stand-in, a representative of something one is frightened of, something in the unconscious beyond one's awareness. Inhibition of achievement may manifest itself in vocational, academic, parental, marital, sexual, or monetary endeavors (4).

Distinct types of success phobia can occur within each of the developmental phases with characteristic manifestations. Rather than reviewing here the clinical issues or developmental origins of achievement and its inhibitions, I will limit discussion to impediments in money acquisition, management, and enjoyment. These difficulties can be identified as fear of autonomy, fear of wealth, fear of risk, and addiction to acquisition of money.

Fear of Autonomy

A fear of autonomy broadly reflects problems of separation-individuation and the vicissitudes of adolescent emancipation into adulthood. Behavior associated with money management can be an outward expression of this fear: wanting someone to take over and make decisions, refusing or retreating from full responsibility for financial or business matters, maintaining financial dependency on someone else, or creating financial crises from which one must be rescued.

If having someone take over and make important decisions is emotionally equated with being loved and cared for, skill at handling money and financial independence risk forfeiting love and nurturance. Adrian Berg summarized the struggle of many emerging women: "Women for whom financial care equals love will see their own financial competence as a disastrous loss of femininity."*

The following vignette illustrates a typical scenario involving autonomy and its monetary expression.

Bob, a young geologist, found himself increasingly interested in investing some of his money. His recent promotion provided him with an opportunity to do so for the first time in his life. He discussed his situation with a neighbor. Rather quickly he was called by the neighbor's friend, who advised him to buy into a limited partnership that owned 250 movies to be shown to cable TV, offshore oil platforms, and made into video cassettes.

Bob bought one-half of a partnership unit for $17,500, borrowing some of the money for his investment. Over the next few months

---

*Personal communication.

he learned that the movies he had purchased were old, unpopular, and poorly marketed, and that he would lose his investment.

Bob examined his important but expensive lesson and his underlying wish to be taken care of. He stated, "I trusted without question my neighbor's friend who brokered the deal." Bob recognized that he was essentially telling this unknown friend of a friend, "Please take care of me—I am a novice investor." He was able to examine a presupposition that had worked quite well for him in his original family, in his work for a large corporation, and in his marriage: if he worked hard and did all the "right" things, he would be treated well, looked after, and have his needs met.

This assumption, however, had no utility in the world of investments and finances. By recognizing his assumption as one that was fashioned for an earlier context, he was able to mourn what he experienced as unmet needs of the past. Without his attempts to recreate his past to get a better solution, he became free to choose assumptions that have utility currently. He decided to become knowledgeable about investments, took courses in money management, and consulted a professional financial planner, rather than hope to be *given* valuable training, leads, and advice.

Some individuals with poor self-esteem spend money to fill loneliness and emptiness, or to contain anxiety in the way that others compulsively eat or drink; they attempt to give to themselves, to be self-nurturant. The illusion of unlimited spending (love) from a charge card is alluring to these individuals. The spender with a diminishing sense of self-worth attempts to demonstrate "worth" in an obvious manner. The motive for spending may be publicity or acclaim rather than intrinsic enjoyment. The compulsive spender may be driven to rectify a sense of inferiority, squandering money to create a self-inflicted poverty which will return him to a state of dependency on someone else. This regression reinstates a superficially economic relationship with a friend or relative which is inwardly rooted in a need for emotional nurturance.

The individual whose foremost, abiding, and obsessive concern is in freedom and autonomy can represent another manifestation of fear of autonomy. Called an "autonomy worshipper" by Goldberg (5), this person with deep dependency needs avoids responsibility, schedules, and demands—anything that restricts independence. He may see money as the currency of freedom, its acquisition ensuring future autonomy. Alternatively, money may be shunned entirely because it (or its pursuit) encroaches on freedom. These are two sides of the same coin; more money provides greater distance from dependency needs, demands, and responsibilities, while attempts to reject money constitute denial of any needs, financially or emotionally. The active protest on both sides reveals the common emotional struggle to bring unsettled and conflicted dependency needs under control.

Fear of Wealth

The following case report illustrates some aspects of unconscious conflict about wealth.

Bryan, a bright and gifted attorney, had a remarkably small income, considering the esteem in which he was held in his community as a reputable subspecialist in a particularly complex area of law. Bryan indicated in one of his analytic sessions how much pressure he was getting from his wife to bring home more money for essentials. He recognized that he was really unconcerned about his billing and fee collection until he was pressured externally to collect bills so that he could pay his own. Often this external pressure took the form of bill collectors approaching him. He fell behind in the payment of his analytic fee. He indicated that his only motivation was panic in response to external compulsions. "If there is no one pressuring me for money, then there is no need to make money," he indicated. He added, "I work only under pressure." Indeed, he had structured his practice so that he continually met a number of externally imposed deadlines, usually involving trial dates. When no deadlines were present, he had extreme difficulty working and concentrating.

Bryan unconsciously wanted someone to direct, guide, and motivate him, yet when someone did urge him to work or to meet a deadline, he felt intruded upon and "crowded"—as if someone else were taking over. To this perception, he felt defiant and rebellious.

Work and achievement for Bryan were very complex issues which were complicated by his experiences with an overly involved and controlling mother who usurped credit for all his achievements. As a boy, he felt so excessively dominated by her that the only way he could emancipate himself from her control was to *not* achieve. He also demonstrated his individuality and independence from his demanding, perfectionistic, socially conscious parents by consistently being bad and getting into trouble. He sensitively perceived that what his parents valued most highly was his good appearance and scholastic preeminence. It was in these two arenas that he rebelled consistently. He recalled a time in his adolescence when he appeared in an elegant restaurant (in which he knew his parents were dining at the time) in tattered clothes with a tin cup begging money, until he was ceremoniously thrown out by the manager.

Although many other pieces comprised his current mosaic, his external point of reference was a persistent theme, with alternating conformity and rebellion. On one occasion when he earned a large settlement in his law practice, from which he received approximately $250,000 as his fee, he had fantasies of giving half of it away and spending the other half very quickly. He recognized in analysis that his motivation to do this was to reinstate an image he had of himself as a "bad kid" who was needy and not successful. That image had been fashioned throughout his childhood when his bad behavior was constantly criticized despite his emotional craving for affirmation and love. He felt loved only when he conformed to his parents' desires and interests.

Squandering a considerable portion of his large settlement recreated the childhood scenario. He was able to sensitively perceive his mother's depression and emptiness; he later learned that she was addicted to amphetamines, which she used in an attempt to elevate her depressed mood. He gave up part of himself—his independence emotionally—to remain entangled with her and try to relieve her depression. When she continued to encourage his childhood dependence, he came to view himself as inadequate and incapable.

Money had become the symbol of his attempted autonomy—something he both desired and feared. He seemed unable to acquire money commensurate with his professional skills. During analysis, he began to bill and to collect for his full professional worth—not the worth he had attributed to himself based on his archaic self-image.

With acquisition of financial worth and reserves, some persons experience paradoxical feelings of unworthiness and guilt about acquiring wealth. A suddenly increased income or a substantial inheritance may engender this response. A financial planner has recognized that "a lot of my clients are young men who have done well early in life. They feel guilty about earning more than their fathers at such a young age. And their guilt translates into immobility" (6).

One manifestation of a fear of wealth is a refusal to acknowledge wealth. This type of denial takes several forms. One man, struggling to make a move to a larger house for his family, suddenly "remembered" an acre of land he had purchased years ago. The property he had "overlooked" was located in what had become an elite development and was worth approximately $200,000. Some people psychologically deny their wealth by failing to write a will, by ignoring investments, or by declining to evaluate net worth or tax bracket.

Charles, an engineer, lectured at a university continuing education course in addition to his regular job. He spent his lecture fees in a foolish and impulsive manner, as if the object were to get rid of it. When he examined his behavior, he recognized that he felt that he did not deserve that money, that it was taboo and unwarranted, since he felt that he was not sufficiently capable or expert in his subject to be a lecturer.

He told his therapist, ''When I recognized that I passed up my father in business, that made me feel guilty. That's why I can't finish things. I also spend money like there's no tomorrow—I get rid of it quickly—it's almost like I don't want to be caught with it.''

Fear of Risk

A writer once remarked, ''I've written a number of articles, and even one book manuscript, but I can't bring myself to send any to a publisher because I'm afraid they'll be rejected.'' He was actively fulfilling his worst fear: rejection. Ambivalence about money and its acquisition can create similar immobility. Individuals may be afraid of doing anything with their money for fear it will be the wrong thing.

Darrell was an entrepreneur who described how he loved to find and pursue different ''deals'': limited partnerships, land syndication, and real estate. He would immerse himself in researching the many aspects of the investment. At the moment of decision about whether to actually commit his money, he would inevitably become afraid and back out. He had never closed a single deal. Despite his substantial means, he had never committed to any investment other than savings accounts. His unhappiness with himself and his situation involved his fear of even a calculated risk. Instead, he wrapped himself in a protective blanket by failing to take a final step. He was disappointed in his resignation and his unwillingness to take a chance.

Darrell's assumptions involved a variety of possibilities, all of which had a negative outcome. The scenarios he imagined did not include positive, productive outcomes. His expectations, attitude, and fantasies allowed him only negative possibilities. From this viewpoint, he responded in a seemingly logical way: by backing out at the last minute, he avoided negative consequences. In his belief system, the *best* that could happen was *avoidance of the negative*. In resolving some of the Oedipal conflicts that resulted in his emotional appraisal of negative consequences of success, Darrell's point of view could then be expanded to consider a full range of potential so that situations could be realistically appraised in the business and financial realm rather than in the emotional.

An inverse manifestation of the fear of risk is the Don Juan of risk—a counterphobic manner of creating risk over and over in order (ostensibly) to master it. High-risk, speculative investments will be sought or challenges will be attempted with money or a job. Gambling on games of chance may be an outlet. Fate is challenged, typically without a clearly rational basis. Risk taking may involve financial or business matters rather than other expressions.

Addiction to Acquisition of Money

Some individuals attempt to equate financial worth with internal value (esteem, confidence). The person who feels empty inside, whose self-esteem depends primarily on the response of others rather than internal references, is committing to a relentless pursuit of external validation: wealth, applause, admiration, and material status symbols.

The frustrating and disappointing conclusion to this misconceived quest is that the accumulation of massive financial worth does not assure enhanced self-worth; confusion and depression can follow this confrontation between the real and the ideal. Some individuals maintain a lifelong illusion that money constitutes happiness and self-validation, continue to look for "the big deal," and believe that it's only a matter of "a little more time." A social equivalent can be seen in individuals who surround themselves with admirers to externally maintain and shore up a sagging self-esteem. Depletion and loneliness occur in the absence of constant emotional regulation by others because they feel incapable of internal regulation.

The unending search is for *more*: more money, success, fame, power. The deep emotional hunger for "more" typically emerges from early emotional deprivation. Success and financial acquisition represent the hope of self-validation. Money is considered concrete proof—evidence—of "worth."

The following case report will illustrate.

Edmund had imagined for most of his 48 years that once he acquired a net worth of one million dollars he would feel secure and his self-esteem would improve considerably. He had worked and saved diligently in order to reach his goal. Shortly before treatment began, he completed a major business transaction that put him well over his goal amount. He came to treatment with all the signs and symptoms of a major depression: a depressed, irritable mood, sleep disturbance, decreased energy, poor concentration, diminished appetite with a 12-pound weight loss, and a waning sexual desire. He was prescribed antidepressant medication to reverse his paralyzing symptoms, and he began in therapy to examine the causes of his profound depression. He was able to reconstruct a scenario of the significant events that brought him to his present emotional state.

His brother, two years older, was athletically and physically superior to him. His brother engaged the full interest of his father, whose attention and response Edmund vigorously, yet unsuccessfully, sought. Disappointed, he retreated to increasing closeness with an already domineering and intrusive mother, who protected him and did things for him that he actually was capable of doing himself. This further eroded his self-esteem and sense of personal autonomy.

At an early age, he vowed secretly to defeat his brother by making more money—by being the first person ever in the family to be worth a million dollars. Surely this would extract from his parents the love and respect that he felt was missing.

His depression, however, occurred decades later (about two months before he first came to treatment), when he recognized that money was only money—that it was not esteem and love. Money had failed to relieve his sense of inadequacy and unworthiness. He had been profoundly dissatisfied for some time with the results of his quest for a million dollars. Although he had attained the long-sought cash value, only his financial statement improved, not his happiness, contentment, or feelings of self-esteem. His disillusionment crystallized into a depression when he achieved the magical million and had to confront its actual value and the irrefutable awareness that money did not replace or purchase the missing parental affection. He now felt helpless, as his one great hope of reversing his chronic depressive outlook was revealed as an ineffective fantasy.

The false equation of money and love, as well as the developmental conflicts that the equation represented, were examined in therapy. Edmund could then observe himself with some objectivity, considering the unconscious determinants of his depreciated sense of self and the developmental factors influencing his behavior for four decades and culminating in a withering depression rather than a life of comforting nurturance, affection, and respect for himself and from valued loved ones.

These impediments in money acquisition, management, or enjoyment are final manifestations of various developmental issues and levels that may need to be explored in considerable detail in treatment. The issues involving money are frequent expressions of difficulties in success and achievement. Some of the more common components are the avoidance of a final step toward success, erosion of successful accomplishment, and ambition without goal setting (7).

REFERENCES

1. Krueger, D. *Success and the fear of success in women*. New York: The Free Press, 1984.
2. Castelnuevo-Tedesco, P. The fear of change. *Can. J. Psychiatry*, 9:67–70, 1984.
3. Krueger, D. Anxiety as it relates to "success phobia": Developmental considerations. In W. Fann, I. Karacan, A. Pokorny, & R. Williams (Eds.), *Phenomenology and treatment of anxiety*. New York: Spectrum Publications, 1979.
4. Ovesey, L. The phobic reaction: A psychodynamic basis for classification and treatment. In E. Goldman (Ed.), *Developments in psychoanalysis*. New York: Columbia University Press, 1966.
5. Goldberg, H. *Money madness*. New York: Signet, 1978.
6. Harris, M. Rebels who get rich. *Money Magazine*, Sept., 1982, pp. 58–60.
7. Krueger, D. Achievement inhibition in contemporary women: Developmental considerations. Presented at American Psychiatric Association Meeting, Dallas, 1985.

2

Classical Psychoanalytic
Views of Money*

Paula B. Fuqua, M.D.

Psychoanalysis has addressed two aspects of the meaning of money. First, there is the matter of how money is handled as an inevitable issue of *technique* for the analyst. If the analyst's technique is facilitating, he sets the stage in treatment for the second challenge: to understand the unconscious *meaning* of money as it appears in the analysand's acts and free associations.

Sigmund Freud's recommendations on technique are clear (1). He saw money as a medium for self-preservation and for obtaining power. Money also frequently symbolizes sexual meanings, and people therefore tend to treat money with the same inappropriateness, secretiveness, and inconsistency with which they treat sex. Under these circumstances, it behooves the analyst to deal with money matters openly and frankly, just as he would deal with sex. The analyst should tell the patient his hourly fee in advance and inform him that he will collect the fee at regular specified intervals. Freud felt the analyst need not be ashamed of an expensive fee because he has an effective method of treatment at his disposal. Nor should he offer free treatment, acting the part of a disinterested philanthropist, since such an offer is clearly unrealistic. Besides, free treatment would be useless since it increases the patient's resistance. The "secondary gain" of receiving a valuable gift of therapy would undermine the

---

*My definition of "classical" has a temporal and a theoretical component. Theory defines classical psychoanalysis as that set of ideas which emphasizes drives, psychological conflicts, and infantile sexuality as motivators of behavior and subjective mental life. Temporally, I consider the classical period to span the intellectually productive years of Freud's life. This encompasses both Freud's work and the ideas of his contemporaries in the same period. Modern theorists who identify themselves as Freudian can be as disparate in their interpretations of Freud as Brenner and Lacan, and I therefore consider them to be *neo*classical rather than classical.

17

patient's resolve to overcome difficulties, face painful affects, and recover from his neurosis. For similar reasons, Freud felt psychoanalysis is rarely effective with the poor. The secondary gain of other's pity toward an impecunious person's neurotic symptoms overcomes any benefit from relinquishing them when he has only to continue to face real poverty whether well or ill.

Issues of technique concern the conduct of the *process* of psychoanalysis, of course, but what of the *content* issue? What is the unconscious psychological meaning of money? The major psychoanalytic view has always linked money with feces in our repressed mental life. Freud first alluded to this in a letter to Fliess in 1897. He told of an old fantasy of his in which he, "a modern Midas," turned objects into filth. He noted that unconsciously the word "miserliness" was associated with the word and idea "dirty." He thus used his introspective and self-analytic powers in a way that was basically empirical.

Freud noted that many myths and fairy tales also bring money into intimate association with dirt and excretory products. He cited an ancient Babylonian idea that "gold is the feces of Hell." In his treatment cases Freud observed an extensive empirical correlation between the patients' interest in money and their preoccupation with defecation. In one instance, the patient's constipation could be cured only after his money complex had been made conscious and analyzed (2).

The association between "money" and "feces" was originally a "word association," in keeping with Freud's level of theoretical thinking early in his career. Later he extended his observations, noticing that his patients' interest in their anal functions was linked more broadly with their characters. The child's pleasure in defecation, which Freud called anal erotism, was a constituent instinct which, in certain cases, was expanded, sublimated, or reacted to in a variety of ways, resulting in a triad of symptoms: orderliness, parsimony (miserliness), and obstinacy. These traits occurred clinically in cases where there was prolonged toilet training (3). Both symptoms and character traits were seen as a result of psychological conflict, and a precise distinction was not made between neurotic symptoms and character disorders at this time.

Freud noted a connection between feces, penises, babies, gifts, and money in the unconscious. While a child's original gift is his bowel movement, he (or she) later learns to extend this offering to the wish to give or have a baby as the anal organization is superseded by a genital one. Derivative gifts of monetary value symbolize the procreative wish in the adult. Freud makes the interesting suggestion that therapists study the gifts they receive from their patients to confirm his findings. He regards this developmental path from anal to genital interests and on to monetary displacements as normal, but it can become pathological if any factor of instinct or experience is too extreme (4). Excessive suppression leads to the obsessive-compulsive triad of symptoms mentioned previously. Ernest Jones points out that if anal erotic drives are given too free a reign rather than excessive suppression, the result is not the triad of orderliness, obstinacy and miserliness, but a too free generosity, a wish to shower one's lover with gifts, and a tendency to overspend, letting cost be no object (5).

Freud's famous case of the "Rat Man" illustrates the connection between money, character traits, and anal erotic instincts.* The patient was an obsessional young man who set himself the task of paying back a debt in a certain ritualistic way in order to prevent harm from befalling his mental image of his fiancée or his father. Freud understood this monetary obsession as the patient's way of binding his hostile and erotic urges. He had suffered an intestinal infestation with roundworms as a child, and this had predisposed him to focus on his bowels and anus. A severe punishment from his father for biting had further set the stage for an anxiety attack when he heard the story of the "rat punishment." The wrongdoer was placed on a chamber pot containing rats, and they were allowed to bite and bore their way through his anus. Upon hearing this story, the patient developed the monetary obsession described. His word associations connected rats (*Ratten*) with installments on a debt (*Raten*) and further with babies and penises. The connection between feces and money became especially clear when the patient, in a heightened transference state, dreamed of marrying Freud's daughter, as his father married his mother, for money and power. His dream pictured Freud's daughter with two pieces of dung for eyes (6).

Sandor Ferenczi expanded on Freud's views from a developmental perspective, using data from both child observation and psychoanalysis. He described a progression of interests in the child which he felt extended to other cultures, so that what was ontogenetic had a phylogenetic thrust too. At first children show a natural pleasure both in defecating and in holding back their stools. The retained feces are their first savings and their first toys. The child comes to enjoy pressing and squeezing his stools and subsequently extends this activity to manipulating mud. In this advance he forgoes the pungent fecal smell and takes a step toward the civilizing limitation of instinct. Later, his interest turns to sand, which is

---

*Anal sadism was considered a subcategory of the anal erotic instinct at this point.

even more socially acceptable, being less moist and dirty. The repressed returns when the child enjoys adding water or urine to his sand castles in moats and lakes. He begins to collect stones with sensual pleasure and enjoys bartering them with other children. The stones become glass marbles, buttons, and finally coins. As cognitive development enhances the child's abstracting ability, the coins are replaced by stocks, bonds, and figures. The sublimated anal erotic pleasure reasserts itself, however, when we see someone enjoy stacking, counting, and "wallowing" in money. Ferenczi felt that our interest in money has a rational as well as an instinctual component because money confers real benefits on us when we possess it. Thus, the "capitalistic instinct" has an egoistic (rational) and anal erotic component (7).

Ernest Jones again takes up the task of describing the vicissitudes of anal erotism in adult characters. He notes the association of pleasure in defecation with sexually excitable alimentary tract mucous membranes. The child often enjoys holding back his feces until the last possible minute, thereby intensifying the pleasure of release. This habit appears later in traits of procrastination and persistence. A self-willed independence often accompanies this and extends to a narcissistic belief in one's exalted personal perfection. Following Freud and Ferenczi, Jones sees the most important fecal symbols in the unconscious to be money and children (5).

Karl Abraham describes these traits further. Gifts are originally fecal presents to one's mother and later become babies given to her or produced in identification with her. Thus, the money one spends for these gifts may represent anal or genital interests. Excessive cheapness and stinginess result from a regression to an anal level because of genital conflicts. Abraham mentions the example of a man who went about his house with his trousers unbuttoned so as not to wear out the buttonholes too quickly. Here we see the shadow of genital conflicts behind the miserly act symptomatic of the anal stage.

Anal characters often equate time with money, Abraham continues, and they may expect themselves to do two or three things at once. They frequently revel in their possessions and save useless or used-up objects like old packing paper and string. They may have difficulty throwing things away, so that they have to "lose" objects somehow when detritus builds up. They cannot otherwise bear to part with anything of some possible use. Money saved up may be spent suddenly in huge amounts, representing a disbursement of withheld feces and a release of libido. An example is the husband who controls his wife's allowance and expenditures, refusing her requests, but generously brings home an expensive gift chosen by himself. Such persons are scrupulous in their accounting of debts owed and paid, yet they may uncharacteristically forget to pay a small sum they owe as their anal erotism breaks through the defenses against it.

Like Jones, Abraham comments on the infantile grandiosity bound up in excretory control and notes that an excessively strict or premature toilet training can result in a too sudden loss of this sense of perfection and power, resulting in massive feelings of inadequacy in later life. It can also lead to an inability to love fully, since one's libido becomes fixed at the level of the *function* of bowel control and is not transformed into an interest in the person for whom bowel control is achieved (8).

Otto Fenichel maintains that the instinctual source of interest in money is enhanced by its social significance. Money conveys real advantages of power and prestige and has survival value in purchasing food and shelter. The interplay of social and instinctual influences is an essential relation. His point of view has interesting Marxist influences. For example, discussing money publicly is considered indelicate not only because of its unconscious identification with feces, but also because promotion of ignorance of financial matters among the disadvantaged is a means by which the upper classes maintain their financial superiority. The authoritarian structure of society is more than a remnant of the infantile Oedipus complex. It serves the purpose of perpetuation of financial authority via a father transference to those holding economic power.

On the instinctual side, Fenichel sees the drive to accumulate wealth as a derivative of infantile narcissism transformed into a more realistic need to achieve power and self-esteem. Money is a source of "narcissistic supply" that originates in an instinctual need for food and for omnipotence. This need becomes a part of the ego—the ego ideal of wishing to become rich. This "will to power" with roots in infantile narcissism is different from the "will to possess," which concerns the wish to control one's own body and its products. In possessing money one bastions oneself against a familiar hierarchy of fears: fear of losses related to weaning, fear of losing control of defecation, and fear of castration. Yet, for Fenichel as for others, anal issues stand out empirically as most important of the three in regard to money.

Consistent with his Marxist-like position, Fenichel takes Ferenczi to task for supposing "ontogeny recapitulates phylogeny." He warns against biologizing and states that anal erotic instincts do not cause the development of a "capitalistic instinct" (i.e., a drive to accumulate money). Rather, rational motives and social pressures *make use* of instinctual forces. External reality plays an important part in this process, Fenichel argues. He sees Ferenczi's ideas as reductionistic.

Fenichel also reminds us that the equation money = feces in the unconscious is far from exhaustive. Money can symbolize anything one can take or give. It can be milk, sperm, baby, breast, penis, protection, a gift, hate, power, or degradation. The patient's associations will tell us which meaning is relevant (9).

In sum, the classical psychoanalytic view of the psychological significance of money very much follows Freud's original contribution. Money tends most often to represent anal meanings unconsciously and tends to be handled with the pleasure and need to control, retain, and release that originally obtain toward one's bowel products. Excessively strict or early toilet training usually influences a person to become stingy, miserly, and acquisitive. Money, as it is unconsciously equated with feces, tends to be regarded as dirty and inappropriate for discussion in polite society. The analyst will be careful to treat these issues straightforwardly and realistically to ensure a proper analysis. Subsequent writing concerns itself more with the relationship between money, anal interests, character, and societal patterns. Fenichel emphasizes the pressures of society as well as the influence of instinct in producing a wish for wealth (9).

A final example illustrates the continued power of these theories in organizing our clinical experience. Mrs. W. is a 48-year-old mother of three who reported being abused as a child when her mother administered inappropriate enemas on several occasions. During the time the enema was given, the patient would concentrate on counting pennies to distract herself. She experienced the enemas as a vicious attack and retained a fear of being stabbed or having her house broken into as an adult. She owed her mother a small sum of money on which she made monthly payments. When her mother did not cash several of her checks, she experienced this potential gift as a hostile intrusion and became momentarily obsessed with paying her debt and regaining control over a "gift" that was really an obligation. The gift was similar to an enema in that something is put inside in order to take even more away. Like the Rat Man, her obsession to repay the money also represented an attempt to bind her own destructive rage toward her mother. This woman enjoyed controlling her world through her own knowledge and found special pleasure in investing her savings and toting up profits and losses. Her characterological need to control and organize all her assets, monetary and psychological, was the remnant of a traumatic infantile anal experience. Mrs. W.'s case illustrates the continued vitality of Freud's clinical insights in the present.

REFERENCES

1. Freud, S. On beginning the treatment. *Standard edition*, Vol. 1 (pp. 126–133). London: Hogarth Press, 1913.
2. Freud, S. Letter 29. *Standard edition*, Vol. 1 (pp. 272–273). London: Hogarth Press, 1897.

3. Freud, S. Character and anal erotism. *Standard edition*, Vol. 9 (pp. 169–175). London: Hogarth Press, 1908.
4. Freud, S. On transformations of instinct as exemplified in anal erotism. *Standard edition*, Vol. 17 (pp. 127–133). London: Hogarth Press, 1917.
5. Jones, E. Anal erotic character traits. In *Papers on psychoanalysis* (pp. 413–437). London: Baillière, Tindall and Cox, 1950.
6. Freud, S. Notes upon a case of obsessional neurosis. *Standard edition*, Vol. 10 (pp. 155–318). London: Hogarth Press, 1909.
7. Ferenczi, S. The ontogenesis of the interest in money. In *First contributions to psychoanalysis* (pp. 319–331). New York: Brunner/Mazel, 1952.
8. Abraham, K. Contributions to the theory of the anal character. *Int. J. Psychoanal.*, 4:400–418, 1923.
9. Fenichel, O. The drive to amass wealth. *Psychoanal. Q.*, 7:69–95, 1938.

3

A Self-Psychological View of Money

David W. Krueger, M.D.

ORIGINAL NET WORTH: THE DEVELOPMENTAL LINE OF NARCISSISM

Children develop a cohesive, positive sense of self when consistent empathic parental responses reflect and validate the child's sensations, feelings, and perceptions (1). The child's developmental needs of empathic mirroring and affirmation exist from the first weeks and months of life.

Kohut has described how the developmentally appropriate "grandiose self" of the first two years of life is nurtured and undergoes transmutation into appropriate and mature self-esteem by parents who reflect the child's experiences from the child's frame of reference, thereby assuring the child of his/her worth (2). Throughout development, the phase-appropriate parental responses of accurate empathy, confirmation, admiration, and limit setting help the child transform and internalize grandiosity and exhibitionism into a more mature capacity for ambitions, goals, and internally regulated self-esteem.

The sense of self (a metaphorical and abstract representation of one's identity and self-regard) is based on an initial formulation of a body self (3). The formation of an accurate and distinct body image emerges from parental mirroring of the developing child's point of reference: parental reflections of internal sensation, and perceptions from the child's experience (rather than the parents'). This attunement to the separate center of the child's initiative, as distinct from the adults', begins in the autistic and symbiotic stages of development, extending in changing forms through separation-individuation phases. A failure to adequately address these development needs in preverbal time results in vague and indistinct body image boundaries; the resultant sense of self is incomplete and incoherent. as there is no solid foundation of body image on which to build (4).

24

An individual with pathological narcissism characteristically experiences a sense of emptiness, lack of initiative, diffuse sensitivity, and vulnerability to others (1). Self-reparative efforts may be channeled into intense ambitiousness and grandiose fantasies to overcome feelings of inferiority and overdependence on the admiration and acclaim of others (5). The narcissistic personality is motivated not primarily by guilt, but by embarrassment and shame. While guilt is a prominent affect in disturbances of object relations, shame is an affect central to disturbances in the sense of self (6). The internal modulation of esteem is difficult for the narcissistic individual. Other people are seen as sources and regulators of esteem, worth, and happiness. Vulnerability is ever-present because the external validators of esteem are not under one's personal control and the internal validation mechanisms are dysfunctional.

With a faulty self-esteem, one must look continually to others and to the environment for confirmation and valuation. When others or the environment fail to reflect the longed-for affirmation and empathy, self-esteem may decline precipitously into devaluation, self-criticism, and depression. One may then attempt to assert absolute control of others and the environment and become harshly and unrealistically demanding of oneself.

If the child's needs are seen only in relationship to the parents' needs, growth of an autonomous self-image is stunted. The child developing under these circumstances remains oriented toward the parents initially and later toward others. Seeking guidance, direction, and initiative solely from others, this child disregards internal signals, devalues his own perception and creativity, and depreciates his own internal points of view. His deeply embedded external orientation stifles the development of mechanisms for the regulation of his own internal standards, values, and feelings.

The need for structure and constant response from others seems essential to maintenance of a positive self-image among individuals whose development has been so affected. Interruption of constant affirmation may precipitate depression or emptiness. For example, formal learning environments, such as secondary school and college, function to maintain feedback, regulation, and structure. The prospect of losing this self-confirming support system upon graduation may be threatening, with a concomitant extreme loss of self-esteem and direction. The common crisis of "needing to find oneself" typically occurs at such developmental junctures.

Money has an overdetermined value for many individuals with pathological narcissism. Money can concretely symbolize confirmation of worth and value, envy and admiration (and thus mastery of one's chronic envy of others), validating power and acquisitive ability. One will desire more and more money as long as nothing challenges the belief that money can command emotional as well as material goods from others who maintain similar belief in its validating power. When one believes strongly that money is able to answer emotional questions, the desire for it is insatiable.

MONEY AND WORK ADDICTIONS
IN THE PURSUIT OF SELF-ESTEEM

Work compulsion is an extreme, unfulfillable internal demand for constant engagement in gainful labor and a corresponding inability or refusal to relax. Inactivity or any activity other than money-generating work may engender guilt or anxiety about inadequacy and self-worth. This compulsion to work attempts to counter such underlying concerns as inadequacy, guilt, and worthlessness. Work is an enabling sacrifice for which others are willing to provide rewards. In a psychoanalytic study of work compulsion, Kramer (7) describes prevalent underlying feelings of imposture, inadequacy, and conflict concerning authority figures. Work may be viewed as the one sphere in which identity can be established and maintained; feelings of importance, recognition, validation, and affirmation may seem available only in work-related activity. A compelling need to work constantly may then emerge, and a lost, restless feeling may predominate when one is not working. Like the mythical Sisyphus, who endlessly pushed a huge rock to the top of a hill, only to have it roll down again, the person with work compulsion cannot rest.

Working passionately, long and hard, and experiencing satisfaction from work, does not constitute work compulsion or addiction. An addiction can be defined as *something one cannot do without*: the person addicted to alcohol or drugs cannot do without them. It is only when the person *cannot do without work* to maintain comfort or a sense of worth that one is addicted. One may experience "withdrawal symptoms" such as restlessness, anxiety, depression, or psychosomatic ailments when *not* working, experience an inability to control the desire for work, or display physical or emotional deterioration as a result of overwork (7).

Profound needs for admiration and self-esteem are the prime motivations in many individuals displaying work and wealth-acquisition compulsions. Immersion in work may be a compulsive attempt to reverse feelings of diminished self-esteem. In those driven by the need to prove themselves powerful and adequate, attention and energy are constantly devoted to new sources of attainment, acquisition, and relentless striving. Although they may attain their vocational or financial goals, individuals so afflicted are not satiated. They recognize that something is still missing. They want more.

If parental approval and admiring confirmation of one's achievements were absent during childhood, one result may be an intense campaign to achieve response and admiration by acquiring the most widely agreed-upon symbol of "worth," money, in the greatest quantities possible and at the sacrifice of any amount of time and work.

Even remarkable successes do not permanently gratify the compulsive worker, and not even result in enjoyment. Each accomplishment may be met, upon completion, with a letdown or even depression, as if the goal were the pursuit of challenge rather than an achievement itself. The disappointment felt upon reaching a goal (or promotion, or other success) reflects a recognition that something is still missing. Some individuals phobically sabotage their own successful completions specifically to avoid this feeling of empty disillusion. They are then able to maintain the belief that the answer is still there, still available to them on the next try. The realization that their discomfort cannot be relieved by outwardly directed effort is the one intolerable disappointment, and elaborate psychological gymnastics are directed toward protecting themselves from this awareness.

The compulsive achiever does not experience gratification with accomplishment. When the goal is achieved, excitement diminishes quickly. Neither joy nor relief is the emotion pursued; more important is the avoidance of anticipated ridicule, rebuff, or shame, and the most recent accomplishment seems to hold them at bay only briefly. The echoes of applause have barely died when this individual is again consumed by emptiness, and a new source of external admiration through material achievement is sought. For these narcissistic individuals, an *internally regulated* self-esteem does not exist: the point of reference is someone or something *external*. They search ceaselessly for admiring approval and affirmation from others to reflect their worth so that they can feel complete, whole, and valuable, and, ultimately, be assured that they exist. Paradoxically, narcissistic individuals wish to be seen as self-reliant, powerful, and idealized by others—not in warm, intimate relationships, but much as an actor is admired and applauded by an audience of anonymous strangers, watching him in the dark from a distance.

Narcissistic individuals perform and feel alive and validated when receiving the confirmation and approval of an admiring audience: employees, clientele, or spouse.

There is a preoccupation with how one is viewed in the eyes of others and an inordinate concern about making mistakes and failing. Situations that are tentative or unpredictable may be avoided to ensure engagement only in successful activities. Very high ambitions and expectations may alternate with low self-respect, fear of failure, and a ready reproach and criticism for falling short of expectations. For some, ambitions and endeavors are pursued only so far, and interest is withdrawn just before the moment of actual commitment. Applications or submissions may be withdrawn at the final moment, or steady pursuit of a goal is abandoned at the final step. This withdrawal is often accompanied by a sudden disavowal of interest in what had previously been a highly invested endeavor (8).

The types of success sought by some individuals with excessive narcissistic needs are those which result in admiration and enhancement of one's perceived esteem, as opposed to those efforts which satisfy intrinsic desires for accomplishment. Narcissistic individuals may feel *entitled* to have rewards flow without disruption. Sudden and intense rage may occur if another person fails to respond to the narcissist's wishes and desires.

If the narcissistic individual senses that positive responses from others are neither wholehearted nor easy to obtain, he may display righteous indignation and withdraw from endeavors (9).

The lifelong irritant of the narcissistic individual is that "No matter how much I have, it's never enough. I want more." This endless pursuit of more, better, and greater is typically confronted by midlife realities and an accumulation of experiences that have forced the narcissist to recognize that wealth, possessions, or position has failed to relieve emptiness and longing for self-affirmation. The illusion of worth and value being determined by external sources is badly damaged. During this period of emotional crisis, the narcissistic individual is particularly vulnerable to imprudent activities such as illicit love affairs, large purchases, risky business deals, and other violations of his own normal patterns as he desperately attempts to withstand awareness that he is his own source of psychic discomfort, and that he, rather than his circumstances, must change if there is to be relief.

MONETARY OR SELF-WORTH:
THE IMPOSTOR PHENOMENON

Some individuals secretly see themselves as impostors despite business, academic, or professional successes. They feel that their accomplishments have been accidental and that they have fooled everyone who perceives them to be capable or successful (8). The "impostor's" self-image is fixed, and any objective evidence of accomplishment is disavowed.

Those who believe achievement is the result of imposture fear being only a step ahead of exposure of inadequacy. These individuals must therefore work incessantly or accumulate as much money as possible before they are "unmasked." They may seek others to reassure and testify to their worth and may stockpile money as an undeniable, concrete evidence of worth to maintain their imposture. They may not even experience themselves as individuals with independent capabilities, but feel as if they are nothing without their spouse, job, title, possessions, or some other significant source of external structure and confirmation. Beneath the external trappings there is a devitalized self without internally generated goals, direction, or belief in one's capabilities or integrity. The behavior patterns of such an individual are typically guided most dominantly by such negatives as fear of rejection or loss of love.

The impostor's choice of employment or profession is heavily influenced by a sense of narcissistic currency (social status, rank, approval) rather than by personal satisfaction with the activity itself. The individual interprets problems as evidence of some grievous basic defect in character which is not correctable. One may bitterly resent any discomfort, including the discomfort of experiencing difficulties in a task, and may respond with rage and the feeling that something unfair is occurring. One protects oneself from recognizing the need to change an outlook or view of oneself by projecting blame for problems onto others and contending that it is not one's own responsibility to correct their defects. This individual appeals to fate, awaits outside intervention, or attempts to discover "tricks" that will make the difficulty disappear. These same forces have made imposture successful. When magic is not invoked, and others do not respond or function in exactly the way desired, intense anger may follow.

The impostor may harbor a picture of general doubt about his capacity; the picture may include a conviction that some central feature necessary for success is missing. Thinking that people have been fooled, an academic, business, or professional position achieved by fraudulent means, dishonesty is experienced despite never having actually committed an outright act of fraud. The impostor may feel that he could only have attained these ends through some special manipulations or by capitalizing on other people's "weakness" or gullibilities. He experiences a strong sense of having been deprived or injured and insists on redress of his grievances.

The impostor is a tangle of contradictions. He feels deeply flawed but perfectionistic. He is narcissistic but bitterly self-critical. He projects self-satisfaction and contentment but is motivated primarily by fear. He uses a variety of strategies to simultaneously satisfy his lofty, perfectionistic ambitions while keeping himself in check. When things are going well, he is likely to be self-deprecating, thus creating in his imagination a great chasm between himself and those he sees as competitors. He may reject favorable information as flattery or the mistakes of others and is likely to attribute accomplishments to luck, to other people, or to virtually anything that will devalue his contribution and allow him to maintain a perception that his successes are not real successes (10).

Work and money are valued to the degree that they satisfy the deep desire to elicit admiration and self-affirmation. Because the needs fueling these desires are insatiable and unremitting, there is the consistent feeling of failing to achieve one's perfectionistic, unrealistic aspirations—and an often inaccurate conclusion of inadequacy.

When the impostor does achieve a significant success, such as accumulating a large sum of money, he doubts that he could do it again. He cannot enjoy his success for very long because he is concerned that at any moment he may be revealed and lose his business or position. A desperate striving creates a reliance and vulnerability on external sources of confirmation and approval.

The following case report depicts a patient who was seen in psychoanalysis at a time when he was growing increasingly depressed as he recognized that he had reached all the monetary and material goals he had set, which he had anticipated would bring him an elusive happiness.

Darrell, a middle-aged businessman, was afraid that once no challenge or risk loomed immediately on the horizon, he would no longer feel useful or motivated or be valued by himself or others. Upon the completion of a major business deal, he would quickly disburse most of his money to trusts and investments, so that it was not available for use, and would spend the remainder in foolish ways. By depleting his available funds, he would create new impetus for himself to renew his efforts and push himself harder.

Darrell stated, "As soon as I achieve something, I lose interest, like I don't need it any more. I constantly create new challenges. I used to work my ass off to make a deal, and afterward would feel horrible, guilty, empty, inadequate—like I needed to blow part of it. I'd wish something bad would happen whenever something good happened. I'll make $250,000 on a deal but instead focus completely on the $1,000 that I didn't make. That kept me from having fulfillment and enjoyment of what I did make." He later added, "Making money is fairly easy. Learning to enjoy it and feel I earned it is hard.''

Although he was quite wealthy and was well respected in his field, he felt as if no accomplishment were ever enough. He could not enjoy any of his achievements because he feared that he would not be able to meet the next challenge, make the next conquest. He worried that he was really an impostor, and that his ineptness would be revealed. Each success was experienced as only an accident or a temporary reprieve from imminent exposure as a fraud. He said that he was afraid of failing, but was afraid to lose that fear, because he might then lose his motivation to succeed. He felt like he was always running from something.

Despite his drive to succeed, Darrell relinquished the *experience* of success by never acknowledging or enjoying it and by plunging unceasingly into constant work, seeking constant challenge.

He stated, ''The thrill is in the struggle, not the accomplishment. I fear enjoying the present—if I did I'd lose my ambition. If I'm not constantly getting laid or doing a deal, I'm empty.'' His handling of money mirrored his difficulty in acknowledging success. He would spend recklessly, gambling or making frivolous large purchases, until he was reduced to a financial level where he once again felt worried and challenged. This scenario ensured his continued addiction to work and to the acquisition of money.

Darrell's parents both worked in a family business when he was a boy, so he saw little of them. Even as a small child, he was alone much of the time and entertained himself. His parents were away most of the evenings entertaining business associates and customers. When they wanted to be with Darrell, however, he had to drop his own interests and spend time with them. He grew to see himself as an extension of their interest and desire, rather than as an individual capable of acting on his own interests and desires. Childhood memories and development of an intense mirror transference in psychoanalysis added depth to the understanding of his current experiences. When his parents did not want or need him, it was as if he didn't exist. He felt abandoned and lonely. These feelings persisted into adulthood; when he completed a business deal, he felt empty, no longer needed. Thus, he searched constantly for a new project or venture in order to escape the awful empty, abandoned feeling. He had to constantly compensate for a still-alive feeling of early childhood. For him, wealth, power, and noncommitment were necessary to successfully counterbalance powerful dependency and narcissistic needs.

Darrell also explored the tremendous sense of guilt he experienced with a major accomplishment. He discovered its Oedipal components and the equation with his childhood desire to be more successful than his father: to have a closer, warmer, more exclusive relationship with his mother than even his father had. His current successes awakened a latent guilt, urging him to quickly liquidate his monetary gains and reinstate his presuccess (pre-Oedipal, dependent) position, to start his compulsive work cycle over again. Working hard had become a punishment of sorts to assuage his guilt at doing so well and figuratively defeating his father.

The narcissistic individual often realizes in middle age that ever-increasing challenges and expansive ambition are limited in their rewards. The hope that ''a little more time'' or a little more money will resolve emotional problems begins to wane. Just as a physical illness challenges one's illusion of personal immortality and omnipotence, financial success can force painful confrontation with the belief that ''more'' will be enough emotionally.

REFERENCES

1. Kohut, H. *The restoration of the self*. New York: International Universities Press, 1977.
2. Kohut, H. A note on female sexuality. In P. Ornstein (Ed.), *The search for the self*. New York: International Universities Press, 1978.
3. Krueger, D., and Schofield, E. An integration of verbal and nonverbal therapies in treating disorders of the self: II. Presented at National Coalition of Arts Therapies Association meeting, New York, 1985.
4. Krueger, D., and Schofield, E. *Body and self: The developmental and clinical role of body image in treatment of disorders of the self*. (Book manuscript in preparation.)
5. Stolorow, R. Toward a functional definition of narcissism. *Int. J. Psychoanal.*, 56:179–185, 1975.
6. Mollon, P. Shame in relation to narcissistic disturbance. *Br. J. Med. Psychol.*, 57:207–214, 1984.
7. Kramer, Y. Work compulsion—A psychoanalytic study. *Psychoanal. Qt.*, 46:361–385, 1977.
8. Krueger, D. *Success and the fear of success in women*. New York: Free Press, 1984.
9. Horowitz, M. Self-righteous rage and the attribution of blame. *Arch. Gen. Psychiatry*, 38:1233–1238, 1981.
10. Rorhlich, J. The dynamics of work addiction. *Isr. J. Psychiatry Relat. Sci.*, 18:147–156, 1982.

4

The Fee as Focus of Transference and Countertransference in Treatment

Rosalea A. Schonbar, Ph.D.

In 1967 I published a paper in which I examined some of the transferential and countertransferential issues that may be involved in fee-setting practices. That paper was summarized as follows:

> This paper examined some of the therapeutic implications of fee-setting practices. Rigorous fee practices based upon Freud's recommendations were contrasted with the more flexible approach advocated by Fromm-Reichmann. Since both approaches are utilized successfully, and since there are no research findings to support any preference for either, this paper explored some of the possible psychodynamic reasons for adherence to each fee-setting system. Some of the therapist variables included cultural considerations, training, personality, and countertransference. The latter was considered both characterologically and within the context of particular therapist-patient interactions.
>
> Those advocating rigorous fee systems predict undesirable resistance and transference reactions if their procedures are not followed. The view taken in this paper is that these reactions will occur regardless of which fee system is followed, and that the reactions will be congruent with the patient's dynamics, as illustrated in two case histories.
>
> For both patient and therapist, money may be a highly charged issue, and may evoke behavior congruent with very central conflicts and with other behavior related to those conflicts. In the therapist, such behavior may, at worst, interfere with the therapy just as do other unrecognized countertransferential trends. In the patient, such behavior may serve to facilitate the therapy by providing an im-

33

mediate and sharply focused paradigm of his distorted interpersonal operations. (1, pp. 284–285)

As I write this chapter, almost 20 years later, I see no reason to change my view that any fee-setting system may represent countertransferential trends for any given therapist, regardless of its presented rationale (or rationalization), especially if there is no variation from patient to patient. One of the implications of this statement, however, is that a rationally developed flexible system is less likely to fall into this category than either a strictly adhered-to rigorous system or a flexible one which does not recognize the psychological as well as the financial characteristics of the patient.

A new search of the literature reveals nothing contradictory to the above conclusion. In fact, the very paucity of more than indirect or passing references to the countertransferential issues is striking, although one psychotherapist (2) has written an article attempting to educate physicians concerning their money-connected countertransferences and how they impact on medical treatment. A common theme is that countertransference is evoked when the patient resists the fee arrangement or violates it (e.g., Paolino [3]), but, except in discussions of the difficulties of beginning therapists, there is little recognition that personal conflicts and neurotic needs of the therapist may be carried into his practice as elsewhere and be expressed in his financial dealings independent of the patient's behavior and in inappropriate ways. One of the few exceptions to this observation is Chessick's (4,5) recognition that a therapist's "greed and vanity" may function to interfere with his empathy and therefore his therapeutic effectiveness.

There has been and continues to be recognition of many ways in which fee paying may serve as a focus around which transferential acting-out may cluster. Statements like "much can be learned about a person's psychic life if we observe how he handles money" (3, p. 169) and "to an amazing degree difficulties in money matters paralleled difficulties in interpersonal relations during the therapy" (6, p. 14) are recognitions of the peculiar status of money issues as an avenue of expression of underlying conflictual issues. For the most part, such recognition is focused on the patient and not the therapist. An exception is Meyers (7), who feels that money is perhaps an even more crucial crucible of both transference and countertransference in a social era in which there are "apparently liberal attitudes toward sexuality" (p. 1460); in such a social era, "underlying transference and countertransference conflicts are more directly manifested in the continued aversion to money" (p. 1460).

Even with the focus on transference, however, it is notable that some recommendations for stringent fee policies give as a reason the avoidance of otherwise inevitable transference reactions concerning the fee; my view is that such transference reactions may well become a valuable source of psychotherapeutic work and understanding, and that the fee is only one avenue for their appearance: if they represent, as by definition they do, conflicts that the patient brings with him into the therapy, then attempting to avoid them is antitherapeutic and doomed to failure anyway. It is striking, in this context, that, as late as 1971, Hilles (8) described her decision to treat a patient's nonpayment of fees interpretively rather than administratively as "experimental," and the treatment thus described as "unorthodox."

THE SCOPE OF THIS CHAPTER

The issues described here arise from the fact that psychotherapists offer their services for pay. And whether the actual transaction takes place between patient and therapist as in private practice, whether the insurance company rather than the patient pays the fee, or whether the therapist is on salary and does not profit directly from the payments of his patients, feelings and conflicts accrue to the matter as iron filings to a magnet. Fee setting, fee paying, nonpayment, fee raising, all of these seem to be administrative details which must be dealt with in any patient-professional relationship. It does not matter if a dentist is greedy or if a client is angry that her decorator charges a lot. And if the patient or client doesn't pay, the dentist or decorator is free to sue or to hire a collection agency. Psychotherapy is different, of course, in that greed and resentment affect the very process and outcome of the professional enterprise. Thus, the office management pamphlets that arrive in my mailbox and the bland advice in many of the professional books addressed to the beginner are equally irrelevant. The psychotherapy relationship is perhaps unique in that even the administrative arrangements are an integral part of the process, whether the therapist handles them himself or delegates them to a secretary.

Given the introduction to the chapter, which emphasized the complexities of this "administrative" interaction, this chapter will deal with some of the deceptively "simple" ideas and practices that impact significantly upon this unique relationship and with the myths with which we have mysteriously surrounded these practices.

WHY A FEE FOR PSYCHOTHERAPY?

For the most part, people in our society who seek services of various kinds pay for such services; sometimes an appropriate government, religious, or private agency provides the services. In any case, the service provider is paid. In our society, this is how the service provider pays his rent, buys his food, goes on his vacations, supports his family, and the like. Professionals like physicians, lawyers, and psychotherapists, who have invested money and many years in becoming competent, also frequently feel that payment for services is an appropriate return on those investments.

Freud (9) stated that the basic reality reason for charging fees is "self-preservation and . . . obtaining power. . . . It seems to me more respectable and ethically less objectionable to acknowledge one's actual claims and needs rather than . . . to act the part of the disinterested philanthropist" (p. 131). Blanck and Blanck (10) comment that "the fee is the only part of the therapy that is legitimately for the therapist" (p. 173).

In fact, the only argument against the legitimacy of a fee for psychotherapy has been offered by Schofield (11). Schofield feels that the services of most mental health practitioners are not available to the most disordered population, but rather to people who are least in need of it—who are "unhappy" rather than "ill." He feels that the functioning but unhappy person might just as well profit from talking to friends, and that the mental health professional has nothing unique to offer such people. Schofield asks, "If prostitution be the oldest of professions, is there any pride to be taken in the fact that the sale of friendship may be the commerce of the newest?" (p. 164).

Schofield's is an idiosyncratic view within the profession, although some patients distrusting or defending against feelings of closeness with their therapists make similar accusations of them. In my experience, patients are seldom "just" unhappy people; usually, they are people in pain who either have no friends or have found talking to friends to be unavailing.

Psychotherapy is not easy work, and I would agree with Freud and Blanck and Blanck that the psychotherapist is entitled to his fee. What I find disturbing, however, is the great frequency with which legitimacy of the fee is justified in the literature, not on the basis of therapist entitlement, but in terms of the detrimental effect of free therapy on the psychotherapeutic enterprise. Freud felt that free treatment increases resistance. Yet he is also quoted by Lorand and Console (12) as having addressed the Fifth International Psychoanalytic Congress in 1918 on the inevitability of eventual free treatment for the poor, based on "the conscience of the community" (p. 59) despite the probable reluctance of governments. They felt, however, that this would place pressure on the analytic professional to adapt his treatment in response. For Freud did feel that, by and large, free treatment would lead to mistrust, resentment, increased dependence on the therapist, increase in resistance, and suppression of negative transference. Nash and Cavenar (13) believe that the free treatment offered by the Veterans Administration interferes with progress, but the only evidence they present is five case histories. Blanck and Blanck feel that an inadequate fee prevents the growth of self-esteem for the patient. There have been predictions of favorite-child fantasies and of the unnecessary development of guilt; it is interesting to note that, on the other hand, Mowrer (14) sees the payment of a fee as an atonement for neurotic guilt. It seems likely to me that any of these reactions might well occur in a patient who has a predisposition to such transference; if he were paying for the treatment, they would still emerge.

Going well beyond the issue of whether a fee is necessary for optimal treatment or whether too low a fee is damaging to the patient, a number of writers on this subject—Menninger (15), Haak (16), Kubie (17), and Davids (18), for example—propose that the fee must constitute a sacrifice for the patient. The ostensible reason is motivational: otherwise, the treatment will become "a matter of indifference" to the patient. These writers are advocates of what I have called a rigorous fee system wherein the fee and the details of payment are presented and enforced as standard aspects of the therapist's practice, including automatic charges for missed sessions; these latter charges are necessary because, according to Kubie (17), for example, the patient would simply skip sessions at painful times without them. Blanck and Blanck (10) take issue with the motivational rationale, noting that treatment frequently goes well even when, for example, a relative pays; they point out that motivation is more profoundly promoted by other means intrinsic to the treatment, and not by "simplistic external devices" (p. 173). They nevertheless see pressure to accept low-cost patients as a denigration of the therapist.

As indicated earlier, I believe the statements of rigorous fee setters that the fee is necessary for the patient's well-being to be at best a myth. There are some data which support my belief. As early as 1958, Lorand and Console (12) reviewed the progress of 59 analysands in a free clinic. Their conclusion was that " . . . the difficulties encountered in this new milieu of treating the patients without charge were very little different from the general difficulties which are found in the office practice" (p. 63).

Given the increase in the number of nonpaying or low-paying patients because of the increase in free clinics and third-party payment, it is striking that more data are not available on this issue, and that the validity of many of the above statements has not been investigated. Other therapists—like Bruch (6), Paolino (3), Chessick (4), and Fromm-Reichmann (19), for example—who are more flexible in fee setting for a variety of reasons do not report damage to the patient or the therapy. Nor, except in very orthodox Freudian psychoanalysis, are there many other areas of treatment in which the emergence of transference is seen as a detriment. In ego-oriented or interpersonally oriented treatment, the patient's idiosyncratic transferential responses are welcomed as data.

The persistence and nonexamination of what increasingly seems to be a myth raises the question that most therapists would raise if their patients held tightly to and refused to examine some deeply held conviction about which some doubts might legitimately arise: what purpose does it serve? Obviously, the more flexible therapists do not present themselves as poverty-stricken or as dissatisfied with their incomes, so it is not simply protection of income. What we may be seeing here is a kind of projection that protects the therapist from his own difficulties concerning money and his own conflicts concerning his entitlement and the meaning of money to him. He simply avoids the possible consequences of having to engage in a genuine interaction in this area. Meyers (7, p. 1460) wonders to what extent simple and unwavering reference to a standard fee "serves to protect senior practitioners from dealing with issues that were not resolved during their own training." Surely, psychotherapists are not immune to the many irrational discomforts aroused by discussion of money and of sale of their services; the rigorous fee system and the unquestioning and frequently false belief that the fee serves not his interests but those of the patient obviate the necessity for him to examine his own conflicts. Menninger (15) rather contemptuously stated that it is unwise to engage in discussion concerning the analyst's expectations in this regard, because the patient wouldn't understand them anyhow. This is indeed a far cry from Freud's comment that the "analyst is therefore determined from the first . . . to treat of money matters with the same matter-of-course frankness to which he wishes to educate them in things relating to sexual life" (9, p. 131). That the therapist's honesty and forthrightness concerning money matters serve as a model for patient behavior is a repeated theme in the literature. Unfortunately, an authoritarian and nonnegotiable stance communicates discomfort, power seeking, and a kind of emotional dishonesty. Surely this model is not desirable. Nor does it avoid the induction of transferential reactions, because that's not possible, even were it a desirable goal.

NONPAYMENT AND MISSED SESSIONS

Setting the fee is, of course, only the beginning of interactions concerning payment. In some sense these other interactions are simply special cases of the issues involved in the fee setting itself. It would therefore be surprising if each of these interactions were not imbued with the same symbolic meanings, conflicts, and behaviors. Thus, the rigorous "by-the-book" fee setters also depend on rules for the handling of such issues as nonpayment of fees and charging for missed sessions. Again, to the degree that these rules are applied without differentiating each occurrence for each patient, one may question what purpose they serve for the therapist. There is, of course, the legitimate need of the therapist for a dependable income, but, again, Haak (16) and others with similar views claim that their practices are based on what is best for the patient and the treatment, in part because nonpayment, especially for missed sessions, would arouse countertransference.

There are situations in which nonpayment or missed sessions arise from reality considerations such as changed economic conditions, financial emergencies, business trips, family responsibilities, or vacation times over which the patient has no choice. Intransigence without investigation seems to me to communicate a lack of interest in the patient's situation. Blanck and Blanck (10), whose general stance in these matters is not entirely classifiable into rigorous or flexible for reasons I shall discuss later, take a relatively rigorous stance here. They state: "In general, the rule that the time must be paid for still holds. In exceptional cases, an individual arrangement may be made. Whether for business, illness, vacation, or the like, it is always useful to raise the question with a patient who is reluctant to pay, 'Who, then, should pay?'" (p. 176). While this has the virtue of at least placing the issue within the framework of what might be called therapist rights, and of calling to the patient's attention the contractual nature of the arrangements, it also seems to me that it raises a question, rhetorical or not, which is not the patient's to answer. It is, in fact, the therapist's problem, and, again, does not avoid transference issues: guilt for some, feeling needed for others, a sense of power for still others. The therapist can free himself or herself of the necessity for asking this question by seeing to it that his or her "standard fee" is designed in the first place to cover such contingencies or by not accepting patients whose health or profession is likely to result in recurrent issues of this sort. Special arrangements on an individual basis are, as Blanck and Blanck point out, also possible.

In any event, the rigorous fee policy in these kinds of instances may well be detrimental to the whole therapeutic enterprise. A colleague of mine described what happened when his wife gave birth to their first child, and he had to miss three sessions with his therapist. The latter charged for those missed sessions, commenting after some discussion of the issue, "I can understand your being upset about this, but you know that that's my policy." My colleague told me that, in retrospect, he realized that he no longer trusted the therapist, particularly with his anger, and that his termination with the therapist three months later was a direct result of this situation.

In instances where nonpayment or missed sessions are not related to such reality issues, or where the reality issues seem to be serving resistance purposes, the more flexible approach allows more easily for exploration of the dynamics and for collaborative consideration of the fee issue itself. After all, these kinds of problems, unlike the initial fee setting, take place within an ongoing process and relationship and may have different meanings at different times even for the same patient, and certainly different meanings for different patients. Let us, for example, look at some instances from my own practice:

1. Ms. A, a married woman in her thirties, was acting out some of the previously repressed issues of early adolescence. One day she simply missed a session, a most unusual event for this patient. She later explained that she had been talking on the phone to the man who had just become her lover. She knew, she said, that she was due to leave for her session, but decided that the phone conversation was more important. When I told her that she would have to pay for the session, she said, "Oh, I know that," gave a sigh of relief, and said, "It was worth it."

This patient was acting out a bit of defiant adolescent behavior in a forbidden (sexual) context. By comparison, the money was a minor issue. Moreover, the sigh of relief indicated a number of things: the charge was indeed a small price to pay for the "deliciousness" of the moment, and it was felt to be an expiation for her guilt. As we discussed her expectation of my possible reaction, we uncovered her fear that I would end our relationship, an expectation based on her mother's refusal to talk to her after she had been "bad."

This incident, then, was a testing of the therapeutic alliance, based on transferential expectations. When she missed a session sometime later because her child had been injured at school and she had to pick him up and get him to a physician, I did not charge her.

2. Ms. B, a counterdependent, highly principled young black

woman, lost her job. While she saw this, in part, as an opportunity for devoting more time to developing a new career enterprise upon which she had been working for some time, she was, of course, concerned about the lack of income. As her savings and severance pay began to dwindle, she became panicky; she had been unable to find a new job, and her new venture was not yet off the ground. Inquiry on my part revealed that she had not applied for unemployment compensation—she saw this as demeaning. Later, when she did, in fact, begin to go to the unemployment office, she also began to experience considerable anxiety and depression. Exploration revealed that, although we had discussed many times, usually on my initiative, what she called "problems in my black identity," her presence among so many unemployed black people at the unemployment office had threatened her unadmitted defensive contempt for blacks, including herself. Of course, we explored this issue; what we did not explore sufficiently was her anger at me for having "placed her in that position."

During this time, I had been seeing her on a deferred, part-payment plan which I had suggested when she had earlier proposed coming less frequently to save money. Eventually, she stated that she "couldn't stand" being in debt, and that she would feel far less burdened were she to stop therapy "for the time being." While this decision was certainly congruent with Ms. B's dynamics, particularly her defensive overindependence, I believe in retrospect that it arose more from her anger at me for having "placed her in the position" of having to face, before she was ready, a really very basic conflict in her life. I think it was that not fully enough explored anger which led to the termination, and not the deferred-payment plan, without which therapy would have had to end even more prematurely than it did.

3. Mr. C, a 23-year-old recent college graduate, has been seeing me for a relatively short period. When I first saw him, he was working at a boring, beginning-level, dead-end job and had a few thousand dollars in the bank—a graduation gift from his parents, about whom he had "complained" that they had always been overindulgent of him. He planned to leave his job, and his plans included either getting a new one in this city, getting one in the city where he had gone to college, going to graduate school there, or going to the city where his parents lived and where "there were more interesting jobs available"; nothing in these plans was specific—no particular kind of job, no field of interest to study in graduate school. As soon as he made a decision in any direction, he immediately unmade it—with one exception: he did leave his job.

When he told his father on the phone that he had resigned, his father became angry and alarmed that the patient no longer had health insurance, and told him that he was coming to this city to make sure that his son would not be without adequate coverage, since he felt that my patient could not deal with this himself. While the patient had mixed feelings of anger and satisfaction about his father's reaction, he saw it as reasonable, since, in the event of some unexpected accident or illness on his uninsured part, payment would "have to" come out of his father's income. He was really shaken when I questioned this conviction.

Since leaving his job, Mr. C has not looked for another because he cannot make up his mind where he wants to be. Recently, I have begun to receive phone calls from him telling me that he is in his college town, trying out the waters there, or visiting his parents to investigate job opportunities in his hometown, and that he will have to miss his session.

In this instance, Mr. C has begun to act out his resistance to commitment and to adult status, his defiance of his father's overdetermined work ethic, and his transferential wish/fear that I, too, will indulge him by accepting his self-indulgence. At this writing, I have enough data to be able to deal with this situation interpretively and to impose the fee for such missed sessions on the basis of their function.

In short, what I do about these fee issues depends in large part on what I see as their message and meaning, and I try to embed my decision on what I understand is going on, so that the major thrust of whatever I decide is therapeutic in intent rather than simply business-oriented or countertransferential.

This is not to say that seeming flexibility cannot also be countertransferentially determined. As Bruch (6) points out, "nonattention to payment may conceal serious defects in the progress of therapy" (p. 15). She describes a psychiatric resident with a "deep interest" and "a warm and protective attitude" toward his patients, who attended sessions regularly. It was eventually discovered that none of them had paid any fees for a year, and that "little of what one might call dynamic therapeutic intervention had taken place with any patient. What had developed was a cozy mutual confidentiality, but without the exploration of any troublesome issues" (p. 15). Similarly, Fingert (20) described a therapist patient of his who "consistently charged low fees to his own clients, ostensibly to be kind, but during treatment he revealed his unconscious fantasy that he was not responsible for his results, because his fees were so low" (pp. 103–104). Obviously, these illustrations are not examples of real flexibility, but rather of neurotic acting-out on the therapists' part that are detrimental to the treatment.

One group of therapists who have an expectable record of undercharging or not collecting are beginning therapists. Meyers (7) studied a group of 20 first- and second-year psychiatric residents who were treating non-Medicaid patients in an agency with a sliding scale. Results revealed a variety of inappropriate attitudes and behaviors: (1) all 20 had at one time or another had patients at least one month in arrears, some not being charged; (2) of the 16 who preferred paying to nonpaying patients, 15 preferred to set the fees themselves, but 19 of the full 20 preferred that the receptionist collect them; and (3) all of them overestimated by two to three times the average fee their patients were paying. Meyers concluded that an educational approach was needed which would emphasize "the myriad transference-countertransference aspects of the patient-therapist financial interaction" (p. 1461). Well and good; however, personal psychotherapy is also necessary.

Buckley, Karasu, and Charles (21) asked supervisors for the most serious mistakes their trainees made; among the top 10 were wanting to be liked by their patients (top rank), stereotyped analytic stance, lack of awareness of countertransference, inability to tolerate aggression, and avoidance of fee setting. Pasternack and Treiger (22) studied the fee behavior of a group of residents in an outpatient clinic because, although many patients were being seen, not much money was being collected; there was a financial crisis. Exploration revealed "extraordinary departures from usual practice." Many countertransferential issues were discovered, and supervisors were instructed to pay attention to all fee issues, so that their dynamics could be clarified. In addition, an administrative setup was initiated which not only increased payment, but which allowed the supervisors and the trainees themselves to identify and discuss problems. The authors did not discuss the issue of therapeutic intervention.

Much has been written about the damaging effect of nonpayment or erratic payment on therapeutic progress. A study by Lievano (23) found therapeutic progress to be related to degree of initial illness and uncorrelated with promptness of payment. However, this is admittedly not a rigorous study, and nothing of the patient-therapist interactions is presented. Nevertheless, the suggestion is again clear that unorthodox payment issues are more related to therapist concerns than to the patient's well-being.

OTHER PERSPECTIVES ON THESE ISSUES

As I have written both in my earlier paper on this subject and in this chapter, I believe that a flexible approach to fee issues is more conducive to productive therapeutic exploration than is the more rigorous approach.

I believe these issues to be inevitable and to serve as a vortex of all kinds of irrational, psychodynamically determined feelings, conflicts, wishes, and fears. Just as money matters are problematic for patients, so they may also be to therapists. As in most other instances of inflexible behavior, the rigorous approach must be questioned in terms of what purposes other than income preservation it may serve. While countertransference may play some part in whatever stance a therapist may take toward fees, an immovable stance, it seems to me, is more likely than a more flexible stance to be countertransferentially determined, especially when it is attributed to patient rather than therapist factors. Such inflexibility may interfere not only with particular therapeutic enterprises, but also with innovative thought and practice which can advance the field as a whole. To conclude this chapter, I would like to present examples of such innovative thought and practice:

1. Freud and his early followers attributed all neurotic money issues to problems arising at the anal stage of development, and many present-day practitioners unquestioningly accept this analogy, despite advances in theory and practice. There are, however, a few who have gone beyond this on the basis of their experience and particularly on the basis of their thinking about the implications of theory.

Allen (24), for example, notes that payment or nonpayment may represent different things on different levels to different patients or to the same patient at different times: "giving or withholding of milk or nourishment, gifts or swearing, a vehicle for control, a phallus, power, or a bribe" (p. 133). It can, according to Allen, be in the service of the ego, the superego, or the id. Gedo (25) suggests that retained payment in the nonpaying patient may serve as a transitional object and thereby serve to deny separateness from the therapist, an interesting notion, although I should point out that transitional objects also serve to enable the infant's separation from the mother.

The most detailed impact of theory on fee practices has been presented by Blanck and Blanck (10). While I have indicated earlier in the chapter instances in which I felt their approach to be inflexible, it actually falls somewhere toward the center of the continuum. Significantly, their fee policies are presented in the context of theoretical consistency. As ego psychologists, they differentiate between the patient with a well-structured ego and the more disturbed patient. The former, they say, can both tolerate frustration and "function at that level of object relations which automatically allows for awareness of reality and for the needs of the other person" (p. 172). For such patients the traditional rigorous approach is strongly recommended and defended by them.

Some more disturbed patients, however, are developmentally unable to fulfill such requirements as regular attendance and payment. These patients seek gratification of their infantile needs. While the therapist cannot offer even the hope for such gratification, neither can he demand more than the patient can fulfill. This poses a delicate problem, because the therapist must be astute enough to set a fee that is neither too high nor too low. The major issue here is that too high a fee is a demand that the patient is too regressed to understand, whereas too low a fee is disruptive to progress. Blanck and Blanck view "tolerable doses of frustration" as necessary for growth because

> it is the experience of frustration that promotes differentiation of self and object representation. . . . The best guideline we can offer is to keep the requirements just slightly ahead of what the patient can fulfill, without insisting upon immediate compliance. This has the advantage of flexibility in relation to level of object relations and, at the same time, proposes that the goal of the therapy itself is the attainment of higher levels. (p. 173)

Thus, Blanck and Blanck really have two fee policies, a rigorous one for relatively well-functioning patients and a more flexible one for more disturbed patients; for the latter, they recommend flexibility for missed sessions and delayed payment as well. What is notable about this is these authors' ability to unite theory and practice in a reasoned attempt to develop an atmosphere in which the more disturbed patient can grow. This is a far cry from Menninger's (15) belief that the imposition of a rigorous fee system with no explanations is desirable because of the fact that patients won't understand the reasons anyway.

2. Hilles (8) found herself in the position of having been assigned a borderline outpatient who had not paid her bills for four years. Hilles wondered what happened to patients with symptoms in money areas. So, although she had been trained in the rigorous-fee tradition, Hilles decided "to deal experimentally with the nonpayment by interpretation, rather than as a reality problem which required immediate realistic solution. The meaning of the nonpayment and, later, of the payment became a major focus of the therapy" (pp. 98–99).

The bill and its nonpayment were discovered to have represented "many significant areas of conflict in [the patient's] life." In the first place, paying the bill meant giving up her negative identity with respect to her mother: "I resist, therefore I am. . . . " (p. 108.) She had a history of being a "bad girl." Not paying was also a way of holding on to the therapist because of what she saw as the clinic's large investment in her; paying would mean surrendering her last barrier against merging when she felt threatened by intimacy with the therapist: "If I did not get mad and throw her out, she herself could always declare the guilt unbearable and quit on her own" (p. 107). Clearly, these were very basic issues for this patient, issues that could never have been touched had there been a power struggle or termination over her "breaking the rules." She began to pay sporadically, stopping again each time significant progress was made.

The treatment ended when Dr. Hilles left town to take a new position. By that time the patient had found intimacy with the therapist unhurtful and had been judged well enough to be terminated and to be responsible for herself. At the end she paid a large bill and commented, "That is not much to charge for saving a life" (p. 108).

This summary does a real injustice to the patient's psychic entanglements with money and payment as well as to Dr. Hilles' patient and courageous departure from tradition, sticking with a difficult patient with the very kinds of problems which, in less creative hands, might have cut her off from treatment.

CONCLUSION

This chapter has been a return visit for the author to the area of the psychodynamics of interactions concerning fees in psychotherapy. In my earlier paper, I had concluded that holding to the traditional, rigorous fee policies was more likely than more flexible approaches to be determined by unsolved conflicts of the therapist.

In this chapter, I have looked at this issue again and have found no reason to alter that conclusion. In fact, the common emergence of countertransferential issues in beginning therapists who frequently go well beyond the flexible into chaos seems to me further evidence in the same direction; unless they deal successfully with the underlying conflicts, the need for rigid structure to counteract the chaos, however rationalized, will impede the exploration of issues in the treatment, thereby rendering it less effective because who the patient is is not taken into account.

It is important to reflect upon one's own approach to this as to any other set of issues, and to evaluate it in the context of one's own dynamics, one's continuing experience, and the rich world of evolving theory.

REFERENCES

1. Schonbar, R. A. The fee as a focus for transference and countertransference. *Am. J. Psychother.*, 21(2):275–285, 1967.
2. DiBella, G. A. Mastering money issues that complicate treatment: The last taboo. *Am. J. Psychother.*, 24:510–522, 1980.

3. Paolino, T. J., Jr. *Psychoanalytic psychotherapy.* New York: Brunner/Mazel, 1981.
4. Chessick, R. D. Ethical and psychodynamic aspects of payment for psychotherapy. *Voices,* 3:26–30, 1967.
5. Chessick, R. D. *How psychotherapy heals.* New York: Science House, 1969.
6. Bruch, H. *Learning psychotherapy.* Cambridge, MA: Harvard University Press, 1974.
7. Meyers, B. S. Attitudes of psychiatric residents toward payment of psychotherapeutic fees. *Am. J. Psychiatry,* 133(12):1460–1462, 1976.
8. Hilles, L. The clinical management of the nonpayment patient: A case study. *Bull. Menninger Clin.,* 35(2):98–112, 1971.
9. Freud, S. On beginning the treatment (Further recommendations on the technique of psychoanalysis I). In J. Strachey (Ed. and Trans.), *The standard edition of the complete psychological works of Sigmund Freud,* Vol. 12 (pp. 123–144). London: Hogarth Press, 1958 (original work published 1913).
10. Blanck, G., and Blanck, R. *Ego psychology: Theory and practice.* New York: Columbia University Press, 1974.
11. Schofield, W. *Psychotherapy: The purchase of friendship.* Englewood Cliffs, NJ: Prentice-Hall, 1964.
12. Lorand, S., and Console, W. A. Therapeutic results in psychoanalytic treatment without fee. *Int. J. Psychoanal.,* 39:59–65, 1958.
13 Nash, J. L., and Cavenar, J. O. Free psychotherapy: An inquiry into resistance. *Am. J. Psychiatry,* 133(9):1066–1069, 1976.
14. Mowrer, O. H. Payment or repayment? The problem of private practice. *Am. Psychologist,* 18:577–581, 1963.
15. Menninger, K. *Theory of psychoanalytic technique.* New York: Basic Books, 1958.
16. Haak, N. Comments on the analytic situation. *Int. J. Psychoanal.,* 38:183, 1957.
17. Kubie, L. S. *Practical and theoretical aspects of psychoanalysis.* New York: International Universities Press, 1950.
18. Davids, A. The relation of cognitive-dissonance theory to an aspect of psychotherapeutic practice. *Am. Psychologist,* 19:329, 1964.
19. Fromm-Reichmann, F. *Principles of intensive psychotherapy.* Chicago: University of Chicago Press, 1950.
20. Fingert, H. H. Comments on the psychoanalytic significance of the fee. *Bull. Menninger Clin.,* 16:98–104, 1952.
21. Buckley, P., Karasu, T. B., and Charles, E. Common mistakes in psychotherapy. *Am. J. Psychiatry,* 136(12):1578–1580, 1979.
22. Pasternack, S. A., and Treiger, P. Psychotherapy fees and residency training. *Am. J. Psychiatry,* 133(9):995–1110, 1976.
23. Lievano, J. Observations about payment of psychotherapy fees. *Psychiatr. Q.,* 41:324–338, 1967.
24. Allen, A. The fee as a therapeutic tool. *Psychoanal. Q.,* 40:132–140, 1971.
25. Gedo, J. A note on nonpayment of psychiatric fees. *International Journal of Psychoanalysis,* 44:368–371, 1962.

5

Fee Practices of Male and Female Therapists

Mary A. Burnside, Ph.D.

Money is an elusive topic in the psychotherapy literature and has been a difficult subject to address (1–5). Mintz (2) suggested that the taboo quality of the subject has resulted from historical, cultural, and personal factors which continue to present barriers to a more open and complete discussion. In his review of the fees and psychotherapy literature, Mintz (2) cited three major surveys of psychotherapeutic practice conducted in 1930–31, 1949, and 1962 and concluded that money was the most difficult subject for the respondents of all three surveys. His tongue-in-cheek summation was that "the most common denominator among various therapists in two different countries, over at least a 30-year period, had been a particular (i.e., reluctant) attitude about monetary transactions with patients" (p. 2). Similarly, in 1968, the American Psychological Association sponsored a survey of fee practices of psychologists which resulted in what was considered to be a very low rate of return (57%) compared to similar requests for other kinds of information at that time (4). Colby (1) has commented that anyone reading the three volumes from the conferences on psychotherapeutic research would never conclude that psychotherapy is done for money. "Either therapists believe money is not a worthwhile research variable or money is part of the new obscenity in which we talk more freely about sex but never mention money" (p. 539).

An equally elusive and unresearched topic is that of the differences in the practices of female and male therapists. There is limited evidence in the literature to suggest that there are differences in the ways males and females conduct therapy, in the way they are perceived by their patients, in the satisfaction of their patients with their therapy, as well as in the improvement of their patients (6–9). Given these differences between male and female therapists, it seems logical to extend this exploration of differences to the subject of fee practices.

This exploration is particularly relevant in light of the findings of an APA survey in 1980 of the annual earnings of all psychologists who were members of the APA (10). Women psychologists, roughly half of whom were clinical psychologists, were found to be paid significantly less and to earn significantly less in total annual income than their male counterparts regardless of employment setting, degree specialization, degree level, or years of experience since receipt of the doctorate. The authors attributed these differences to pervasive subfield segregation and pay inequities for women. Bureau of Labor statistics for 1983 show a similar difference in weekly earning for male and female psychologists ($417.60 for men versus $366.53 for women) (11). If a woman is used to being paid less and to receiving less total annual income than her male counterparts, what will the fee be when it is the female clinician alone who sets her rate of compensation in private practice? Ancedotal evidence (M. L. Bristow, personal communication, October 31, 1984) has indicated that a woman will set a lower fee than her male associates and will refuse to raise her fee even when her male colleagues urge her to bring it in line with theirs.

STUDY 1

The Public Information Officer of the local psychological association in a major city in the Southwest listed 53 clinical psychologists who received referrals for psychological services through the association. Requirements for placement on the list were state licensure at the doctoral level, membership in the local organization, and proof of malpractice insurance. When the executive committee of the association changed its policy early in 1983 and decided to encourage its members to provide low-cost services to people in need, the psychologists on the referral list were asked whether or not they would accept referrals for reduced-fee services. At that time, this change was not made a requirement for inclusion on the list. Responses to this request cannot be considered a random sampling of psychologists in practice. However, participants on the referral list represented a wide range of practice and years of experience.

All 53 psychologists on the referral list responded. Twelve of the thirty male therapists (40%) said that they would reduce their fees while 15 of the 23 female therapists (65%) said that they would be willing to reduce fees in cases of need ($X^2 = 3.3$, $p < 0.1$). Although the data did not produce a significant difference between male and female therapists in their willingness to reduce their fees in accord with patient need, there is a trend toward difference. Since this sample could not be considered random and information was extremely limited, a further investigation of fee practices of male and female psychologists was warranted.

STUDY 2

A random survey of fee practices of psychologists was undertaken approximately one and a half years later. Eighty psychologists (40 male and 40 female) in the city were randomly selected from the state roster of licensed psychologists and, in a brief telephone interview, were asked to state their fees for private practice work, their years of experience in psychological practice, and the circumstances under which they would reduce their fees. A single female undergraduate student blind to the study's hypothesis conducted all interviews during a two-week period. The interview process was discontinued when 30 males (29 of whom quoted their fees directly) and 30 females (all of whom quoted fees) had been contacted and provided information to the interviewer.

Male therapists charged significantly more for their services than female therapists ($t = 2.07$, $p < 0.05$). There were, however, no differences in interviewer ratings of male and female therapists' willingness to make reduction in fees on an 11-point scale ranging from $+5$ (very willing to alter fee) to -5 (not at all willing to consider a fee reduction) ($t = 0.866$, NS; see Table 1). Since less experienced therapists are reputed to be more flexible in their fee structures so that they can build up their practices, length of time in practice was examined. There were no differences in experience levels between male and female psychologists which could have accounted for the fee differences found ($t = 0.23$, NS; see Table 1).

An examination of the range of fees charged is also relevant. As shown in Figure 1, fees for the male therapists were tightly clustered in the range of $80–$90 per hour with a fair number of therapists charging $100 or

Table 1
Analyses of Means

	Males		Females	
	x	SD	x	SD
Fee charged (in $ U.S.)	86.0	9.81	79.67	13.39
Rated willingness to adjust fee (−5 to +5)	−0.133	3.07	0.533	2.78
Experience level	10.67	4.69	10.28	7.67

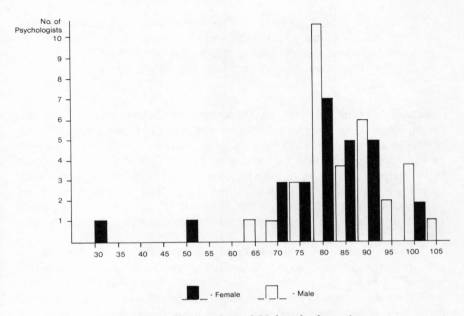

Figure 1. Fees of 30 male and 30 female therapists.

more.* Women therapists set a much wider range of fees, and many charged quite a bit less than the norm for their therapeutic "hour." Although information on standard length of session was not requested, a number of the respondents volunteered this information. It is interesting to note that the men reported more 45-minute sessions than 50-minute sessions (4 : 2) while the women conducted fewer 45-minute sessions than 50-minute sessions (2 : 7). The men seem to be charging *more* for *less* time spent with their patients.

DISCUSSION

The results of these studies can be summarized as follows:

1. Female clinical psychologists charge less than males in this southwestern city.

---

*Lest the readers gasp at fees for psychotherapy in this city, let me explain that it has long enjoyed a reputation as a city where rates were much higher than the national or the state average. Speculation about this deviation has centered around the low supply of mental health professionals versus the total population. This ratio has changed rapidly in the past few years with a dramatic influx of all manner of mental health personnel into the city. Fees have been fairly stable for the past few years.

2. Although, initially, it seemed that males and females might differ in their willingness to alter fees in case of need, there were no
differences found in interviewer ratings of openness to fee reduction.
3. It seems that male therapists conduct slightly shorter sessions than
females.*

Schofield (4) has posited that the avoidance of the subject of fees and,
by implication, low fees for psychotherapy is related to self-doubt or lack
of confidence, or, conversely, self-confidence and worth. Traditionally,
as a group, women have suffered from low self-esteem (12). Perhaps it
is not surprising that women psychologists in this city charge less than
their male counterparts. After all, there is a well-documented history of
pay inequity in the field which continues today (10,11); why would women
expect, and therefore ask for, as much remuneration for their services as
men?

Does this finding mean that women psychologists are accepting the sex
role stereotypes and "second-class citizen" myths which remain in our
culture? That was the conclusion that the male therapists reached when
their female colleague refused to match their fees—even though she enjoyed a professional reputation equal to, if not better than, theirs (M. L.
Bristow, personal communication, October 31, 1984). Nevertheless, factors other than sense of self and one's own beliefs about one's worth go
into the setting of a fee.

Women are reputed to be more empathic and to be better prepared
culturally for the role of helper and healer than men (8). As culturally conditioned *and* professionally prepared helpers, some women may be more
attuned to being good helpers rather than making money. The lower fees
of women may be related to altruism as opposed to lowered self-esteem.
Likewise, sympathetic understanding of the financial drain of psychotherapy may cause women to ask for somewhat less than men.

In addition, many female therapists, particularly feminist therapists,
tend to have practices that are entirely or almost entirely female. Since
women as a whole tend to have less purchasing power than men by virtue of their own reduced earning power, it may be that women therapists
charge in accord with what they believe these women will be able to
afford.

---

*Shorter sessions can have major implications for earning power. The traditional
50-minute hour (favored by women in the survey) allows for patient appointments every
hour with a short break for the therapist. If he forgoes his breaks, sessions every 45 minutes
allow the therapist to schedule more appointments in the day. The clock divides easily into
45-minute segments but not 50-minute ones.

Finally, it seems possible that the general population as a whole may devalue the services of women psychologists, thereby forcing women to charge, and therefore receive, less for their therapeutic hours. Pheterson, Kiesler, and Goldberg (13) demonstrated that women and men alike devalue the work of the female professional when she is an artist. It seems likely that this could be equally true of the female therapist. If a female therapist is devalued in general, it not only immediately affects her fee in terms of what she thinks she can charge, but it also has long-term effects on her practice. There will be significant competition among female therapists to get and keep the segment of the population "willing" to consult a female, also to get and keep the referral sources "willing" to refer to women. These groups of potential patients and referral sources are restricted compared to those available to men. With the resultant increased competition among the women psychotherapists, fee reduction seems likely in an attempt to get an edge on the market.

In explaining the findings of this study, it has been useful to postulate differences in financial opportunities attributable to gender (e.g., prejudices of patients and referral sources), sex differences in intrapsychic functioning (e.g., self-worth), as well as differences in professional practice that are gender-related (e.g., altruism, value on help over financial compensation, concerns about escalating medical costs, etc.). Although the scope of these surveys could not address any of these hypotheses directly, future investigations which ask practitioners how they establish their fees and fee practices would yield some answers with implications for these hypotheses. One word of caution, however: the psychological reasons for some of these practices may not be consciously determined and, thus, evident via self-report survey. Nevertheless, a multicity survey that gathers information on the characteristics of practice (including length of sessions) of male and female therapists from all the psychotherapy disciplines should be undertaken to extend this preliminary work.

REFERENCES

1. Colby, K. M. Report to the plenary session on psychopharmacology in relation to psychotherapy. In J. M. Schlein (Ed.), *Research in psychotherapy*. Washington, DC: American Psychological Association, 1968.
2. Mintz, N. L. Patient fees and psychotherapeutic transactions. *J. Consult. Clin. Psychol.*, 36:1–8, 1971.
3. Pope, K. S., Geller, J. D., and Wilkinson, L. Fee assessment and outpatient psychotherapy. *J. Consult. Clin. Psychol.*, 43:835–841, 1975.
4. Schofield, W. Psychotherapy: The unknown versus the untold. *J. Consult. Clin. Psychol.*, 36:9–11, 1971.

 5. Shipton, B., and Spain, A. Implications of payment of fees for psychotherapy. *Psychotherapy: Theory, Research and Practice*, 18:68–73, 1981.
 6. Gibbs, M. S. The therapist as imposter. In C. M. Brody (Ed.), *Women therapists working with women: New theory and process of feminist therapy*. New York: Springer Publishing Co., 1984.
 7. Kirschner, L. A. Effects of gender on psychotherapy. *Compr. Psychiatry*, 19: 79–82, 1978.
 8. Mogul, K. M. Overview: The sex of the therapist. *Am. J. Psychiatry*, 139:1–11, 1982.
 9. Zeldow, P. B. Sex differences in psychiatric evaluation and treatment. *Arch. Gen. Psychiatry*, 35:89–93, 1978.
10. Russo, N. F., Olmedo, E. L., Stapp, J., and Fulcher, R. Women and minorities in psychology. *Am. Psychologist*, 36:1315–1363, 1981.
11. Bodger, C. The sixth annual salary survey: Who does what and for how much. *Working Woman*, pp. 61–77, 1985 (January).
12. Sanford, L. T., and Donovan, M. E. *Women and self-esteem*. Garden City, New York: Anchor Press/Doubleday, 1984.
13. Pheterson, G. I., Kiesler, S. B., and Goldberg, P. A. Evaluation of the performance of women as a function of their sex, achievement, and personal history. *J. Personality Social Psychol.*, 19:114–118, 1971.

6

Complexities in the Psychology and Psychotherapy of the Phenomenally Wealthy

Peter A. Olsson, M.D.

It is easier for a camel to go through the eye of a needle than for a rich man to enter the kingdom of God!—Matt. 19:23.

INTRODUCTION

Almost all human beings covet phenomenal monetary success in conscious or unconscious fantasy. Relative financial success, while not equal to happiness or contentment, is certainly one important ingredient in both. Mentally healthy wealthy people apparently proceed to enjoy and adjust to their financially fortunate position. When wealthy, powerful, or influential people suffer from emotional illness, we clinicians soon realize the unique and unusual problems they encounter in the treatment process. We also encounter the complexities and problems in our own emotional responses during their often difficult psychotherapy or psychoanalysis. Unprocessed countertransference and therapists' envy and subtle condescension can add to the isolation of the wealthy mentally ill.

In his by now classic article, Weintraub (1) defines "VIP" as "any patient who has been able either through personal influence or professional status to exert unusual pressure upon the staff of the psychiatric hospital." The phenomenally wealthy clearly overlap and entwine with the VIP. Weintraub describes in rich detail the incessant quest of these patients to be treated as "important" and "special," and he gives practical suggestions for their clinical care and administrative handling in the hospital setting.

In this chapter I will attempt to provide a social, psychological, and psychodynamic theoretical framework within which the phenomenally wealthy patient can be understood. I will then proceed to discuss particular challenges for psychotherapeutic technique with these patients. A final section will deal with the conundrums of countertransference.

A CASE HISTORY ILLUSTRATIVE OF TYPICAL PROBLEMS

Tom is the middle child between two academically, socially, and vocationally successful older brothers and two academically successful younger sisters who have superficial but calm marriages to financially prominent men. Tom's father is a cool, aloof, quick-witted, "self-made" man of phenomenal wealth. Tom's mother is strikingly beautiful, in her sixties, and comes from a family of enormous inherited wealth. She is emotional, intelligent, but educated only in artistic, literary, and social areas.

Tom was first seen by a psychiatrist at age 17 when he attacked his older brother at a lavish family Christmas gathering during an acute crescendo of a paranoid psychosis. He was hospitalized for two months and never completed high school after this eruption. In the hospital, Tom was initially difficult with threats of violence toward staff and other patients. Soon he began to settle down, his hallucinations and delusions quieted then faded, and he began to trust and even grow close to his psychiatrist-therapist.

The family, however, after initial expressions of relief and benevolence, began to pose difficulties. The father would never approach the unit staff regarding Tom's passes, privileges, or family conferences. Rather, he had his administrative assistant call Tom's psychiatrist or the hospital director for reports. He would call himself to present demands or pose difficult questions which then had to be carried to the hospital conferences about Tom by the director. Tom's father insisted on late-night or off-hours visits "because of his busy work schedule." He offered to pay Tom's psychiatrist twice his usual hourly fee so that the psychiatrist "could be on call at special hours in light of the family's extensive work and social commitments." The psychiatrist politely refused this, and the hospital director refused a huge donation to "the charity bed program." Tom's father was visibly offended and acted slighted by the hospital. He became more distant from Tom's treatment. He never seemed to be able to schedule time for the family therapy sessions. Tom's parents often were gone on long weekends for "working trips" with business acquaintances to retreat houses throughout the world.

Tom's mother would infrequently arrive on the unit with her entourage and propose athletic activities for Tom such as lacrosse, cricket, and water polo, offering the hospital free equipment for those activities. She seemed to worship Tom's athletic prowess saying, "His father would have been a good athlete but his studies and work always prevented it." The therapy team was distressed at having to turn down some of her offers because Tom was indeed a good athlete and had achieved some positive self-esteem from his accomplishments in athletics.

In his therapy sessions, Tom told of his uneasiness at his mother's overinvestment in his body and athletics. He described how she had not been around during his boyhood "except at our championship games." He had really been raised by several kindly but permissive "nannies" whom he could manipulate. A kindly but firm chauffeur had once been fired by his father "because he had been too authoritarian with Tom."

Tom had begun study for his return to high school and was active at last in peer group therapy when his father abruptly withdrew him from the hospital, to allow Tom to go to Tibet for a lengthy mountain-climbing expedition "to build a positive self-image and become independent." The father would not listen to the psychiatrist's objections and barely accepted his pleas that Tom remain on medication. This disruption of flowering treatment was to recur on seven subsequent occasions when relapses of psychosis occurred. During several of these hospitalizations the father was either a patron of the institution or knew several members of the boards who aided his disruptive but benevolently couched "grand moves" for similar geographical-athletic cures. Between these episodes a diluted out-patient therapy was conducted by a "prestigious" psychiatrist, who was, at best, supportive and, at worse, infantilizing in his complicity with the family's control of Tom's treatment.

Finally, at age 32 Tom had a particularly florid, paranoid, and violent psychosis during which he held several family members at dangerous gunpoint before being subdued and narrowly avoiding tragedy. It was at this time that the original psychiatrist was again called in consultation. The psychiatrist managed to have a family lawyer draw up a written agreement of noninterference with treatment which legally appointed a guardian to administer Tom's resources until treatment was complete or solidified. Tom has since made modest progress, but still shows the sadness and loneliness of the psychologically underprivileged young man of phenomenal wealth. As Tom said, "One man's golden dream is another's prison."

THEORETICAL, DIAGNOSTIC, AND PSYCHODYNAMIC CONSIDERATIONS

Phenomenal wealth and its frequently attendant power, prestige, influence, notoriety, and accomplishment are like the proverbial emperor's new clothes. A closer, in-depth evaluation of the psychodynamics of money and great wealth will give us a feel for the texture of these golden garments.

TOWARD A SOCIAL PSYCHOLOGY OF MONEY AND THE QUEST FOR GREAT WEALTH

How do we account for the human quest toward the accumulation and preservation of money? Pulitzer Prize winner Ernest Becker provides a framework for us to address this question. To begin, he joins Tolstoy's lamentation:

> What will come of my whole life. . . . Is there any meaning in my life that the inevitable death awaiting me does not destroy? (2, p. 24)

Becker (3) proceeds:

> What man really fears is not so much extinction, but extinction with insignificance. Man wants to know that his life somehow counted, if not for himself, then at least in larger scheme of things, that it has left a trace, a trace that has meaning. (p. 4)

Let's examine in more detail the crisis conference Tom's effective psychiatrist held with his aging parents and his siblings. It became gradually apparent that feelings of affection or family love were overshadowed by family financial concerns for the future. The integrity of the family's lines of inheritance, future financial planning, and the related legalities were the most potent practical considerations that convinced the family to stand behind a solid boundary for his treatment plan.

Becker would view these current social and legal procedures as rituals specific to a society and culture and as "religious" in a broad sense. They act as vehicles for the transcendence of death. Becker (3) continues:

> The point I want to make is simple and direct: that by means of the techniques, ritual men imagined that they took firm control of the material world, and at the same time transcended that world by fashioning their invisible projects which made them supernatural, raised them over and above material decay and death. (p. 4)

This sets the scene for a social psychologist to view man as working for economic surplus of some kind in order to have something to give. Becker agrees with Rank (4) and Brown (5) that man has a core psychological motive for living in a group. Primitive economics rests on social organization as a vehicle for shared guilt. Society becomes a dramatization of dependence, an exercise in mutual safety, and an opportunity to achieve heroism and expiation at the same time (3, p. 32), "like the dutiful son who brings home his paper-route earnings and puts them in the family coffer" (3, p. 37).

Becker then leads us to "the origin of inequality." In his chapter by this title, he points out that even primitive man recognized differences in talent and merit that led to special privileges among men. Prowess in hunting, war, and later economics naturally led to tokens and trophies of durability power or immortality power. Becker (3) paraphrases Rank:

> This is the basic role and function of the hero in history: he is the one who gambles with his very life and successfully defies death, and men follow him and eventually worship his memory because the hero embodies the triumph over what they fear most, extinction and death. (p. 43)

Millionaires are remembered as begrudged or worshipped heroes of history as well as generals, political leaders, artists, scientists, etc. As Becker (3) says:

> Power is the life pulse that sustains man in every epoch, and unless the student understands power figures and power sources he can understand nothing vital about social history. The history of man's "fall" into stratified society can be traced around the figures of his heroes, to whom he is beholden for the power he wants most—to persevere as an organism, to continue experiencing. (p. 45)

Presidential financial advisers and stockbrokers suddenly became modern heroes who are psychologically kin to the epileptic who seizured and then "returned to life" in ancient times, or the shaman of primitive society. A shaman is a hero who "died" and is reborn unfailingly to regularly act out man's triumph over death. Becker maintains that one additional, unavoidable factor of human nature besides death is inequality. Becker asks us, "Why are men so eager to be mystified; so willing to be bound in chains?" (3, p. 50).

Becker's answer is that "man carries within him the bondage that he needs in order to continue to live" (3, p. 43). In essence, "men fashion unfreedom as a bribe for self-perpetuation" (3, p. 51). Becker uses a broad social context for the psychoanalytic notion of *transference* to account for man's basic ambivalence about freedom. In his applied psychoanalytic notion about transference, Becker holds that "people take the overwhelm-

ingness of creation and their own fears and desires, and project them in
the form of manna onto certain figures to which they then defer. They
follow these figures with passion and with trembling heart" (3, p. 50).
Heroes can be priests, lawyers, politicians, therapists, or economists, and
they were originally parents or, more accurately, their heroic imagos;
Kohut (6) would say, the idealized potential imago.

Becker (3) uses Rank (4) and Brown (5) in a brilliant synthesis toward
his final points about money.

> The record of the taming of man is found in the "immortality sym-
> bols" that men have used and discarded across the face of history.
> Unlike Freud, Rank argued that all taboos, morals, customs, and
> laws represent a self-limitation of man so that he could transcend
> his condition, get more life by denying life. (3, p. 65)

Earlier men figured out they could gain a kind of immortality by leaving behind earthly sons or daughters; now they became aware that they
could leave behind vast accumulations of other physical mementos of their
imagos (3, p. 74). As money evolved in the life of society and the average
man, gold became the new immortality symbol. Hocart (7) suggests a common origin for the gold coin, the crown, and the halo, since all three represent the sun or moon's disks. Becker (3, p. 79) points out that originally
gold, silver, or stone was in the actual image of a god; later, the tradition
with coins or paper money had been to imprint the images of divinities,
kings, presidents, and other heroes on the money. Through money, fantasies of divinity, cosmic power, and a new universal immortality became
the property of everyman in the marketplace. The coin or money seems
to link up with potential expanded narcissism and grandiosity, as well as
immortality in fantasy. Here a link occurs between the grandiose self of
the marketplace and immortality of the gods. In the collective "social"
unconscious, an ultimate paradox pervades an evolving unconscious
equation. Brown (5) spells it out:

> These accumulations of stone and gold make possible the discovery
> of the immortal soul. . . . Death is overcome on condition that the
> real actuality of life passes into these immortal and dead things;
> money is the man, the immortality of the estate or a corporation
> resides in the dead things which alone endure. (p. 286)

Money is too close to us and so much a part of our life that its deepest
significance escapes conscious effort, much like a fish being the last creature to discover water (3, p. 76). Grandiosity and narcissism link up silently in our unconscious meanings around money.

In summary, money is a special ritual of the group of living animals called man. It evolves out of a social structure of shared guilt, helplessness, dependency, and denied terror of mortality. At its deepest essence, money symbolizes and condenses our quest to deny death. Money is sacred immortality power. The core of the intrapsychic motivational dynamic of great wealth lies in the unconscious linkage of *immortality power* and the grandiose self. Money acts as the symbol of immortality power in the external world and the dynamic of unbridled narcissism in the intrapsychic world. These two are an intimidating combination of forces for a therapist to deal with.

Our complex theoretical journey now leads us to a place where we can understand the unique intensity of the dilemmas of the very wealthy.

> In its power to manipulate physical and social reality *money* in some ways secures one against contingency and accident. —Most of all, it can be accumulated and passed on, and so radiates its powers even after one's death, giving one a semblance of immortality as he lives in the vicarious enjoyments of his heirs that his money continues to buy. (3, pp. 81–82)

We will soon rejoin our patient, Tom, to illustrate some of Becker's final points. Tom also will help us study some of the dynamics and diagnoses of his colleagues among the super-rich.

DYNAMICS AND DIAGNOSES AMONG THE PHENOMENALLY WEALTHY

Any psychotherapy is a persistent, compassionate effort to change diagnosis, so this section will also by implication be discussing difficulties or potential impasses in the psychotherapeutic treatment of wealthy people. Some of the major problem dynamics mentioned in the literature are: 1) extreme ''narcissism,'' 2) sociopathy, 3) maternal deprivation and anaclitic depression, 4) paternal deprivation, 5) impaired identity formation, 6) geographical mobility or elusiveness, 7) weakened family structure, and 8) special problem dynamics around fees. Stone (8) writes cogently about these areas and cites depression, narcissistic character disorder, and sociopathy as the most frequently encountered diagnoses among children of the super-rich (9, pp. 332–337).

After his treatment program finally stabilized and his psychosis was in remission, Tom explored his conundrums about money. Even though he was of above-average intelligence, he was painfully aware that he could never master the spectrum of intellectual or social skills necessary to manage businesses or huge amounts of investment money. At times, he made brilliant suggestions that even impressed his father (quite a task), but these were spotty in occurrence. Long after the family had cognitively accepted his severe illness and limitations, he would repeatedly experience subtle rejections from his father's facial expressions, words, and deeds. At the other extreme, his father and particularly his mother would suddenly light up with talk of another mountain climbing, canoeing, hunting, or fishing challenge for him in some exotic corner of the world. During a tearful session he exclaimed in painful frustration, "I'm good athletically, but not great—never as great as my mother's brilliant stories of my trumped-up exploits. I'm sick inside; I would never be good without their guide and great white hunter friends!" His parents had just been confronted about how ill-advised a raft trip in Chile would be at a time when he was entering an advanced vocational course in welding. Tom had hoped to combine this with his excellent scuba-diving skills for a well-paying career in offshore oil rig repair technology.

In his discussion of money as immortality symbol Becker said:

> The new patriarchy passes on not only family immortality to the son, but accumulated gold, property, and interest—and the duty to accumulate these in turn. The son assures his own self-perpetuation by being "greater" than the father: by leaving behind a larger mark. (3, p. 74)

Tom's brothers were very able and active in this fulfilling process of self-perpetuation. Tom was not. He suffered the inner isolation, brooding, and empty despair so typical of the mentally ill and less successful son of the unempathic man of great wealth. In Tom's words, "I can see it in Dad's eyes. He looks away, fighting off disgust. He will never respect me because of what I will never be able to be." Tom did gain insight into his hatred of his brothers though and could understand why he had assaulted them in a murderous rage during his psychotic episodes.

EXTREMES OF PATHOLOGICAL NARCISSISM

Why do wealthy people have such a preponderance of narcissistic problems? Or, do narcissistic people simply gain more money? Classic analytic theory (10) proposes several reasons for fixations of personality during early development. One reason is *excessive gratification* at a stage of development so that the level is renounced only with reluctance. A second is *excessive frustration* at a given level causing the organism to refuse to go further, demanding the withheld satisfaction. A third reason is the *coexistence* of confusing excessive gratifications and frustrations. A fourth is *abrupt shifts* from excessive satisfactions to frustration. The final and most common cause of fixation is *satisfaction* of a drive and concomitant security against anxiety (10, pp. 65–66).

In Tom's situation we could document numerous instances of all five reasons for fixation at a level of the grandiose self or the idealized parental imago. He was traumatized by both his mother's absences and her unpredictable, overstimulating seductive attention to his body self and its athletic prowess. In simple terms, all children can be "spoiled" more easily in recent decades, but the phenomenally wealthy can do a more thorough job (8, p. 17).

In addition to classic formulations and self-psychological themes of explanation, Becker's ideas regarding *immortality power* deepen our understanding of the potential grandiosity and unbridled narcissism of the very wealthy. Further dynamic issues relevant to this subject will be presented in the sections on parental deprivation.

SOCIOPATHY

The core issue here is the capacity of a wealthy family to "bail out" their child when he or she is involved with antisocial or illegal behavior. Stone comments, "Wealthy parents, if they themselves are disdainful of social norms, may go to extraordinary lengths to nullify the usual corrective processes mobilized by society to contain or counteract antisocial behavior" (9, p. 334). Therapists' interpretations of these acting out issues are easily brushed off by wealthy patients with arrogance or aloofness.

In the later phases of Tom's treatment the psychiatrist learned that one of his psychotic episode's stress triggers involved Tom's finding out that his father had used some of Tom's liquid funds to enter a business venture of shady ethical proportions. Tom's violent verbal confrontations of his father led his father to have Tom committed to a psychiatric hospital!

MATERNAL DEPRIVATION

Stone (9) noted a strong depressive cast to the personality of many of his very wealthy patient sample and refers to them as reminiscent of Spitz's anaclitic depression of institutionalized children (9, p. 328). Stone notes a multigenerational pattern in the following observation:

In many families of the very wealthy, especially where the parents themselves had little emotional rapport with their parents, the mothers parentify their husbands, devoting inordinate time and attention to them, and correspondingly little to their children. The husbands, in these instances, are being utilized as mother surrogates, making up for the deprivation experienced years before by their wives. (9, p. 327)

Stone's further observations provide a probable causal association between the related issues of maternal deprivation, narcissistic personality disorder, and sociopathy.

In those families of the super-rich where it is meaningful to speak of maternal deprivation, narcissistic character disorders are usually noted in the mothers. Great wealth may attract great beauty, and some women who enjoy the latter are vain, self-centered and more accustomed to receiving adulation than to bestowing tender concern toward others, including their own children. (9, p. 328)

Tom's sister confirmed many of these traits in her mother when she "told all" at a family session.

PATERNAL DEPRIVATION

In the recent decade psychoanalytic theorists have begun to stress the importance of the preoedipal father. Munder Ross states:

Theorists have highlighted the role of the father as inviting children to separate from mother, discover their individuality, assume their gender identity and modulate and control the derivatives of their drives, especially their aggressivity. The effort has been to offset the relegation of fathers to the one dimensional tyrant of Oedipal fantasy and to flesh out the shadowy figure on the periphery of the mother-child dyad. (11, p. 170)

Tom's father was absent both physically and psychologically during his childhood years, and Tom was permitted few surrogates. Phenomenally wealthy fathers, in Becker's sense, often choose the road less traveled and pursue gold as an immortality symbol rather than the generativity issues with their own offspring.

IMPAIRED IDENTITY AND AUTONOMY FORMATION

Wahl advises:

Actually it is an important part of the analyst's sociological education to discover that the rich, being members of a small minority,
display many of the apparent identification difficulties that are generally characteristic of any minority group. (12, p. 75)

These traits of suspiciousness of outsiders, loneliness, and isolation cause
problems particularly during the rapport-building phases of therapy and
later when the analytic patient needs to identify with positive superego
traits of the analyst or therapist.

If very wealthy parents have a child with very subtle mental disorders,
they may regard the child with anger and scorn for years without realiz-
ing he was not lazy but was prepsychotic. This experience was particularly
vivid for Tom, and what little potential for autonomy he had was threatened by his father's scornful demeanor. The old adage "To whom much
is given, much is expected" can be a bitter curse to the offspring of the
super-rich.

GEOGRAPHICAL MOBILITY AND ELUSIVENESS

The phenomenally wealthy country-hop for many reasons. They share
with theater and movie stars the problem of irregular therapy sessions,
and the very continuity they need in the therapeutic relationship is ham-
pered by vagaries of schedule. It is not just the therapist's inconvenience
that gets involved but, as Stone points out: "In treating younger patients,
it is often the doctor's ability to establish personal contact and a good rapport with the family that spells the difference between success or failure"
(8, p. 27). In Tom's case it always seemed that his parents were in another
country just when he and the therapy team needed them most.

WEAKENED FAMILY STRUCTURE

Again the very wealthy share a common dilemma with the very poor.
Multiple marriages or extramarital affairs seem to be part of the life-style
of wealthy people. If the children are witness to or involuntary agents in
affairs of their parents, they may experience silent anguish and loneliness.

This is particularly so if infidelity or multiple marriage is not common among their friends' families. What is narcissistic entitlement to fathers is narcissistic injury to the children. A final issue in these situations is the difficulty of scheduling sessions and working with the complicated dynamics of his, hers, ours, and nobody's situations.

SPECIAL PROBLEM DYNAMICS AROUND FEES AND MONEY

As Stone points out, the family who pays for a member's treatment may always become obstructionistic, but the very wealthy tend to be more so in both degree and kind (8, p. 18). Tom's father's maneuvers of offering the psychiatrist a higher fee and donating to the hospital are typical efforts to control the therapist. The independent spirit and benevolent control a good therapist needs can be threatened in ever so subtle ways, as Stone (8) abundantly illustrates. The very wealthy, often because they can afford the "best," formulate a notion of the "best therapist" which may often hinge on glamorous trappings or social contacts rather than genuine competence (8, p. 25).

Stone makes two pithy statements here: "Awe and respect of physicians is by no means so common among the wealthy" (8, p. 33) and "Self-made men may, as they ponder the magnitude of our fee with the intangibleness of our 'product,' regard the psychiatrist as an incompetent charlatan at best, or an unscrupulous Shaman at worst" (8, p. 33).

Tom's father actually used some of these very words as he devalued the family therapist–psychiatrist who was trying to confront some of his ruthless manipulations of Tom and the family.

An often unexpected dilemma for the beginning therapist are the subtle phenomena of "hospitalitis" (8, p. 35) and "therapyitis." Here I refer to the tendency of some of the very wealthy families to want to keep the patient in the hospital or therapy indefinitely because they can afford to do this, whereas families of ordinary means or with limited insurance coverage cannot. In effect, this maneuver is to hire the therapist and/or hospital as the subtly devalued substitute caretaker, parent, nurturer, etc.

COUNTERTRANSFERENCE CONUNDRUMS
WITH THE SUPER-RICH

Wahl was told the following by a celebrity patient, about her two previous and unsuccessful therapists: "Both of the doctors were more like friends than doctors. They fawned on me, seemed to want to know me as a friend and one of them even asked me for an autograph for his daughter'' (12, p. 71). This illustrates how such a posture would never allow a transference to develop or be resolved. Wahl emphasizes how uniquely solitary, lonely, and depriving our work as therapists is. In light of this vacuum for recognition, praise, and sharing, it is possible to understand how easy it is for therapists to gossip, ''name-drop,'' or even cultivate friendships among wealthy patients. The therapist's unconscious unresolved sibling rivalries or old peer rejections are displaced upon the colleagues whom ''the great one'' has *not* chosen as therapist.

A particular reaction formation spectrum of countertransferences occurs when the patient is both very wealthy and a ''sex symbol.'' The therapist often moves into a chivalrous and quasiseductive behavior and dodges the steady work of interpreting the sexual symbolism in the patient's behavior. The therapist often merges in fantasy with the wealth, beauty, and immortality power of the patient. Another risk in this situation is an overly strong Oedipal and incestuous transference that is too intense to be interpreted (12, p. 73).

A third countertransference problem is the therapist's envy of the rich. Wahl states, ''Our education has often been obtained at the cost of great privation and sacrifice. If so, it is possible to preserve even into analytic adulthood an animated, if covert, hatred or envy of the rich'' (12, p. 74). The counterreaction to envy can be to treat the very wealthy patient as special. This often includes various forms of differential behavior on the therapist's part, for example, rearranging appointments too easily and with very short notice compared to other patients; greater efforts at gentleness and avoidance of interpreting embarrassing material; and finally a more ingratiating demeanor (8, p. 38).

Stone discusses the therapist's contempt for wealthy patients. This is usually a reaction formation to envy, but it may also result from the wealthy person's reflex ''pulling rank,'' self-protection devaluations of professionals, and sense of entitlement conveyed by Stone's pithy statement ''Among the very wealthy, some feel they do not have to adjust to life; they make life adjust to them'' (8, p. 41).

In general, many of the countertransference reactions to wealthy patients are those typical of reactions to the narcissistic transferences of idealization-devaluation or merger-twinship as they are described by Kohut (6, pp. 260–295). Basically Kohut advocates acceptance of admiration and idealization is an empathic but neutral way (6, p. 264). He advocates sympathetic understanding toward the mirror transferences and an effort to avoid boredom, impatience, and emotional distancing which are natural countertransferences to such twinship-merger transferences (6, pp. 272–275).

In fact, the transmuting internalizations that occur during the working-through process are analogous to a lot of lost time with an empathic parent in early childhood.

SUMMARY

I have explored the psychology of the phenomenally wealthy with a special emphasis on the unique contribution of Ernest Becker's Rankian view of money as immortality power. This view, when added to classic psychoanalytic theory and self-psychology, provides a refined theoretical vantage point from which to view the dynamics of great wealth. The core motivational dynamic of phenomenal wealth lies in the association and linkage at an unconscious level of immortality power fantasies (4) and the grandiose self (6). Money acts as the symbol of immortality power in the external world and unbridled narcissism as the intrapsychic presence of this intimidating dynamic combination.

This unique blending of Rank and Kohut might shed increasing light on the often bewildering states of pathological narcissism of the very wealthy and their problems with depression, subtle deprivation, sociopathy, and weakened family structure. I explored specific dynamic problems in working with the super-rich and discussed the enormously complex area of countertransference in the psychoanalytic therapy of the phenomenally rich and their families.

REFERENCES

1. Weintraub, W. The VIP syndrome: A clinical study in hospital psychiatry. *J. Nerv. Ment. Dis.*, 138: 181–193, 1964.
2. Tolstoy, L. *A confession*, 1882. London: Oxford University Press, 1961 ed., p. 24.
3. Becker, E. *Escape from evil* (pp. 4, 32, 37, 43, 50, 51, 65, 74, 76, 79, 81–82). New York: The Free Press, 1975.
4. Rank, O. *Will therapy and truth and reality*, 1936. New York: Knopf, 1945, 1-vol. ed.
5. Brown, N. O. *Life against death: The psychoanalytical meaning of history*. New York: Viking, 1959.
6. Kohut, H. *The analysis of the self*. New York: International Universities Press, 1971.
7. Hocart, A. M. In Lord Raglan (Ed.), *The life giving myth* (p. 99). London: Methuen, 1952.
8. Stone, M. Treating the wealthy and their children. *Int. J. Child Psychother.*, 1:15–46, 1972.
9. Stone, M. Upbringing in the super-rich. In J. Howells (Ed.), *Modern Perspectives in the Psychiatry of Infancy*. New York: Brunner/Mazel, 1979.

10. Fenichel, O. *The psychoanalytic theory of neurosis.* New York: W. W. Norton, 1945.
11. Munder-Ross, J. Oedipus revised: Laius and the Laius complex. *Psychoanal. Study Child,* 37:169–200, 1982.
12. Wahl, C. Psychoanalysis of the rich, the famous and the influential. *Contemp. Psychoanal.,* 10:71–85, 1974.

7

A Psychoanalytic View of
Personal Bankruptcy

*Lawrence M. Ginsburg, J.D., and
Sybil A. Ginsburg, M.D.*

Bankruptcy is a millennia-old sanction. Although the Bible (Deut. 15) provides for release of debt every seven years, a stigma is still associated with bankruptcy in most societies. Dickens wrote poignantly about the psychological toll exacted from family life in Victorian England by the debtor's prison of the day (1). Our federal Constitution, by contrast, at its inception specifically authorized the enactment of laws relating to bankruptcy.* Economic and social factors, peculiar to the United States, probably account for the historically higher incidence of formal recourse to insolvency proceedings than in other jurisdictions. The advent of lawyer advertising has in some measure conditioned our public to the acceptability of filing bankruptcy.

Society ultimately shoulders a significant share of the bill for debtors in deep default who develop health and marital problems. Caplovitz found that 50% of such debtors developed health problems as a result of their situation. Divorce, because of debt problems, ensued for 9% of those he studied (2). An individual hopelessly in debt is overwhelmed by the attendant pressures, which often operate as the psychological equivalent of a debtor's prison.

Jacobson wrote about the psychological effect of imprisonment on female political prisoners. Certain concepts advanced by her (3) confirm the prison memoirs of Sieverts (4),† who compared "the tremendous trauma

---

*The Bankruptcy Act of 1800 was the first federal legislation in the United States promulgated pursuant to the grant given Congress by Article 1, Section 8, Clause 4 of the Constitution: "to establish . . . uniform laws on the subject of bankruptcies throughout the United States."

†Incorrectly referenced by Jacobson as "R. Sieverts."

70

of arrest'' (even when clearly anticipated) with ''a catastrophe in nature or a sudden bankruptcy.'' Sieverts is quoted by Jacobson as having correctly described certain symptoms (''the initial state of 'helpless stupefaction' with 'blurred feeling and thinking,' 'anxiety and restlessness' and its 'transition to depression' ''), which Jacobson characterized as ''the outcome of a complicated psychological process'' (3, p. 334). '' . . . In the foreground,'' according to Jacobson's assumption, ''stands the sudden violent attack on the narcissistic safeguards of the captive whose personality is threatened by the executive power of the state . . . '' (3, p. 334).

It seems noteworthy that the psychology of bankrupts has been almost completely overlooked in the psychoanalytic literature. A number of hypotheses are suggested by this paucity of attention to such a fundamental and emotionally significant occurrence. Perhaps therapists are reluctant to address ''pocketbook'' considerations that they cannot remedy. A practitioner may argue that he is motivated by humanitarian concerns to mute or table the gravity of a patient's overextended debt load. Empirical observations do not support the altruistic purity of such a rationale.* Both participants in the therapeutic dyad are susceptible to insulating themselves from the reality of impending financial failure. Clinical case material demonstrates that certain core issues associated with insolvency are psychologically linked to resurrected fears about death and narcissistic injury.

A recent paper by Schafer described the treatment of a ''successful attorney'' who ''specialized as a consultant on bankruptcy problems'' (5). Clinically presented was the following constellation of psychodynamic factors:

> Analysis established that unconsciously he had chosen this realm of work because, among other things, it represented dealing continuously and only half-hopefully with death, the threat of death, and the making of reparative efforts, all matters with which he had been chronically concerned in an intensely anxious and guilty way. Analysis also established two of the leading reasons why he preferred the role of consultant: first, being only a consultant restricted the extent of his personal involvement with clients who, considering their extreme circumstances, could be expected to be highly emotional and demanding, and it restricted the extent to which he would have to be in on the often inevitable demise of their business ventures . . . . (5, p. 79)

Schafer's case illustrates the psychodynamics of an attorney who attempted

---

*See judicial reasoning and cited authorities in H. Jon Geis, P.C., v. Betsy Landau, 117 Misc.2d. 396–403 (Civil Ct. N.Y.C. 1983).

to master his conflicts about death and reparation by means of carefully balanced approach-avoidance involvements with bankrupt clients.

Bankruptcy arouses the terrors associated with both body and ego dissolution: it is the financial disintegration of the self. Psychological practitioners must be capable of mobilizing viable paradigms within themselves to confront these issues. Otherwise, they are vulnerable to defensive deflection while warding off the emergence of latent anxieties (i.e., correlatable with images of death, visions of physical mutilation, and other mental configurations of disaster). A conspiracy to ignore the patient's increasingly dismal financial situation may result. When the bankruptcy actually occurs, the denial may be superseded by shock and a judgmental attitude.

Case 1 and Case 2 presented below were law clients of the first coauthor. Case 3 was a psychotherapy patient of the second coauthor. None of the individuals involved were both law client and psychotherapy patient of the respective coauthors. The illustrative case material has been evaluated from a necessarily bifurcated frame of reference (legal and psychoanalytic) with the respective limitations of each branch.

Despite current advertising that urges beleaguered debtors to cancel debts for a "clean slate" in life, a high incidence of repeat behavior indicates that the advertised "economic rebirth" thesis, while operating as a defense against the anxiety provoked by the financial disintegration of the self, actually often proves illusory.

CASE 1

A 45-year-old entrepreneur, who overextended himself after a series of initial successes, voluntarily declared bankruptcy when confronted by numerous business creditors. Because ancillary legal proceedings were widely covered by the local television media, he opted at first for "on-camera" interviews against the advice of counsel. He welcomed the opportunity for such public exposure. He argued that it provided him with a forum to justify his questionable business techniques before a regional audience including his teen-age children, who could then view "the other side of the story." However, as the myth that he had been "forced" into personal bankruptcy by circumstances beyond his control disintegrated, appearances were scheduled in distant courtrooms where semiprivate entrance and exit pathways were available to spare him further television exposure. In conversations with counsel about lessons learned after his final appearance in federal court, the bankrupt flippantly commented: "What is good for a du Pont of Delaware is all right for me!"

This client utilized narcissistic defenses of omnipotence and grandiosity reinforced by rationalization and intellectualization. He was able to maintain these shields, along with a denial of responsibility for his predicament, throughout the entire experience. Painful superego conflicts involving guilt and shame were seemingly avoided.

CASE 2

An attractive and vibrant 34-year-old mental health professional, whose husband had deserted her and their four children, declared bankruptcy soon after she received a wage garnishment. She had been a twice-a-week psychotherapy patient over the preceding three-year period. Third-party insurance coverage reimbursed her psychiatrist for a substantial share of his fee. Outstanding balances in the low four-figure range not covered by insurance were partially reduced on a sporadic basis from income tax refunds as they became available. One of her children was in simultaneous treatment with another psychotherapist. When the patient's psychiatrist received a bankruptcy notice as one of many creditors, he contacted her counsel with shock and dismay, expressed as follows: ''I knew she was experiencing some financial difficulty. . . . I always thought of her as a plucky person. . . . But why me?''

In this case, the therapist colluded with his patient's transference and was seemingly unaware of their mutual defenses. The balances for that portion of the treatment not covered by insurance steadily increased, but were apparently never questioned. Throughout the course of treatment, the patient had been badgered by extratherapeutic creditors. Yet discussion of the extent of her overtaxed financial resources was avoided. When an outstanding bill for treatment surfaced in his patient's bankruptcy proceedings, the therapist voiced feelings of betrayal. Clarification of whether full payment for treatment constituted a manageable burden had never been made. Her bankruptcy declaration came as a surprise; the prospect of his unpaid bill on an equal footing with those of non-therapeutic creditors was anathema for him.

One may hypothesize that the pact to avoid confronting traumatic reality allows both patient and therapist to maintain feelings of omnipotence. The patient's belief that ''it can't happen to me'' is reinforced by the therapist's sidestepping of a central area of concern. At the same time, the therapist risks indulging in rescue fantasies and in a belief that his therapeutic repertoire is so great that he need not consider reality issues. This ''partnership of silence'' about impending financial disintegration is necessarily dissolved by personal bankruptcy. The patient's grandiose image of the therapist is broken. The latter rapidly becomes degraded, undeserving, and responsible for the failure. The therapist, in turn, is swept with negative countertransference commensurate with the degree to which he had been formerly gratified by feelings of omnipotence. Such negative countertransference, in the continued absence of minimal recognition of his own complicity, irrevocably ruptures the treatment relationship and the potential for postinsolvency empathy.*

CASE 3

An outside salesman in his thirties sought therapy because of depression. He expressed feelings of worthlessness and shame as a result of an inability to progress beyond supporting himself, his wife, and their two children in modest circumstances. He reported repetitive involvements in money-making schemes which ultimately failed. Although initially lethargic and self-deprecatory, he soon became hopeful and energetic. This change in mood corresponded with the announcement that he had embarked upon another business venture which, he was certain, would solve all his economic woes. Interpretations were made about the defensive nature of his excessive optimism. The patient was reminded of how he had repetitively coped with past feelings of failure by thrusting himself anew into ostensibly promising ventures which invariably proved unrewarding. Some insight was achieved as he reinforced the psychotherapist's interpretations by describing how his sexuality fluctuated in a manner that paralleled his financial prospects. Failure was perceived as emasculation, whereupon he ceased to perform sexually. Hope of projected success then operated to relieve his impotence followed by demands for frequent and often anal sex from his habitually submissive wife.

The motivation for insight, however, was not sustained, and the interpretations were soon disavowed with the assertion that "this time will be different!" The patient's credulity matched his need to negate the possibility of failure. In a hypomanic mood, he attempted to sell the latest venture to his psychotherapist: "You, too, should invest!" He characterized her as the one who was "ignoring the knock of opportunity." The new promotion drained every financial

---

*Biographical extracts of two famous personalities (the Wolf Man and Harry Stack Sullivan) that unveil some of the transference and countertransference reactions to financial insolvency have been examined elsewhere. See Ginsburg, L., et al., Some clinical and psychobiographical aspects of personal bankruptcy: A psychoanalytic inquest, *J. Psychiatry & Law*, 11:25–27, Spring/1983.

resource at his command. Eventually, he acknowledged that it was his wife's secreted wages from her own gainful employment which sustained them thereafter.

The patient paid his psychotherapist's bill promptly after each of the first three months he was in once-a-week treatment. By the end of the fourth month, it became apparent that he could no longer pay his obligations as they accrued. At the patient's request, further sessions were "temporarily" suspended until his "boat came in." He was certain the interruption would be brief in duration. Meanwhile, his wife had suggested that he pay a small amount of his overdue psychotherapy bill each month. No further word or remuneration was forthcoming from him during the succeeding months until his former psychotherapist, among other creditors, received notification that he had declared bankruptcy.

This patient struggled to fortify himself against the terror associated with financial disintegration of the self. He utilized a series of narcissistic shields, including denial and grandiosity and seesawed between elation and despair.

SUMMARY

Personal bankruptcy can be a traumatic burden for all involved, including the family and society; and its tragic outcome commonly includes blame, loss, renewed denial, and repetition. Professionals may be drawn into a defensive network designed to cope with private terrors aroused by financial disintegration. Illustrative case material has been presented to demonstrate the dynamics and defensive structure of bankrupts and the pitfalls for professionals working with them. The temptation for therapists to collude in denial of impending financial disaster, as well as the scarcity of psychoanalytic literature addressing the subject of personal bankruptcy, is probably attributable to resurrected fears about death and narcissistic injury, creating a taboo for all concerned.

REFERENCES

1. Dickens, C. *The works of Charles Dickens*, National Edition, 20 Vols. New York: Collier & Son.
2. Caplovitz, D. *Consumers in trouble: A story of debtors in default* (pp. 280–285). New York: The Free Press, 1974.
3. Jacobson, E. Observations on the psychological effect of imprisonment on female political prisoners. In K. R. Eissler (Ed.), *Searchlights on delinquency: New psychoanalytic studies* (p. 344). New York: International Universities Press, 1949.

4. Sieverts, R. *Die Wirkungen der Freiheitsstrafe und Untersuchungshaft auf die Psyche der Gefangenen*, Hamburgische Schriften zur gesamten Strafrechtswissenschaft, Heft 14. Mannheim: J. Bensheimer Verlag, 1929.
5. Schafer, R. The relevance of the ''here and now'' transference interpretation to the reconstruction of early development. *Int. J. Psycho-anal.*, 63:77–81, 1982.

II

MONEY IN THE THERAPIST-PATIENT RELATIONSHIP

8

Fee Policy as an Extension of the Therapist's Style and Orientation

Alan B. Tulipan, M.D.

As is true of so many aspects of psychotherapy, consensus is lacking regarding the theory and practice of the exchange of money—a ubiquitous transaction, to be sure. Controversy exists about such questions as how to collect fees, whether to charge for missed sessions, when to increase fees, and whether to vary fees for patients of differing levels of affluence.

Not only is there no consensus, but before this book was written, no determined effort had been made to bring some order into this most important and ever-present aspect of the therapeutic encounter. Since the literature about fees has been scant, the conclusion must be drawn that there is a general unwillingness to deal openly and actively with a transaction that may be justified within the context of the modern commercial world, but which carries, for some, an undesirable mercenary connotation. Psychotherapists tend to want to nurture their image as beneficent purveyors of good rather than as individuals who are at least partially involved in commerce. The result has been a gap in the literature that can only be the result of some degree of "selective inattention," more than likely arising from difficulties in facing up to the attendant conflict (1,2). It seems that each therapist has maintained his or her own idiosyncratic protocol—routinizing the practice of collecting monthly payments.

But the wide variety of operations surrounding fee collection makes it mandatory that we pay more attention to the process, either to formulate a methodology that can transcend differences in theory or, since this is not a likely possibility, to formulate an orientation that allows for individuality in the fee process, whereby variations are tolerated, but justified as an outgrowth of each therapist's integrity. That is, a therapist would validate a personal theory and practice regarding fees through their authenticity as a logical extension of individual style and orientation.

HISTORICAL CONTEXT OF FEE POLICY

Freud (3) clearly stated that he adhered rigidly to the principle of leasing a definite hour. "A certain hour of my available working day is appointed to each patient; it is his, and he is liable for it, even if he does not make use of it." He cited a threat to the therapist's livelihood if this were not so. In emphasizing the needs of the therapist, Freud courageously advertised that the physician is not only a selfless minister, whose altruism supersedes other more mundane considerations. Freud was partly forced to this conviction because he had, indeed, many expenses, brought about by a large family, a precarious practice, and a worrisome situation in Vienna in 1913 (4). "Gratuitous treatment," he said, "means much more to a psycho-analyst than to other medical men—namely, the dedication of a considerable portion (an eighth or a seventh part, perhaps) of the time available for his livelihood over a period of several months" (p. 352).

He also said that patients' resistances might increase enormously were they to pay no fee, sometimes forcing treatment into a stalemate. Thus, aside from the therapist's need for maintaining creature comforts, Freud was convinced that fees were necessary for eliminating deleterious interferences with therapy.

However, subsequent to these remarks, Freud himself flouted his own rule and, on his second therapeutic contact with the famous "Wolf Man," did see him for an extended period without charging him. In fact he collected from colleagues and pupils considerable sums in order to sustain the patient and his family—for a period of six years (4). True, the Wolf Man had returned from Russia stripped of everything and penniless, but the implication is that Freud was not above breaking his own rules. And nowhere did he indicate that therapy deteriorated as a result.

The cultural reference point for Freud's stated conviction that charging fees is a necessity was the Western ethic at the beginning of the century, when success, achievement, and affluence were closely allied, and when the patient's motivation for change was therefore considered likely to increase through the outlay of money. It was the reason for the conception, still held by many, that charging "'til it hurts" is a good propellant for change. It did, indeed, serve as something of a motivation, and still does at times. But as much as satisfaction and a sense of well-being accrue from financial gain, the outlay of money is by no means the only motivator in life—or in therapy. The pain of despair, an uncontrollable symptom, the intrusion of thoughts that interfere with productivity, the passivity that reduces one to mediocrity and loneliness—all serve as motivators as well. The very need to mitigate unhappiness can be the incentive that overcomes resistance to change.

It is questionable, at best, whether we do our patients a service by furthering the message that money is indeed a propellant and motivator by adopting the philosophy that it is therapeutic to charge until it "hurts."

THE RANGE OF FEE POLICIES

There is no question that charging a lowered fee, charging nothing, or accepting third-party payments changes the character of therapy. The patient will respond in consonance with other personal issues, such as dependency, self-esteem, relationship to authority, and inadequacy. The therapist will have to cope with personal feelings of resentment, condescension, martyrdom, power, and sanctimoniousness.

But the nature of the change, or its extent, is subject to widely differing opinions (1,5–10). Furthermore, any generalizations deserve careful scrutiny when one considers the infinite variety of reactions and attitudes within therapist-patient interactions. What is true in one instance may not be so in another. Not only do therapists differ in orientation, but each therapist will respond differently toward different patients, or differently toward the same patient at different times.

A therapist who has a firm belief in one therapeutic "technique" and follows therapeutic protocol assiduously is likely to have a set practice for charging fees. In the wide spectrum of therapeutic functioning, the other end of the scale would be exemplified by therapists who are "experiential" in orientation. This position might result in a broader stance regarding fees. The integrity of neither position ought to be impugned, as long as the therapist has a conceptual framework which is consistent with therapeutic principles and is consistent with therapeutic style and with the individual therapist as a person. That is, the therapist's messages and approaches should be free of personal and professional conflicts. Firm methodology in practice is fine with a mathematical-minded person. More flexibility is valid in one who tends toward free participation in a felt role as participant-observer. The former needn't be pejoratively labeled "rigid" nor the latter "sloppy."

It has been agreed that lowering fees—or even not charging at all—is likely to have an effect on the *process* of therapy. The question arises as to whether it has a deleterious effect on the *quality* or the ultimate *results* of therapy. Freud said, in discussing dreams (11), that if something is missed for either lack of time or difficulty in interpretation, the therapist need not worry, since the same material will surely show up in other dreams or in other contexts. That same principle will hold true relative to other issues. Problems—even problems with money—are not solely a function of whether or not one receives services for nothing. Psychodynamics are much more pervasive, for both patient and therapist alike. Money problems are closely tied to questions of dependency, inadequacy, competitiveness, status, prestige, and authority, and much will emerge in therapy referential to them. The therapist needs to regard the problems and proclivities of the patient regarding these issues and their relationship to money, as well as the therapist's own (12). Charging high fees means something. Charging low fees also may carry its burdens, not the least of which is a self-inflated sense of beneficence toward the less well endowed—a potentially condescending intrusion at best.

THERAPISTS' RESPONSES

Most often patients want very much to believe in their therapist and, no matter what, can frequently build their own set of defenses to prevent awareness of flaws, inconsistencies, and discrepancies. They may miss the mixed messages. However, when such inconsistencies are there, they register consciously or unconsciously and can become further evidence that this is the way people are, as they've been in his past. The experiential aspects of the therapeutic interrelationship confirm the patient's view, e.g., that dishonesty or fraudulence is a fundamental "given" among people. It is then a confirmation of a need to be wary, perpetuating the retention of defenses accumulated over a lifetime.

To avoid any such pitfalls, therapists need to examine very carefully not only their words and responses during therapeutic sessions (as assiduously as in student supervisory days), but other details of the encounter as well, including handling of fees. Thus, activities within the therapeutic encounter can encompass other extraverbal aspects of the relationship as well. The treatment experiences then enhance growth through their influence on the "corrective emotional experience" (13).

THEORETICAL ISSUES

Certain issues concerning the payment of fees have been left unaddressed in the literature, and practices remain questionable because of it. One seems at first glance to be simple—namely, is the fee a payment "for services rendered"? According to all other commercial transactions in our society, if the service is not rendered, no fee is paid. If one calls up the masseur and says that he's not well and won't get his massage that day, he certainly is not charged for the massage as if it were given. Frieda Fromm-Reichmann addressed this when she said that it is not the therapist's privilege to be exempt from the general cultural standard of not being paid for services not rendered. She goes on to say that "to a productive personality, such free time may be of the essence'' (14). It is this last conception that has led some therapists to split the fee with the patient as an arbitrary compromise, based on the fact that the therapist himself gains something because of a cancellation.

Freud justified, in principle, the mandatory charging of fees on the basis that otherwise it might constitute ''the dedication of a considerable portion of the time available for his livelihood over a period of several months'' (3, p. 352). He needed his fees because of the reality of his circumstances at that time. But what if another therapist, at the same time, were to have been independently wealthy? On those grounds promulgated by Freud, would this therapist have no justification for charging for missed sessions? Or suppose another therapist, not excessively wealthy, but satisfied with an ambiant life-style, chooses not to charge for cancellations and has simply averaged out the loss incurred in the projection of yearly income. In these cases, Freud's rationale does not stand up, unless other rationales are introduced, based on other principles, such as therapeutic efficacy.

Another problem arises when the therapist has to make a decision as to whether the reason given by the patient for a missed session is justifiable or not. How does one rank the excuse of a head cold next to an attack of renal colic? If there's a funeral to be attended, what about the relative merits of that of a first cousin, a best friend, a sister? And if transportation to the therapeutic hour is bogged down because of a severe snowstorm, is that any more valid than the problem of a flat tire? Are we really so perspicacious and wise as to be able to be judge and jury on these matters? Some escape conflict by charging no matter what. Others will relent at times, basing their judgment on an assessment of the validity of an excuse.

Still another theoretical difficulty arises when the therapist assigns a higher fee to one patient, a lower fee to another. This is often based on the capacity to pay. But how does the therapist justify this? Certainly not on the basis of a specific ''fee for service,'' for this would not then be putting a particular monetary value on a unit of service. If a patient being seen at a regular fee suddenly loses his job, or is separated from a spouse and burdened with outrageous legal fees, is treatment discontinued? Or does the therapist lower the fee, or charge nothing for a while because of therapeutic commitment to the patient? Is it out of beneficence? Charity? Altruism? An identification with the medical model of the indigent who reports to the local clinic for help? Perhaps. But if so, the therapist must be aware of possibly intrusive attitudes of condescension, the need for gratitude, one-upmanship, and guilt provocation. It's easy to fall into the trap. How can we get around all this? The best way is to start from scratch and examine fundamental attitudes toward therapy. The fee posture flows from this. The following is an example of the development of a particular position.

FUNDAMENTAL ASSUMPTIONS REGARDING FEE POLICY: AN ILLUSTRATION

Psychotherapist Y. is an interpersonalist. He believes thoroughly in the principle of participant-observation, and his participation is active and often spontaneous. He eschews rigid, formularized methodology because he is convinced that each relationship is different and has to be experienced anew. He would like (though he knows it is not completely possible) to eliminate all preconceptions and open himself to the uniqueness of the patient and the surprises in the therapeutic encounter. He believes in meticulous observation of the interaction, including his own reactions, but he tends to observe the *in vivo* process essentially postconceptually rather than with preconceptions which he feels might contaminate the reality of the encounter. In other words, he observes things within the context of the spontaneous immediacy. Truths and insights arise largely from the drama of the here and now—the past serving as corroboration and a means of establishing a cognitive understanding of the psychodynamics. The patient's present life, within and without the therapeutic relationship, provides the means for a compelling delineation of interpersonal patterns. In short, therapist Y. tends toward an interpersonal-existential-phenomenological orientation. Much of the patient's growth arises from his cognitive understanding. But just as much arises from the experiential aspects of treatment—the "corrective experience."

Central to Y.'s posture in therapy is directness, honesty, openness, spontaneity, confrontation. He is himself, with a sense of concentrated responsibility that compels him to focus exclusively on his and the patient's experience in the context of the encounter. He classifies his material along interpersonal lines.

How does this influence his fee policy? How is that policy justified theoretically?

He does not see the financial exchange as a "fee for service." True, he has background, training, discipline, and experience, and they all bear on his ability to help the patient in his quest for a satisfying life. But he feels that his main vehicle for effecting this is his own self—committedly, consistently, wholly. In individual sessions he might be querulous, confrontational, irritated, bored. He might say a little or a lot. This may not always arise from "skill" or from a preconceived therapeutic imperative, but rather from an immediate felt response, from a hunch, from intuition, from an acute observation of his responses, and from the interchange itself. Being his own self surpersedes, quite often, the ministration of technically "proper" offerings.

He has come to the conclusion that the patient's fee is best looked upon as a way of subsidizing him, the therapist. The money he receives, in the amount his patients can afford, provides him with a reasonably comfortable and stimulating life, free and devoid of the cumbersome details necessary for one who might otherwise have to compete in the marketplace. All his patients, as it were, "chip in"—some more, some less—so that he can have a relatively "clean" encounter with them, largely uncontaminated by undesirable artifacts (2). This concept of "patient subsidy" makes valid a number of his operations around fees which would otherwise be theoretically baseless.

For example, it provides a rationale for a variation in fees when, by chance, the patient's circumstances make it impossible for him to afford the "regular" fee. It eliminates a conscious or unconscious "preference" for one patient over another, or earlier termination for some, or a skewed approach toward the frequency of office visits. The interpersonal field remains intact, and since the life comfort of the therapist is cared for, he can give himself committedly to each of his patients.

It also allows for a greater flexibility regarding the matter of charging for missed sessions. Therapist Y. actually does not normally charge for them. He has taken into consideration that in the course of a year a certain number of hours will be missed, and by and large this will average out among his patients. He has developed a fee scale that allows for this, and he does not feel he suffers thereby. He has two reasons for his policy. First, he does not feel he has the wisdom to judge the validity of a given excuse for a missed session. He certainly wants to find out the reason, for it may carry significant therapeutic messages. And certainly if it appears to be happening with some frequency, he'll need to deal with that in the therapeutic context, and it may, indeed, result in a revision of the policy with a particular patient and be mutually agreed upon. But generally, the therapist does not feel exploited, deprived, or aggrieved because of an occasional missed hour.

There is a second reason for not, as a rule, charging for missed hours. An alternative to making arbitrary decisions is to charge uncompromisingly for all cancellations. But therapist Y. cannot do this according to his orientation. He does not see psychotherapy as being adversarial in nature, a struggle between a patient who is determined to remain embedded in his neurosis struggling with a therapist who is trying to extricate him from

it. Rather, he characterizes therapy as a mutual attempt at moving toward
a goal in the context of a fundamentally trusting relationship. He does not
deny the presence of resistances, but if trust is to pervade the encounter,
it has to go both ways. Therapist Y. would tend to value the patient's
reason for missing a session, rather than viewing it as a defensive retreat.
He may, indeed, be proved wrong. But his initial assumption of pre-
sumptive trust flows from his basic approach.

He bills by mail, rather than handing out statements directly to his patients at the end of the month. This is because he's found that his immediate involvement with his patients at that end-of-the-month hour often
causes him to become forgetful about handing out the bill, and he has to
encumber himself with what he feels to be the burden of remembering
it next time. He recognizes that he may miss a reaction or two regarding
the patient and money, but as has been said, the psychodynamics are
more than likely to arise at another point in therapy anyway.

He upgrades his fee scale from time to time, to care for his own needs,
but he is flexible enough to keep certain of his patients at their former scale
if they cannot afford the increase. He feels strongly that he has made a
serious commitment to them, and he won't let their inability to pay the
extra amount interfere with that commitment. His increased fee is primarily designed for any new patients he may see. The "patient subsidy" concept outlined previously is sufficient rationale for this.

In the end, his particular fee structure provides him with relative peace
of mind, so that he doesn't have to spend a lot of emotional energy worrying about the well-being of his family or himself. It provides him his
comforts as well as the opportunity to travel, to enjoy his leisure time,
to pursue his interests, to attend meetings when he feels like it, and to
be sick without financial concern. He also knows that he doesn't have to
work any more hours than would be compatible with the kind of atten-
tiveness and responsibility he owes his patients.

CONCLUDING REMARKS

This is but one of many possible ways of looking at fees. It flows inex-
orably from one therapist's posture regarding psychotherapy itself. But
it also emanates from his personal style, an attitude toward his life, and
it is congruent with his felt needs as a practitioner as well as needs for
leisure, family interaction, and a stimulating life in and out of the office.

It would be well if therapists were to examine carefully their own
policies, to determine whether their professional activities are at one with
other parts of themselves. Psychotherapeutic routines are often estab-

lished thoughtlessly, by emulation of a respected therapist, or a "guru," or a "how-to" text. The simple assumption of a process, concerning fees as well as a number of other transactional processes, can prove to be inimical to a productive therapeutic relationship. A better atmosphere is generated through a reexamination of the congruence of practice and its roots in personal style and theoretical orientation. The resultant overall consistency will prove most salubrious to both patient and therapist alike.

REFERENCES

1. Chodoff, P. Psychoanalysis and fees. *Compr. Psychiatry*, 5:137–145, 1964.
2. Tulipan, A. B. Fees in psychotherapy: A perspective. *J. Am. Acad. Psychoanal.*, 11:445–463, 1983.
3. Freud, S. Further recommendations in the technique of psychoanalysis. On beginning the treatment. The question of the first communications. The dynamics of the cure (1913). In *Collected papers*, Vol. II. London: Hogarth Press, 1949.
4. Jones, E. *The life and work of Sigmund Freud*, Vol. 2. New York: Basic Books, 1955.
5. Lorand, S., and Console, W. A. Therapeutic results in psychoanalytic treatment without fee. *Int. J. Psychoanal.*, 39:59–65, 1958.
6. Gray, S. H. Does insurance affect psychoanalytic practice? *Bull. Phil. Assoc. Psychoanal.*, 23:101–110, 1973.
7. Chodoff, P. The effect of third-party payment on the practice of psychotherapy. *Am. J. Psychiatry*, 129:540–545, 1972.
8. Menninger, K. A., and Holzman, P. S. *The theory of psychoanalytic technique*, 2nd ed. (p. 31). New York: Basic Books, 1973.
9. Nash, J. L., and Cavenar, J. O. Free psychotherapy: An inquiry into resistance. *Am. J. Psychiatry*, 133:1066–1069, 1976.
10. Halpert, E. The effect of insurance on psychoanalytic treatment. *J. Am. Psychoanal. Assoc.*, 20:122–133, 1972.
11. Freud, S. The employment of dream-interpretation in psycho-analysis (1912). In *Collected papers*, Vol. II. London: Hogarth Press, 1949.
12. Singer, E. *Key concepts in psychotherapy*, 2nd ed. New York: Basic Books, 1970.
13. Alexander, F., and French, T. *Psychoanalytic theory: Principles and applications.* New York: Ronald Press, 1946.
14. Fromm-Reichmann, F. *Principles of intensive psychotherapy.* Chicago and London: The University of Chicago Press, 1950.

9

The Effect of Fees on the Course and Outcome of Psychotherapy and Psychoanalysis

James Raney, M.D.

In 1912 Freud recommended a particular fee arrangement as most appropriate for psychoanalytic therapy (1). The fee, according to Freud, should provide the therapist an adequate living and should be charged for all scheduled appointments with the exception of those that the analyst cannot keep. The "material existence" of the therapist as well as the integrity of the therapy should be protected. Freud noted that missed sessions, even those missed because of illness, become infrequent with this arrangement. Modern methods of assessment and validation of unconscious mental functioning have demonstrated that Freud's original recommendations continue to be correlated with optimal therapeutic outcome in a wide variety of psychotherapies.

PSYCHOANALYTIC ASSESSMENT AND FEES

Patients in any therapy, when they are permitted to speak, reveal unconscious meanings of the actions of the therapist and the conditions of the therapeutic situation in accordance with consistent psychological mechanisms (2). Aspects of perceptions are problematic or conflicted and therefore are relegated to unconscious mentation. These aspects appear as *derivative* expressions (3–7). Derivatives are disguised, indirect allusions to important perceptions and thinking that is unconscious to the patient. The ego or adaptive "organ" of the mind keeps some part of the perception of the therapist unconscious and modifies the ultimate expression of these perceptions and thinking to make them acceptable to the conscious awareness. Derivatives are compromises or an amalgam of images that suit the patient's mental structures and objects as well as the patient's perception of the dangers in the external world (4,5). Patients allude via derivatives to these unconscious aspects of the perceptions that they make of actions and intentions of their therapists. Both the meanings and the particular images that constitute the derivative expressions of these perceptions are colored by the patient's individual personality and prior experience.

The patient may unconsciously perceive and work over the actions and intentions of the therapist in contradistinction to the therapist's view of his or her own intent and action or intervention. This dichotomy may occur *even when the patient shows symptomatic improvement*. For example, patients may welcome advice, suggestion, medication, and a forgiving fee arrangement. At the same time they may unconsciously feel and express derivative images of being invaded, abused, or mistreated. While lack of symptomatic improvement is a good indication that the therapy is failing, symptomatic improvement *per se* is not a reliable sign of successful psychotherapy (6).

The importance of attention to the fee in psychotherapy is based on the need to close off an avenue of action that can interfere with interpretation and understanding. The fee is a part of the therapeutic frame (8,9) which is the vehicle for the introjection or "taking in" of the therapist. Introjection of the therapist and therapeutic process seems to be an important determinant of favorable therapeutic outcome.

Short-term (10,11) studies of the effects of therapeutic procedures have shown that therapists influence patients by what they do as well as what they say. In long-term (i.e., several years after psychotherapy) follow-up former patients report a sense of a benevolent and neutral presence (the "memory" of the analyst) and an ability to self-analyze and solve problems with a greater sense of confidence (12). These findings seem to contradict the analysis of resistance as the *sine qua non* of psychoanalytic therapy. With the advent of ego psychology the "removal" of resistance has been replaced by "analysis" of the resistance, but the belief persists that interpretation is the critical factor in successful outcome. This belief is supported by symptomatic "cures" that can be variously explained. Nevertheless, because it is not mentioned, the effect of the fee arrangement on the outcome has yet to be measured in long-term outcome studies (12,13). For that matter, no long-term outcomes or cures have been explained or correlated with any other interventions or specific therapeutic activities that have been made during the course of the therapy.

In the past few years a few authors have applied psychoanalytic assessment to their fresh clinical anecdotes as well as case reports from the previous literature in which fee arrangements can be identified (5,14). Studies have not been limited to psychoanalytic therapies. Similar reactions and meanings of the fee appear in many different therapies and settings (15–18). Evidence in all of these studies supports conjectures made by earlier writers that the fee presents an especially important and, when it is varied in some respect, problematic element in the therapy situation.

In cases where the fee is adequate at the beginning and handled in the standard fashion, very little can be identified in the derivatives that refer specifically to the fee. Patients more often affirm the overall management of the secure therapeutic frame of which the standard fee is one element. The fee becomes apparent and significant when there is a problem. Because no long-term follow-up studies have been made of the effect of the fee, long-term effects of any fee arrangements must be extrapolated from the more immediate results that have been discerned during the course of therapy. As these periods during the course of therapy can be months or years, lasting effects beyond therapy termination would seem likely. Negative or positive "short-term" (i.e., during therapy) effects can be hypothetically correlated with corresponding long-term outcome.

DYNAMICS OF THE ADEQUATE
FEE ARRANGEMENT

Psychoanalysts have for the most part agreed with, although not necessarily followed, the standard fee recommendations since Freud wrote of them (19). A few conjectures have been made about the dynamics of the basic arrangement. For example, the adequate fee arrangement has been justified on the grounds that the patient must feel some sacrifice (20,21) in order to benefit. There is more recent support for another concept that sacrifice is not as important as the meaningfulness of the fee. The money paid is, on one hand, symbolic of the patient's worth. On the other hand, both the patient and analyst know that the fee becomes a significant part of the analyst's livelihood. The basic fee arrangement is a statement that a commitment is expected from both parties. The therapist endeavors to adhere to his or her side of the commitment, for example, by minimizing absences other than the usual vacations that are announced well ahead of time.

In addition, the "rigorous system of payment" can also symbolize the analyst as a person who dares to accept the aggressions of the patient without the fears that have characterized prior figures in the patient's life. The patient can examine the pathogenic aspects of his parental objects in the light of this new person as well as experience the related impulses, drives, and/or their vicissitudes in comparative safety. The therapist can also be perceived as one who dares to defy the general hypocrisy about money as he takes good payment for all the appointments. The patient may utilize this characteristic as a component of an introjected new object.

The adequate fee arrangement can have an effect on passivity and masochistic and aggressive conflicts that may not be as efficiently addressed with interpretations alone. The frustration of dealing with a therapist who knows what he wants and will not be compromised, directed, or frightened addresses passive and masochistic tendencies in the patient. Although the patient may still suffer under the regime, the consistent alternative of the autonomous therapist introject makes this position difficult to maintain. The patient is unable to injure the analyst or exhaust his patience via the fee. An adequate fee is sufficient compensation in reality for the inevitable aggressions that are part of successful treatment. The patient has no further realistic debt of gratitude, or gratitude's darker companion, guilt (19).

Case 1

A patient was not charged for missed appointments. After he canceled an appointment, he alluded to images of betrayal, to his mother who once remarried in his absence, and to other disturbances. After a second cancellation, he alluded to clients who waste his time. He had decided to bill one of them for the time spent. He missed having an appointment last time. He mentioned a spoiled colleague who kept everyone waiting at meetings and who finally was told to keep the schedule because he was interfering with the work of others. A dream of a pile of Christmas presents awakened him in a cold sweat. He spoke of spoiling his children with gifts and "buying them off." When the therapist linked these images to the cancellation without charge, the patient recalled worrying at the time of the first cancellation that his time would be filled. A firm contract and not getting just monetary gifts was important. Gifts made especially for him were the most valuable (a reference perhaps to the interpretation). The patient then suggested that he be charged for canceled sessions (17).

Case 2

A patient has been allowed, because of financial troubles, to defer paying a prior fee, although he pays each month for his current analysis. The analysis seems stagnant. Over several hours the patient has alluded to efforts of others to get him to perform. People try to get his money. Up to this time the analyst had not interpreted anything about the ongoing debt. In one hour the patient told how angry he had been at a drunk who had tried to "dun" him and said he would not pay him a cent. When he described this, he felt very anxious and uneasy, as if he were slipping on banana skins. When the analyst made an interpretation that connected these images as references to the unpaid fee, the patient paid the debt and the analysis appeared to begin to move again (14).

DYNAMICS OF VARIATIONS IN THE STANDARD FEE

Early writers (20,21) worried that fees paid by foundations or government might make the analysis "a matter of indifference," of little value and therefore ineffective. Low fees or free therapy produce feelings that the therapy is charity or a sense of guilt that the patient is taking up time that could be used by someone else more needy (22). In patients of low social class no fee or fees paid for with coupons reinforce a perspective of second-class social status.

Case 3

A patient chafed at her need for free clinic treatment with an allusion to a friend who had been nice to her. She could never repay the friend nor could she speak freely to her, especially about money. Her free therapy was like food stamps, the sign that she was a second-class citizen. She did not feel that the therapist accepted her. She has to give up a lot and would like to be in private therapy that she paid for so she could say whatever she wanted (15).

This example resembles other studies of middle-class clinic settings in which patients view themselves as special cases or favored children when their fee is proportionately too low to provide the therapist with a living (23).

CAN MODIFIED FEES BE "ANALYZED"?

Both psychoanalysts and other therapists argue that modifications can be analyzed without returning to the basic secure therapeutic frame of psychotherapy. Some say that low fees and third-party payors have little effect or can be analyzed (24,25). Despite these assertions, there is little evidence that useful interpretations can be made of variations in the standard fee arrangement. Interpretations may appear to be validated if the patient's associations are taken only at their face value. Grateful patients, especially where fee modifications are involved, obligingly provide responses that are compliant, intellectualized, gratifying, and therefore quite reinforcing to whatever the therapist has done. The therapist who listens for derivatives, however, hears implicit meanings of the derivatives that contradict the manifest responses. Images of seduction, of people who cannot be trusted, people who will take advantage, or who want to benefit at the expense and detriment of others are common. Excessive fees or fees accepted in advance evoke similar images.

Nash and Cavenar (22) were in partial agreement in their conclusion that patients with overt sexual identity problems could not be treated for no fee. Such patients harbor the belief that the therapist wants sexual favors in lieu of the fee. This belief seemed unresponsive to interpretation alone. They concluded that the absolute fee was not an issue as long as some fee was charged. Nash and Cavenar provided no evidence for their assertions. Other studies, utilizing case vignettes that include, but are not limited to, patients with sexual identity issues, confirm the idea that the fee must be charged, but they also show that charging an appropriate fee, one that adequately compensates the therapist, frees the patient of obligation, compromised self-worth, and concerns about what else the therapist may want.

Case 4

Hodges (16) gave an example that appears to have included a substantial fee, but it was paid in part by third parties. Allusions to homosexuality and interrupted motivation seemed related to the fee. Derivative images suggested an unhealthy alliance that was taking place unbeknown to the participants.

In this case a therapist accepted payment from the patient's parents. In one session the patient referred to continued drug use and images of threesomes and things that needed to be fixed. The therapist's intervention linked the patient's continued drug use to some aspect of the therapy. No response was discernible, and the patient paid the therapist with another check from his parents. This time the therapist left the check out in the patient's view at the next session. The patient asked about the check and was directed to see what came to his mind. He said that he continues to use drugs and should stop. Sometimes he comes to his sessions "stoned." His parents always bail him out of jams with money. He should get a second job so he could pay for his own car repairs. His boss offers him beer and marijuana during work. A girl friend got government checks that supported both of them, which was bad because it encouraged both not to work. He doesn't feel that he is getting any better.

The therapist suggested that the images referred to mutual dependency on an outside financial source and the therapist may be much like his boss, dependent and incapable of providing good solutions to problems. Furthermore, some of the images suggested a need for more self-control by the patient's managing the finances of the therapy himself. The patient replied by doubting that he could do that and recalled a time when he and a friend got drunk and something homosexual may have happened. He nevertheless wants to continue the therapy. The patient brought his own check to the next session and described his improved control over drugs and alluded to people who were helping him by example (16).

Case 5

In this instance homosexual anxiety and fantasy disappeared when the fee was raised from a discounted to a full fee.

The fee of a young man in four-times-a-week analysis had been negotiated to about half the analyst's usual fee because of finances. After two years of analysis the patient reported that each morning he imagined that the analyst would anally rape him. This fantasy was so vivid that he would pull up his pants with his back to the bedroom wall so no one could get behind him. The patient had increased his income significantly in the two years. The fantasy persisted despite interpretations about homosexual wishes, feeling helpless in several situations, and the possibility that the fantasy may express a fear that the analyst might exact the balance of the fee through sexual favors. The analyst raised the fee, and no further fantasies were reported until shortly before termination when he reported one or two brief recurrences (14).

The disappearance of the fantasy suggested that it was the manifest expression of the unconscious fear (wish) that he was indebted by the low fee and thus attached via his anus to the analyst. The low fee and fantasy of attachment via the anus seemed to be an uneasy narcissistic truce. The patient endeavored to create financial independence, which was ambiguously the means for independence from the therapist. To *have* money would be a way of holding therapist/mother within him (in his bank account). With the fee discounted, the money he saved or withheld was in reality the therapist's property and, in fantasy, a part of the therapist. To relinquish the money was to free himself, but, in another way, to separate from the therapist with "no strings." This independence, although desired, also threatened separation and loss of the analyst object. The brief fantasies at termination were evidence of the latter.

No evidence of anything similar to homosexual rape was obtained in this man's history, but the theme of pathological attachment via guilt to his mother, her manifest disappointment in his father, and her use of the patient as a confidant were common themes. His mother's periodic psychotic depressions and production of several more babies during his first decade implied real neglect with anal phase stimulation and excitement, conflict, and fixation. These may have been the "palette" for the construction of the fantasy that was triggered by the discounted fee.

Variations in the fee arrangement can be analyzed only when a full fee has been reestablished. The sufficient fee seems to remove the reality basis for obligation and acting out, with the fee, the gratifying privileged position or the discouraging nonprivileged second-class status. Wishes, resentments, and self-concepts as well as views of the world/therapist can be expressed and interpreted more freely in the context of an adequate fee.

THIRD-PARTY PAYMENT

Not surprisingly, studies of insurance-supported psychotherapy mainly show that, when insurance is available, people tend to use it to pay for their psychotherapy. For example, the well-known West German study (26) utilized relapse rates, hospitalizations, and self-descriptions of patient satisfaction to conclude that psychoanalytic therapy conducted with insurance support improved the pretreatment states of the patients. These manifest results give no idea of the internal changes of the patients. Noninsured therapy was not compared in this study. These and similar studies indicate only that psychotherapy reduces symptoms, but nothing about the influence of insurance in the therapeutic process. No studies have been done that compare individuals or populations with only the payment method as the variable. It is feasible to make comparisons with and without insurance in the study of single patients. A few anecdotal examples of these comparisons, rare in the published literature, appear in this chapter.

At the time of this writing there are also no studies of third-party payment by agencies, government, insurance, or relatives that separate the reporting, diagnosing, confidentiality breaches, and assumptions that the patient is untrustworthy (by requiring the therapist to sign the claim, for example) from the payment method alone. These other aspects of third-party payors, whether insurance carriers or relatives, create such over-shadowing evidence of indignation, intrusiveness, and other reactions that the fee payment factor cannot be clearly discerned (14).

Third-party fee arrangements seem to lead to indifferent or flat thera-pies with only vague allusions to the reasons for the paucity of progress. Patients are loath to progress when fee variations are followed by allu-sions and images of unconsciously felt gratifications, bonuses, or gifts, even if the patient receives no direct monetary benefit. Patients also pro-vide images of getting something for nothing, stealing, and the like. Pa-tients may take action or react with inaction. They may, for example, at-tempt to ignore their insurance company and remove themselves from any responsibility. Others experience conflict when information is requested and resist the request for information that the insurance company makes. Attempts to persuade the doctor to misrepresent the dates of treatment (24), diagnoses, or other information are common and reflect the un-conscious view of the arrangement as corrupt. At the same time, these efforts may also reflect the patients' desires for privacy. Patients may in-terpret fees paid by others as manipulations and respond with obstruc-tionistic reactions (18). The net effect is impaired therapeutic progress.

Case 6

> A patient's fee was paid by the patient, the patient's mother, and insurance. In his hours the patient appeared passive and helpless, often invoking suggestions from the analyst. The analyst's sugges-tions, including those about the fee, were met with anger. The pa-tient described trying to make his parents aware of his sister's re-sistance to their rigid expectations. His sister ultimately became independent of the family for her psychiatric assistance (27).

Although this is a summary of a summary, the story of the patient's rigid parents who were unaware of his sister's independent strivings, their failure to her and him, and ultimately her successful independence of them for her psychiatric therapy could be reflections or derivatives of his struggle with his own therapist, who made suggestions and did not ap-parently interpret or rectify the fee, the tangible symbol of his dependence. The fee and money seemed to become a direct issue of control between the patient and the analyst. The patient seemed to resolve the issue by giving his analyst gifts that he had made himself (academic papers and woodcuts). These were apparently not interpreted. The gifts served as an alternative to the fee that he did not pay. They symbolized his worth and worthiness. The woodcuts continued after termination of the formal analysis, perhaps indicating the lack of closure of this issue.

Case 7

In another example (13) a patient directly expressed a wish to pay for the analysis out of her own income. Although references are brief, she apparently arranged to do so. The first reference to another source of funds was signaled by a failure to endorse her check (14). She signaled her discomfort with the source of the fee months later by again failing to endorse the check. She complained that strength always seems to come from someone other than herself. By her account the analysis had a beneficial outcome, but hints of a splitting of her analyst as a good object and a prior therapist as a bad object were apparent in the follow-up interview. Synthesis of good and bad objects into a neutral whole did not seem to have been achieved. The fee issue was only a part of the complexity of issues in this analysis.

Case 8

Halpert (28) provided an unusual example in which the patient appeared to have avoided a third-party insurance payor. The patient maintained a secure frame but avoided further analysis in the same move.

This man learned that his therapy would be eligible for insurance reimbursement in the near future. The patient terminated therapy before his new insurance coverage could be used manifestly because the insurance would not pay as much as he had wanted (28).

The example is unusual because more commonly patients manifestly welcome the opportunity to use insurance to pay all or part of their fee. A more subtle problem in this therapy may have contributed to the premature departure. Halpert had made a genetic interpretation that connected the insurance, the patient's mother, and his analyst. This may have created resistance to the potential of uncomfortable connections between the insurance, earlier experiences, and his wishes. Why, then, did he not continue? He probably anticipated that the therapist would accept the new arrangement with the insurance. The interpretation may have opened just enough of a possibility that the gratification of the insurance, if it were to be used, would become an intolerable regression. An option, in lieu of a safe neutral therapist, is flight.

If acceptance of the insurance provisions is not acted upon by the therapist and useful interpretations are made instead, a few patients will continue therapy without insurance even when it is available. They will unconsciously validate this alternative as therapeutically correct. By stopping, this patient succeeded in maintaining a secure frame in regard to the fee. The genetic interpretation may have been correct but premature, creating "resistance" (29). Indeed, the reference to the insurance as not paying what he expected might have been a derivative of his unconscious awareness that the insurance/mother/analyst interpretation was also a surprise and not what he had expected (5).

Had Halpert begun by connecting the anticipated insurance to the therapy experience or to himself and made some conjecture in that arena first, before making a genetic interpretation, the meanings of the insurance as a derivative of some drive activating circumstance (30) or adaptive context (5) might have been teased out. "As I have not made my position clear, you may be concerned that I might accept the insurance payment" would be a possible intervention. Later, depending on the development of the patient's derivatives: "My acceptance of the insurance and going along with their requirements could be similar to treating you as a dependent child. This is disturbing because it reminds you of your mother's babying you" could be a subsequent interpretation. This interpretive sequence would begin at the "surface" and avoid the too-much-too-soon that evokes resistance and defensiveness (29). The patient would then more likely have stayed and not used insurance had Halpert interpreted the distress around the prospect of an infantilizing treatment situation.

COUNTERTRANSFERENCE

Harmful countertransferences are problems with changeable fees, fees that are too low, or fees not paid in a timely fashion. Untoward aggression against the patient in response to the hurtful (to the therapist) fee variations is common, even if the variations have been permitted or encouraged by the therapist.

Modified fee arrangements are very attractive to both patient and therapist, often irresistibly so. These attractions and direct interest in the fee by each party in the therapy interfere with objectivity in both professional practice and scrutiny of the consequences (30).

ANALYSIS OF MENTAL LIFE OR OF REAL LIFE?

The psychoanalytic therapist analyzes the patient's mental processes, not his real life. Diversions into descriptions of events as real issues rather than as derivatives or components of current "here-and-now" thinking and adaptive processes serve as major resistances (31). Accordingly, to modify a fee in response to some statement about the patient's real life, whether it is to lower a fee or forgive a fee for a cancellation, sets a precedent that leads away from the primary analytic task. Reacting to some exigency of the patient's real life, rather than attempting to fully understand the exigency, the patient's response to it, and the relation of the interaction to the therapy, is antithetical to psychoanalytic psychotherapy.

Assuming a tactful manner on the part of the therapist in setting up the fee arrangement, the patient may respond with a manifest complaint or disagreement or may say nothing directly. An unconscious validation expressed through derivatives may be heard. With the adequate fee, derivatives will contain allusions to firm parental figures, courageous or bold actions, serious intentions, commitments, and the like. If nothing else, the affirmation of the setting of an adequate fee is unconscious because it is incongruous with the manifest wish of the patient.

CONCLUSION

The fee arrangement in any psychotherapy is significant. Clinical evidence shows that correction of a modified fee to a standard adequate fee that is collected for all scheduled sessions has a distinctly positive effect on the course and outcome of psychotherapy. While therapies that continue with modified fees can have symptomatic improvement, when the standard adequate fee arrangement is used, either from the outset or corrected in response to derivative communication of unconscious perceptions, optimum ego structural change is the result.

REFERENCES

1. Freud, S. Recommendations to physicians practising psycho-analysis (1912). In *Standard edition*, Vol. 12. London: Hogarth Press, 1957.
2. Langs, R. Modes of "cure" in psychoanalysis and psychoanalytic psychotherapy. *Int. J. Psycho-Anal.*, 62:199–214, 1981.
3. Langs, R. The patient's unconscious perception of the therapist's errors. In P. L. Giovacchini (Ed.), *Tactics and techniques in psychoanalytic therapy*, Vol. 2: Countertransference. New York: Jason Aronson, 1975.

4. Langs, R. *The therapeutic environment*. New York: Jason Aronson, 1979.
5. Langs, R. *Psychotherapy: A basic text*. New York: Jason Aronson, 1982.
6. Brenner, C. *Psychoanalytic technique and psychic conflict*. New York: International Universities Press, 1976.
7. Gill, M. M. The analysis of the transference. In R. Langs (Ed.), *Classics in psychoanalytic technique*. New York: Jason Aronson, 1981.
8. Milner, M. Aspects of symbolism in comprehension of the not-self. *Int. J. Psycho-Anal.*, 33:181–195, 1952.
9. Langs, R. Framework, misalliance and interaction in the analytic situation: three encyclopedia articles. In R. Langs (Ed.), *Technique in transition*. New York: Jason Aronson, 1976.
10. Langs, R. Validation and the framework of the therapeutic situation. In R. Langs (Ed.), *Technique in transition*. New York: Jason Aronson, 1977.
11. Glover, E. *The technique of psychoanalysis*. New York: International Universities Press, 1955.
12. Schlessinger, N., and Robbins, F. P. *A developmental view of the psychoanalytic process*. New York: International Universities Press, 1983.
13. Dewald, P. A. *The psychoanalytic process*. New York: Basic Books, 1972.
14. Raney, J. The payment of fees for psychotherapy. *Int. J. Psychoanal. Psychother.*, 9:147–181, 1982–83.
15. Cheifetz, L. G. Framework violations with clinic patients. In J. Raney (Ed.), *Listening and interpreting: The challenge of the work of Robert Langs*. New York: Jason Aronson, 1984.
16. Hodges, A. G. The Langsian approach to acting out. In J. Raney (Ed.), *Listening and interpreting: The challenge of the work of Robert Langs*. New York: Jason Aronson, 1984.
17. Keene, C. Framework rectification and transient negative effects. In J. Raney (Ed.), *Listening and interpreting: The challenge of the work of Robert Langs*. New York: Jason Aronson, 1984.
18. Silverstein, E. A. Langsian theory and countertransference. In J. Raney (Ed.), *Listening and interpreting: The challenge of the work of Robert Langs*. New York: Jason Aronson, 1984.
19. Greenson, R. R. *The technique and practice of psychoanalysis*. New York: International Universities Press, 1967.
20. Haak, N. Comments on the analytic situation. *Int. J. Psycho-Anal.*, 38:183–195, 1957.
21. Menninger, K. *Theory of psychoanalytic technique*. New York: Basic Books, 1958.
22. Nash, J. L., and Cavenar, J. O. Free psychotherapy: An inquiry into resistance. *Am. J. Psychiatry*, 133:1066–1069, 1976.
23. Goldensohn, S. S., and Haar, E. Transference and countertransference in a third-party payment system (HMO). *Am. J. Psychiatry*, 131:256–260, 1974.
24. Pasternak, S. A., and Treiger, P. Psychotherapy fees and residency training. *Am. J. Psychiatry*, 133:1064–1066, 1976.
25. Rudominer, H. Peer review, third-party payment, and the analytic situation: A case report. *J. Am. Psychoanal. Assoc.*, 32:773–795, 1984.
26. Sharfstein, S. S. Third party payors: To pay or not to pay. *Am. J. Psychiatry*, 135:1185–1188, 1978.
27. Gedo, J. E. *Beyond interpretation*. New York: International Universities Press, 1978.

28. Halpert, E. A meaning of insurance in psychotherapy. *Int. J. Psychoanal. Psychother.*, 1(4):60–68, 1972.
29. Glover, E. The therapeutic effect of inexact interpretation: A contribution to the theory of suggestion. *Int. J. Psycho-Anal.*, 12:397–411, 1931.
30. Eissler, K. R. On some theoretical and technical problems regarding the payment of fees for psychoanalytical treatment. *Int. Rev. Psycho-Anal.*, 1:73–101, 1974.
31. Gray, P. Psychoanalytic technique and the ego's capacity for viewing intrapsychic activity. *J. Am. Psychoanal. Assoc.*, 21:474–494, 1973.

10

Money Issues That Complicate Treatment

G. A. Williston DiBella, M.D.

Money issues always complicate treatment and can appear throughout all encounters with patients.

Freud wrote: "Money questions will be treated by cultured people in the same manner as sexual matters, with the same inconsistency, prudishness, and hypocrisy" (1). More than 70 years after he wrote this, many can talk of sexual matters yet have more difficulty talking about money matters. Nearly everyone is susceptible to feeling considerable emotional discomfort and conflict over openly dealing with money issues.

Therapists have experienced the same societal pressures and upbringing as everyone else, and their prevailing ethics still seem to dictate that openly dealing with money would be distasteful. The training of therapists generally fails to include guidance for the therapist toward dealing with money issues even though monetary dealings are ubiquitous in life in general, including during psychotherapy.

To increase therapists' awareness, this chapter touches on the ways money issues appear in patient contacts, and it attempts to provide some guidelines toward working through distress over money and mastery of these issues. What follows is based on previous explorations of this issue (2), the author's supervision of therapists, recent readings, more than 15 years of psychiatric practice, and the development of a Category I continuing medical education seminar to reduce difficulties with money in treatment.

SIX MAIN COMPLICATIONS

Ambivalence, conflicts, and dysphoria about money issues with patients are detrimental in at least six significant ways (2). Most important, treatment is incomplete and less efficient. Transference and countertransference are less understood because money issues are neglected. The patient fails to get help in working through money problems in his day-to-day life. Few things besides money can so completely symbolize conflicts. Thus, whenever therapist and patient do not examine money issues (including fees), they are missing a superb opportunity to succinctly highlight such conflicts as the following: dependency versus adult self-reliance, giving versus receiving, responsibility versus infantilization, exploitation versus altruism, pride versus guilt and obsequiousness, to mention a few. There often seems to be a direct correlation between neglect of money issues by the therapist and poor management of other features of treatment. Despite the integral role money plays in life, it is also remarkable that the therapist in his initial history taking usually does not include investigating the source and amount of the patient's money and how the patient goes about budgeting and spending.

Second, some clinics and practitioners just barely survive; this occurs in part because discomfort over money interferes with collection of fees. Pasternak and Treiger showed this, and they went on to demonstrate that there was a fourfold increase in clinic revenues after residents were helped to examine and resolve conflicts about fee setting and collecting (3). The therapist feels unnecessary disappointment, resentment, and frustration when anticipated fairly earned income fails to come in.

Third, when the therapist conducts his money transactions wih the patient poorly, he does the patient a disservice since such transactions become a significant source of ill will, annoyance, distrust, and misunderstanding.

Fourth, adverse resentful feelings about a practitioner's money transactions can then lead to retaliation by patients. This may take the form of fee withholding, suing doctors, and generally declining good will toward the helping professions from the public, and to other constrictions. An example of the latter is the change in Medicare reimbursement put into effect in the United States in 1984. The new laws single out physicians as the only professional group in the United States to have rules against them raising their fees for services.

Fifth, when therapists fail to be concerned about costs of treatment (whether because of fear of seeming greedy or idealism), they may be contributing to the now unacceptably increasing costs of treatment in many countries. Therapists have to share society's burden of becoming cost conscious and helping to put a realistic and affordable limit on medical expenditures.

Sixth, when transferences and countertransferences over money are ignored, these often turn into an unspoken conspiracy. This may occur if both participants are afraid of facing some painful (real or imagined) viewpoint. For example, the patient may secretly conclude about a lowered fee, ''I must not be good enough to pay a full fee,'' and the therapist says, ''I am unworthy of being paid much for my professional services.'' The therapist/patient relationship may become like a love-buyer/love-seller one; however, when a therapist fails to deal with money forthrightly while pretending to give love, he may actually seem to be practicing a form of prostitution or robbery.

THREE STAGES TOWARD MONEY MASTERY

First Stage

The first step to take is the willingness to contemplate money issues. Even simply getting close enough to contemplate a conflicted issue is likely to cause anxiety to surface, as many chapters of this book attest clearly to the deep emotional significance of money. Therapists will need to steel themselves against these anxieties and be prepared to expend considerable emotional energy to contain themselves and prevent premature closure, judgments, or diversion. An open, exploring mind is needed while recalling that contemplation does not require any commitment or action.

It may be best also that the therapist not tackle this issue alone, since it is quite hard to self-scrutinize emotionally laden areas without a supervisor or trusted colleague with whom to discuss these issues.

Second Stage

What is needed is a clear awareness of the many phases of treatment in which money complications are most problematic and arise most evidently. Then the therapist can carefully examine, understand, and master these issues. Otherwise, it is probable that unexamined feelings will appear in disruptive ways.

The one underlying conflict that seems to rise in all phases is the struggle between good and bad. ''Bad'' is essentially any monetary concerns that might impair delivery of quality medical care. ''Good'' seems to be an all-giving parentlike provision of care with nothing expected in exchange, except perhaps obedience and emotional gratefulness. Thus, the therapist feels good when (s)he is only consciously concerned with the health and increasing well-being of patients, and (s)he feels guilty and ashamed about any commercial interest in getting money in exchange for professional time/expertise or in keeping costs down. In conclusion, many therapists would really prefer to avoid even appropriate money awareness (2).

The phase of discussing and setting fees. Too often therapists have a tendency to avoid involvement with fee setting. To bring up fees, therapists find the task of describing themselves in money terms and often find this most distasteful. Therapists tend to hesitantly ask about fees from their colleagues (who actually only rarely reveal these with complete frankness). Then the therapist mindlessly uses the same or lower fees. Buckley et al. showed that avoidance of fee setting was among the top 10 mistakes of beginning therapists (4). Such avoidance fails to provide a foundation that can stand up to the emotional hurricanes that arise out of the therapist/patient relationship.

Fee setting includes deciding on whether to have an unchanging standard fee or one that varies. Both methods may affect the therapist and patient adversely. For example, if the therapist feels worth a certain fee and yet lowers the fee because of fear of appearing mercenary, this beneficence may turn into a resentment of being deprived by the lower-paying patient or may turn into condescension. The ways these feelings might show themselves include denigrating the patient, withdrawal, forgetting appointments, delayed response to phone calls, cutting short the therapy hour, etc.

Little experimental work has been done on the effect on the patient of charging a full fee versus eliminating or reducing the fee; nonetheless, strong opinion has been expressed from both sides on the importance of a fee (5). In addition, "there is no question that charging a lowered fee or charging nothing at all changes the nature of the therapeutic relationship" (6). The following are examples of lowered fees being detrimental to one or another patient. A patient might learn that the only way to get special consideration or favors is by being disordered and neurotic. A patient's sense of self as incompetent might be reinforced by the therapist acting on a view of the patient as not able to pay the standard fee. A patient's unhealthy desire for dependency or special treatment compared to others may be reinforced. Another patient might suspect that the therapist will demand some other compensation, such as sexual favors, and the patient might precipitously leave therapy. Other patients will feel so pressured by guilt or gratitude that they will not dare seem ungrateful by showing anger at the therapist.

The optimal discussion of fees is usually not done by therapists who have discomfort over money matters. For example, when a passive-aggressive patient and the therapist both are uneasy over money exchanges, the discussion may be hurried and the fee seemingly quickly accepted. This misses an opportunity to interrupt the patient's surface malleability, yet covert resistance. Another time the therapist might become defensive and try to rush the fee discussion by curtly responding to a patient's concern about the fee with something like "You really should understand that you only get what you pay for. You really must show an intense willingness to sacrifice if you are ever to get better."

During times of emergency and severe illness, conflict over money can be intensified. It is considered horrible, unloving, or disloyal to bring up the costs of such expensive treatment. But if there is the pressure to spare no expense, the costs of care mushroom, and society and/or the family finds itself in unacceptable debt. Therapists are expected to be leaders and guardians of welfare; they may then be held to blame for the high costs and debts, especially if they do not initiate a full discussion of fees/costs before therapy is begun.

The phase of raising fees. If the issue of a fee raise is brought up, it again forces the therapist and patient to see the therapist as interested in money or selling time for money, and as aggressive enough to be demanding more from the patient. This might clash with the therapist's wish to be a benevolent healer and friend, who might then avoid legitimate fee raises. Resulting tense concern and conflict are likely in both patient and therapist; subsequent countertherapeutic acting out is not unlikely.

The phase of collecting fees. In many ways the therapist may indicate that money matters should not be brought up, with subsequent decrement of the patient's ability to deal with money. For examples, some therapists cannot stand to be handed a check and signal the patient to drop it on the desk. Many have to distance themselves from money by using a go-between such as the mail or a secretary.

There tends to be a positive correlation between the therapist's distress and a lesser frequency of billing. Such delays often result in uncollected bills (7).

Bill-paying problems occur frequently; these include balances unpaid after the end of treatment, bounced checks, and lateness in paying. Given the great symbolic importance of money, it is surprising how often lateness in payment is not brought out into an open discussion by either patient or therapist. The therapist can hardly be helping the therapeutic process if he or she does not speak up because of fear of angering the patient, of seeming greedy, or of losing the patient's adoration and love, or because of masochism. The therapist is also likely to harbor some building resentment at not receiving payment as agreed. How will this resentment come out? Regarding the patient, the patient may be gratifying some unhealthy wish for special treatment. Another part of the patient is aware of an obligation and may worry silently about how the therapist is reacting. Subsequent patient conflict and anxiety would be typical, perhaps with premature termination.

The patient must be wondering whether the therapist is allowing non-payment out of love, low self-esteem, desire to get something else instead, etc.

Third Stage: Developing Better Procedures and Attitudes

Over several weeks the therapist should keep a diary on the many times tensions about money arise with patients. This will convince the therapist that money issues constantly arise, and he can then decide whether or not these need better management.

Facing facts of life. Hopefully the above step will motivate the therapist to face the following realizations. First, normally, the therapist cannot completely eliminate exchanging his expert time for money.

Second, therapists do benefit moneywise from helping patients who are sick and in pain, but this is not the same as exploiting the patient.

Third, each therapist must work out a logical, coherent point of view toward monetary inequities in life. Since one person may have more money and material possessions than another, how much inequity is fair and just? One viewpoint is that all persons are equally deserving and valuable as human beings; thus, each should have essentially the same income as another. On the other hand, one might say that one has to accept that life is never totally fair, just, planned, and rational. In addition, how much money should anyone get? Is it reasonable or realistic that a servicing person gets paid relative to time and energy expended, the amount the recipient of benefit is willing to pay, and perceived value of the producer's time, achievements, and product?

Fourth, how can the therapist both attend to legitimate self-interest and still encourage the patient toward realism and responsibility? Perhaps each adult should have the opportunity to try to select how (s)he wants to live, the amount of money to earn, and how to spend it. Similarly, the therapist has a right to pick out an earning rate, and it seems inappropriate to give this up in the face of a patient's unhealthy demand that someone else be a keeper or parent. An adult should not be infantilized. There is no one right or wrong answer to the above issues, but each therapist should carefully think out these issues and work out a personalized, solid philosophical foundation congruent with each individual therapist's personality, needs, and approach to therapy. The patient needs the therapist to be a whole, consistent, integrated person, not one who, for example, pretends to be uninterested in fees yet who is covertly worried about whether (s)he will be paid.

Specific suggestions for handling fee discussions. How to set fees: The therapist may consider written answers to the following questions: (1) What income will I find satisfying? (2) What money value do I put on all my activities in the day: e.g., on an hour with my family versus an hour of patient care? How many hours of patient care daily is right for me? (3) What do other therapists feel is a fair fee? (4) How do I want to make a monetary differential for each type of professional effort, since one effort may require more time, training, concentration, and burden than another?

Having a standard fee with possible exceptions requires the therapist to write down answers to the following: (1) Do I feel obligated to give charity to patients? If so, how many should I accept at a lowered fee? (2) How much monetary sacrifice might I make for an especially "interesting" patient? (3) Can I truly be free from unhelpful feelings (such as condescension or annoyance) by receiving a fee lower than I feel I am worth? (4) What basis do I feel there is for charging one patient more than another? Does the value of my professional time go up because a client is wealthy? (5) Can I avoid being solicitous or guilty if I were to charge a well-to-do patient more? Each therapist should write down why (s)he is getting paid. For example, one therapist might write, "Every relationship involves an exchange of value, and I charge a fee in exchange for devoting varying periods of an expert professional relationship. The money given to a producer for his or her time should be the amount recipients are willing to pay and directly proportional to the participants' perceived values of the therapist's time and achievements and output." Another example is provided by Tulipan in detail (6).

How to initiate discussion of therapy expenses: To help achieve comfort with fees, the therapist may find it useful to keep the following in mind just before starting the discussion of fees (2). First, the therapist should focus more on the patient's anxiety that always needs assuaging, rather than his or her own. When the therapist brings up fees in a frank, nonapologetic, self-confident, structured way, the patient's anxiety is decreased. Second, the therapist is being a good model for the patient and providing a valuable therapeutic experience around money by a calm, candid fee discussion. Third, the therapist needs to earn a living while at the same time respecting the patient and trying to expect the best of the patient by giving the patient an opportunity to be an adult who can engage in an appropriate give and take.

Optionally, fee policies and treatment costs are discussed frankly and thoroughly in the first one or two visits. These are best discussed in person, except for the fee for initial consultation; some reasons for this follow.

First, the issue of fees is complex and involves matters other than purely financial consideration; thus, there should be a complete evaluation of the patient's situation. Second, the therapist could help to make a better referral if the patient cannot afford the standard fee. Third, an exception to the usual fee should be done after deliberate, careful evaluation, not as a result of squeamishness over money. Fourth, a patient's resistance to treatment may make the fee a rationalization for avoiding treatment, and the patient may do better in giving highest priority to health if he had face-to-face support from the therapist to do so.

Initial discussion of fees should include a cost/benefit analysis, including risks. Patients need this to provide the required informed consent. Treatment should be indicated and not result from wishful thinking.

Toward the end of the discussion the therapist would do well to encourage the patient directly to express reactions to the discussion of fees. The therapist needs to be especially alert to hints of dissatisfaction and vagueness by the patient so that negative reactions are not left to smolder covertly.

Miscellaneous procedures. All aspects of fee policies should be written out and made logical and internally consistent and compatible with the therapist's style. Many of these may be put into a patient information brochure, since this is appreciated by patients (7). Fee policies would cover how and when bills are paid, raising fees, third-party payments, canceled appointments, telephone calls, vacations, lateness, house calls, etc. Regarding raising fees, enough advance notice should be given. Generally, four to six weeks is sufficient.

In conclusion, both therapist and patient have problems dealing with money. Overcoming these problems requires some intense efforts over enough time so that money no longer causes dysfunction. Wholesome attitudes to money should be incorporated into good daily practice by carefully thought-out and written-down philosophy and procedures followed by repeated performance to assure a calm proficiency. Thus, therapists will be best able to help in their main goal of assisting "people with problems" toward functioning at an optimum, including in the area of money.

REFERENCES

1. Freud, S. Further recommendations in the technique of psychoanalysis; on beginning the treatment (1913). In P. Rieff (Ed.), *Therapy and technique*. New York: Collier Books, 1963.
2. DiBella, G. Mastering money issues that complicate treatment: The last taboo. *Am. J. Psychother.*, 24(4):510–522, 1980.

3. Pasternak, S., and Treiger, P. Psychotherapy fees and residency training. *Am. J. Psychiatry*, 133:1064, 1976.
4. Buckley, P., Karasu, T., and Charles, E. Common mistakes in psychotherapy. *Am. J. Psychiatry*, 135:1578, 1979.
5. Yoken, C., and Berman, J. Does paying a fee for psychotherapy alter the effectiveness of treatment? *J. Consult. Clin. Psychol.*, 52(2):254–260, 1984.
6. Tulipan, A. Fees in psychotherapy: A perspective. *J. Am. Acad. Psychoanal.*, 11(3):445–463, 1983.
7. McCue, J. *Private practice: Surviving the first year.* Lexington, KY: Collamore Press, D.C. Heath and Company, 1982.

11

The Effect of Third-Party Payment on the Practice of Psychotherapy

Paul Chodoff, M.D.

An issue of the *Journal of the American Medical Association* (1) contained a letter from a psychiatrist asking for guidance about a sticky situation with which he had been confronted. He was treating the mistress of a married man who asked the psychiatrist to make out the bill in his name as if he were the patient. It had occurred to the psychiatrist that the married man's purpose was not only to keep the relationship secret but also to collect insurance payment for the services. What, dear editor, the psychiatrist prayed, was his duty in the face of this thorny ethical and legal conundrum?

This tidbit illustrates that when we accept the participation of an otherwise uninvolved third party in the financial aspects of the psychotherapeutic contract, we have come very far from the simple and uncomplicated situation in which the purveyor of the psychotherapeutic services is paid directly either by the recipient of those services or by someone, usually a relative, who has a personal interest in and responsibility for the patient or client.

However, the issues raised by the increasing use of impersonal third-party payment mechanisms such as health insurance for psychotherapeutic services far transcend in scope and importance the doctor's dilemma described above. In those areas of the country in which this method of payment has become a significant factor in the financial transactions between the two parties involved in psychotherapy, a host of unexpected problems has appeared, either as a direct result of the new mode of payment or because problems previously dormant or glossed over have begun to surface with an urgency demanding answers in terms of dollars and cents rather than theories.

To suggest the range of these problems, I could mention that third-party payment has brought into question such issues as confidentiality, the therapist's allegiance, diagnostic and reporting practices, and transference-countertransference relationships in the therapy. Professional identity confusions appear as the therapist becomes less a priest and more a businessman and the organizations to which he belongs become involved increasingly with guild and political concerns rather than with purely professional ones. Ultimately the third-party interest raises questions about the applicability of the medical model to psychotherapy.

Third-party payment, of course, occurs not only in the private practice of psychotherapy but also when psychiatric care, including psychotherapy, is provided in state and federal hospitals and in outpatient psychiatric clinics and community mental health centers funded by various means. However, in this discussion I shall confine myself to the setting with which I am most familiar—that is, the office practice of private psychotherapy—and I will draw to a considerable extent on the experiences of myself and my colleagues in the Washington, D.C., area, where the Federal Employees Health Benefits Program has provided a substantial portion of the income of psychiatrists treating government employees and their families.

MEDICAL VERSUS NONMEDICAL MODEL

For the federal employee in the Washington area whose major medical insurance coverage provides 80% payment for outpatient psychotherapy, the third-party influence may first be felt at the point when a prospective patient seeks a therapist. Of course in those cases in which he is referred to or seeks out a physician specializing in psychiatry, the problem I will delineate does not arise. But the potential patient may instead be considering treatment with a nonphysician, such as a psychologist. If he is paying for the services out of his own pocket he can choose between the psychiatrist and psychologist on the basis of what he knows about the kinds of services these two disciplines provide and his feeling about the particular individual. However, if the insurance carrier is paying a substantial portion of the fee, there will usually be an advantage in choosing the psychiatrist instead of the psychologist since the former will be treated by the insurance carrier like any other doctor and will receive his payments accordingly, as long as he lives up to certain requirements. The psychologist, however, is not an M.D. and he will therefore be in a somewhat ambiguous and unclear position as a potential recipient of payment for medical services. If the patient is insured by the largest local carrier, the

Blue Cross and Blue Shield plan covering federal employees, the psychologist therapist will have to submit himself either nominally or substantially to the supervision of a psychiatrist physician before his services become eligible for insurance payment; this will affect both his self-image and his relationship with the patient.

The magnetism of financial advantage inherent in this situation will have a differing effect on psychiatrists and on nonmedical psychotherapists. The former group includes a substantial number who in the past have not been reluctant to emphasize the ways in which they are dissimilar from other physicians. Such attitudes are likely to be reversed as psychiatrists respond to the economic spur of third-party payment, prodding them to mend their medical fences and reestablish their allegiance to the medical model; this obscures some of the real problems about its applicability to their psychotherapeutic practices. The nonmedical therapist, on the other hand, may find himself on the horns of a dilemma since, although his heart may be with the behavioral change model, his pocketbook may push him toward at least grudging acceptance of the medical model. That is, in order to fall within the purview of medical insurance, he will have to acknowledge that he is treating disease rather than changing behavior.

He may choose the alternative of seeking a basic change in the criteria used by the insurance companies, that is, to try to convince them that psychotherapeutic treatment by psychologists should be accepted as parallel and equal to that by psychiatrists (2). This course, which is being pursued by the American Psychological Association, raises very fundamental questions about the use of medical insurance for purposes that could be considered nonmedical and may also tend to widen the breach between medical and nonmedical psychotherapists, already illustrated by the recent conflicts within major psychoanalytic organizations about the admission of certain non-M.D.s as full-fledged members. Although real and substantive differences are involved in this dispute there also appears to be a hidden agenda present in the form of economic guild issues, one of which is the fate of psychoanalysis under present insurance plans and, even more, under a future national health insurance program.

CONFIDENTIALITY

Let us assume now that the therapist has been selected and that he is a physician. The contract between patient and physician must now include provisions for complying with certain requirements of the third-party insurance carrier. With the approval and knowledge of the patient, some facts about the patient will have to be conveyed to the insurance company by the psychiatrist. But if this requirement is complied with, what about the ideal of absolute confidentiality in the psychiatrist-patient relationship? This is an emotionally laden area for many psychiatrists, inducing a great deal of anxiety and resentment and, along with this, certain defensive maneuvers. Some psychiatrists, choosing to disregard the axiom that he who pays the piper calls the tune, may go so far as to deny that the insurance company has the right to any information about the patient for whose treatment it is authorizing payment; these psychiatrists may then engage in conflicts or obfuscating maneuvers with the carrier.

Even though the majority of psychiatrists recognize the legitimate need of the insurance carrier to have certain facts about the cases for which they are authorizing payment, they may be troubled by this requirement and by its possible effect in breaching the trust the patient must have that he can say anything at all to his therapist without fear of disclosure. To obviate this uneasiness, psychiatric organizations in the Washington area have worked with the insurance carriers to define and keep to a minimum the information the carriers require to carry out their obligation to their policy holders and to ensure that such information remains only in authorized hands.

But the uneasiness among psychiatrists, justified or not, remains. One of the ways in which it is manifested is in the diagnostic reporting of the condition for which the patient is being treated. Although I have no data on this matter, it is my impression that the most common diagnoses submitted on insurance company forms are anxiety neurosis and depressive neurosis: such DSM-II (3) diagnoses as alcoholism, schizophrenia, and homosexuality are made so infrequently as to suggest that patients suffering from these conditions may be receiving other diagnoses.

If this kind of mislabeling is occurring, two sets of reasons could be advanced for it, both at least partially the result of the influence of third-party payment. The first (already mentioned) is the psychiatrist's uneasiness about the confidentiality of the information he is transmitting to an impersonal bureaucracy, where leakage cannot be ruled out; this leakage, including the diagnoses I have just mentioned, may be harmful to the interests of the patients under his care. In this case, incidentally, there is no doubt that the psychiatrist's allegiance is to his patient rather than to the insurance company, so that conflicts about whose interest he is representing would not arise as they might in other instances of third-party payment such as the military service, where a psychiatrist might have a real conflict between his allegiance to his patient and to the military organization of which he is a member.

But fears that confidentiality may be breached are not the only reason for the diagnostic reporting practices I have suggested. A second factor is the difficulty in conforming some patients to the diagnostic scheme of DSM-II (3). This is not a problem in the case of all or even most psychiatric patients receiving psychotherapy; most fall quite comfortably into medically oriented diagnostic rubrics, whether or not the psychiatrist chooses to employ them. However, especially among patients who are being treated by intensive psychotherapeutic (including psychoanalytic) techniques, there are a certain number whose problems, although real, cannot be adequatedly described in medically oriented diagnostic terms. These are the people whose difficulties in such interpersonal areas as family, work, and social relationships result in relatively little disability in the ordinary medical use of this term. When such individuals pay for their own psychotherapy, the troublesome question of whether they conform to the medical definition of a ''patient'' need not be a matter of concern to themselves or to their therapists. If the need and the suffering are sufficient, treatment will be undertaken regardless of diagnosis or of whether the sufferer is a ''patient.'' However, medical insurance requires medical diagnoses, and unless this requirement is altered for certain categories of patients seeking psychotherapy, the psychiatric profession is under the increasing necessity of somehow coming to terms with the problem of diagnosis.

EFFECT ON TREATMENT PATTERN

Having agreed to undertake a psychotherapeutic enterprise together, the two parties involved must now also agree on the frequency of visits, a decision that is of major importance in determining whether the psychotherapy will be at the supportive end or the more intensive, psychoanalytically oriented end of the spectrum of possible approaches. When substantial third-party financial assistance is available, this choice becomes relatively free of financial hindrances so that it may be dictated more by the therapist's judgment about what would be best in this particular case than by the patient's means. Such a payment arrangement provides an opportunity for individuals otherwise not able to afford it to receive skilled and experienced psychotherapeutic help.

However, although substantial help in paying for psychotherapy is clearly beneficial in allowing a freer choice of treatment modality, there may be other consequences. For instance, the absence of clear-cut indications for various types of psychotherapy might influence therapists to choose the kind of therapy they prefer to do rather than to make a deci-

sion on the basis of more objective criteria; an increase in the more intensive types of treatment might well result. This danger is not unique to
psychiatry; it has been pointed out as a general trend in medicine that the
existence of third-party payment provides "little incentive for efficiency.
Instead, the trend is to use the higher cost facilities and services and to
make as many of these available as possible" (4). On the other hand, it
is likely that one of the factors stimulating the present popularity of the
various varieties of group therapy is the availability of insurance payment.

It is also clear that as long as there is a discrepancy in the amount of
insurance coverage in different geographical areas, more psychotherapeutic services will be dispensed where insurance coverage is substantial. For
example, in the Washington, D.C., area the organization previously known
as the Baltimore Psychoanalytic Society has changed its name to the
Baltimore-D.C. Psychoanalytic Society, since more of its activities are taking place in Washington than in Baltimore, where insurance coverage of
mental disorders is much less extensive. Such a differential will tend to
disappear once the uniform provisions of a national health insurance program have been agreed upon and implemented; the effect of third-party
payment on the choice of psychotherapeutic modalities will then be determined by the amount of coverage for outpatient psychotherapy contained
in such a program.

I will now turn to the effect of third-party payment on the course of
the psychotherapy itself, that is, its influence on such treatment dynamics
as transference-countertransference issues, resistances, fantasies, defense,
motivations for treatment, etc. This subject, which merges with the general effect of payment on psychotherapeutic transactions, although rich
in its implications for psychotherapy, has to the best of my knowledge
not been sufficiently treated in the relevant literature. Such discussions
of the subject as exist are found mainly in regard to intensive psychotherapies, and especially psychoanalysis, since it is in these forms of
therapy where a scrutiny of the relationship between therapist and patient is of such importance that these issues find their fullest play and are
most likely to be affected by financial transactions.

THE ISSUE OF FINANCIAL SACRIFICE

As far as psychoanalytic psychotherapy is concerned, the paramount
question posed by the increasing availability of third-party payment is
whether and to what extent such treatments are crippled when regular,
direct payments are not made by the patient to the therapist. In a paper
written in 1964 (5), I summarized the classical psychoanalytic position as

holding that the analyst must require sacrificial fees from his patient because they provide the patient with motivation, generate analytical material, and are beneficial to the countertransference. However, reports of actual experiences with free and low-cost analysis available at that time suggested that such a payment milieu was not fatally inimical to treatment; rather, despite theoretical preconceptions and individual examples to the contrary, the evidence indicated that psychoanalysis can proceed success-fully in the absence of fees or with low fees. This finding supported the view that motivation for patients to work at psychoanalysis (or in psycho-therapy generally) is not simply a function of the willingness to spend money for treatment; such a willingness is an evidence of motivation but it cannot provide motivation. There is ample experience that motivation to work in psychoanalysis may very well be present in high degree even when the treatment does not represent a financial sacrifice. It appears that the fee is a more important source of motivation for the therapist than for the patient.

Since 1964 third-party payment has become far more common than formerly, and a considerable amount of experience has accumulated on the effects of third-party insurance payment on psychoanalytic and other forms of psychotherapy. A recent report by Halpert (6) sounds a warn-ing note, on the basis of two cases, that insurance payment may offer a focus for resistance, making the analytic task more difficult.

There is also a school of thought which holds that no form of psycho-therapeutic treatment in which payment is not a private matter between therapist and analysand can be considered psychoanalysis. This repre-sents an example of classification by definition and if it is accepted, one will have to find a new name for what many fully qualified psychoanalysts with impeccable credentials are doing with patients from whom they receive third-party payment under the mistaken notion that they are prac-ticing psychoanalysis.

My own experience and that of the colleagues with whom I have dis-cussed this matter seems to support the view that when payment is made partially through a third party, some problems appear in the psychoanal-ysis or other intensive psychotherapy that otherwise would not be pres-ent. Some are like the ones cited in Halpert's cases, where the narcissistic gratification the patients were reported to have received in the form of fulfillment of fantasies of omnipotence from the fact that they themselves did not have to pay for the treatment was sufficient to interfere with their motivation to work in their analyses.

However, fantasies of this kind often appear in analysis and are sub-ject to interpretation and working through like any other kind of fantasy.

It sometimes may even be an advantage to the analysis to have the patient feeling that he is getting something for nothing mobilized by the fact that he does not have to pay, in exactly the same way that other fantasies may be mobilized and must be interpreted when the patient must make regular payments. At any rate, the practice of psychoanalysis and other intensive psychotherapy with third-party payment is flourishing where such payment is available, and there is no reason to believe that the results of such psychotherapy are in any way inferior to those produced in direct-payment settings.

THE TREND TOWARD GREATER ACCOUNTABILITY

In making the above statement, I am aware that I am venturing on rather shaky ground because of the uncertainty that pertains to the whole field of outcome studies in psychotherapy. The reasons for this state of affairs are complicated. The most important may simply be the extreme difficulty of the task, but it also seems likely that practitioners of psychotherapy have not been particularly motivated to scrutinize their work and that of their colleagues in a manner approaching scientific standards. However, this is a situation that inevitably will change under the economic spur of third-party intervention as the various carriers increasingly supplement the monetary carrot with the stick of accountability. Insurance officials and their actuaries are going to want to know what they are paying for, whether patients are being treated under proper indications, and whether psychotherapeutic practices are being abused. They expect this kind of accountability from surgeons, and although somewhat confused by the differences between psychiatry and the other medical specialties, they are not likely to regard psychiatrists as any more sacrosanct or immune from questioning than other medical specialists.

Also, we are undoubtedly entering an era when organizations of psychiatrists and other psychotherapists are going to have to negotiate contracts with various insurance carriers, and in these negotiations the representatives of psychiatry will have to answer such questions if they wish their services to be included under insurance coverage. Thus we see that an already troublesome problem—the criteria for various forms of psychotherapy and evaluation of their effectiveness—has been given a new urgency by the increase in third-party payment.

A relatively new development in psychiatry is the peer review committee, which makes recommendations about such matters as fees and indications for type and duration of treatment when these are called into question in individual cases. It is difficult to imagine that monitoring agencies of this kind would ever have been considered necessary or useful before the interposition of a third-party payment mechanism between patient and therapist. There is little doubt that the near future will see an increasing use of such quality control methods; the real question is whether they will be adequate and acceptable or whether such functions will be taken out of the sole control of psychotherapists. Whether this latter eventuality, with its far-reaching effects, ever comes to pass is dependent on the attitude of psychiatrists who specialize in psychotherapy not only toward peer review committees but also toward all the other issues involving third-party payment that I have raised.

If they take the position that everything which happens between their patients and themselves is nobody's business but their own, they will be in a difficult and anxiety-provoking situation in dealing with third-party requirements; they may be better off refusing to accept patients who pay their bills by such means. If, however, they accept the queen's shilling of insurance payment for part of their patients' financial obligations to them, they will have to come to terms with some of the hard questions I have touched upon.

REFERENCES

1. Married man asks to be billed for psychiatric care of mistress. *JAMA*, 218:1443, 1971.
2. Psychologists bid for inclusion in health insurance legislation. *Psychiatric News*, Dec 1, 1971, p. 1.
3. American Psychiatric Association. *Diagnostic and statistical manual of mental disorders*, 2nd ed. Washington, DC: APA, 1968.
4. Bevan, W. The topsy-turvy world of health care delivery. *Science*, 173:985, Sept 10, 1971.
5. Chodoff, P. Psychoanalysis and fees. *Compr. Psychiatry*, 5:137–145, 1964.
6. Halpert, E. The effect of insurance on psychoanalytic treatment. *J. Am. Psychoanal. Assoc.*, 20:122–133, 1972.

ADDENDUM: 1985

This article was written in 1972 at a time when the major carrier for the Federal Employees Health Benefit Program provided benefits of 80% of payment for psychotherapy sessions up to an overall total of $100,000. As described here, under these conditions the practice of psychotherapy flourished in the D.C. area generally, and the use of intensive and psychoanalytic forms of treatment was encouraged. At that time also, there was a distinct advantage to being a psychiatrist rather than a psychologist as far as ease of reimbursement was concerned.

Since that time the situation has changed drastically in the Washington area. Beginning in 1983 benefits have been provided for 80% of the cost of each psychotherapy session but only up to a total of 50 visits per year. This development has had a negative effect on the attractiveness of Washington as a place to practice psychotherapy, particularly the more intensive, psychoanalytically oriented variety. In addition, psychiatrists are no longer in a better position than psychologists to receive direct reimbursement from the insurance carriers. This is true throughout the country. The cutdown of benefits for outpatient psychotherapy is evidence of the generally grudging and suspicious attitude of medical insurance companies toward psychotherapeutic services. These insurance attitudes and actions have generated countermoves by organized psychiatry for legislative redress against the barriers psychiatrists feel exist between coverage for psychiatric and other medical services. In addition, marketing and public relations initiatives by organized psychiatry have burgeoned. The trend mentioned in the 1972 article for a rapprochement between psychiatry and the rest of medicine has become more firmly established.

The confidentiality-accountability conflict mentioned in the 1972 article continues to pose problems, possibly somewhat less sharply now, since by cutting down on the total amount of their coverage as a cost control measure, the insurance companies are no longer as interested in the divulging of patient information before claims will be paid. The third-party influence has also had an effect in the discussions leading to DSM-III. The formulations in this manual may have been influenced by a need to apply a "medical" label to every condition treated by a psychotherapist in order to make the insurance claims of such patients reimbursable.

The possibly deleterious effect on the psychotherapeutic treatment process of third-party interference no longer seems to be a live issue. Whatever third-party influences are present have been accepted and incorporated into the treatment situation apparently without disruptive effects on results of psychotherapeutic treatment.

12

On Negotiating Fees with Psychotherapy and Psychoanalytic Patients

Daniel H. Jacobs, M.D.

Despite Freud's (1) advice to "cast off false shame" (p. 131) on the subject of money, a full exploration of the fee and its effect on the psychotherapeutic process is often overlooked in our work with patients. At the beginning of treatment, the negotiation of fees with the patient is often given short shrift, as though it were not an integral part of the treatment process that can yield valuable information about the patient-therapist relationship. There are several reasons why these negotiations are often ignored. In the first place, fee arrangements are usually made at the onset of treatment. The setting of the fee before its meanings to the patient can be fully explored may imply to both therapist and patient that the subject is somehow outside the province of full analytic inquiry, especially in those instances in which the patient readily agrees to pay the fee proposed by the therapist. Second, since the therapist's decision to charge a certain fee for his or her work cannot be analyzed, but only reacted to by the patient, the fee's influence on the treatment may not be addressed by patient or therapist. Third, the therapist may not always view his or her own attitudes toward money and fees as important in the analytic process, particularly in relation to countertransference feelings that arise during treatment. As a result, it too often happens that during treatment, in Eissler's words (2), "the whole complex matter of money is rarely treated in a satisfactory or sufficient way" (p. 95).

The literature on the subject reflects ongoing differences of opinion in how fees may best be negotiated and how the meaning of the fee to the patient and to ourselves may best be understood. Freud (1) suggested that the hour be leased to the patient and noted that without a fee patients

121

might be deprived of a strong motive for bringing treatment to an end. He cautioned, furthermore, against agreeing to a fee that was not in keeping with the financial needs of the analyst. "It seems more respectable," he wrote, "and ethically less objectionable to acknowledge one's actual claim than . . . to act the part of the disinterested philanthropist—a position one is not, in fact, able to fill with the result that one is secretly aggrieved, or complains aloud, at the lack of consideration and the desire for exploitation evinced in one's patients" (p. 131). Freud also noted that setting a very low fee does not enhance the value of the treatment in the patient's eyes. Haak (3), elaborating on Freud's statements, maintained that a reasonably high fee was a necessary condition of successful and meaningful treatment. The high fee, he felt, was necessary to counteract the feelings of guilt in the patient arising from his attacks on the analyst. It also helps avoid countertransference situations in which the analyst is not charging enough because he is masochistic, or in love with the patient, or afraid of him. Borneman (4) points out that all money belongs to someone already. The taking of it is a form of aggression sublimated, hopefully, in the therapist's request for a reasonable fee. However, to deny the wish to take money from the patient to satisfy one's own needs is to imply that such wishes are unacceptable and that the patient could not himself have them or expect to gratify them through others.

Freud, however, did not always follow his own advice about leasing the hour. He treated the Wolf Man for free, at times, and even raised funds for him when he was destitute. He felt, furthermore, that psychoanalysis "should be accessible . . . to the great multitude who are too poor themselves to repay the analyst for his laborious work" (5). For years, in both Berlin and Vienna, members of those psychoanalytic institutes saw some patients gratis. Lorand and Console (6) report that free psychoanalytic treatment affords no insurmountable obstacle to successful outcome, although they noted that free treatment in clinics lasted longer than treatment in private practice. Favreau (7) has suggested that there are some patients who are definitely unable to pay any fee because of the unconscious meanings of money to them. They are, nevertheless, good cases for free treatment if it is carried out in a clinic and not in the consulting room of the analyst. Lievano (8) observed the same for patients in psychotherapy, indicating that the success of treatment did not seem affected by whether or not they paid their clinic bill. It seems to me, however, that in the situations that both Favreau and Lievano describe, the analysis of certain character traits would seem likely to be circumscribed unless the patients' needs for free treatment were thoroughly analyzed and, at some time in the treatment, a fee was either requested by the therapist or offered by the patient.

The disagreement and confusion over how best to think about fees in relation to the psychotherapeutic process have made it difficult for many clinicians and patients to freely and fully discuss the setting of the fee in the context of a developing relationship. Thus the transference and, particularly, the countertransference meaning of the monetary exchange may escape scrutiny. This is unfortunate, for it is in the establishment of the fee, its payment, and its receipt that the mutual nature of the therapeutic endeavor is often most clear and takes its most concrete form. The patient needs the skills of the therapist to aid in self-understanding. The therapist needs to be reimbursed for his skills in order to support himself. Thus for therapist and patient, issues of setting a value on the treatment, of giving and withholding, of autonomy and control, of need gratification and need frustration may come up around the fee for both patient and therapist as the transference develops (9,10), and when countertransference feelings arise. Furthermore, in setting a fee, the therapist must explore how much he values his work and wants to do it apart from its monetary rewards. This is particularly true at a time when insurance coverage for psychodynamically oriented psychotherapy is increasingly limited and when the number of patients who are willing and can afford to undergo costly, intensive psychotherapy or analysis is decreasing.

The fee for psychotherapy or psychoanalysis has multiple meanings in the unconscious of the patient and therapist. Their different symbolic meanings at different levels of psychic development will often reveal themselves during the course of treatment, provided sufficient attention is paid to them. The psychological significance of money and the fee to the patient may shift during the course of treatment. Thus, at one point, as Gedo (11) has indicated, the withholding of fees may be an attempt to deny separateness from the analyst, the fee withheld representing a transitional object and connecting link to the analyst. At another point in the treatment, the fee may represent nourishment offered to the analyst by a loving patient. Or it may represent sustenance which the patient feels he himself needs but must surrender to the depriving analyst. At still another stage, it is a precious anal gift presented in exchange for love and approval. It may also be associated with powerful phallic strivings and the wish to exhibit or hide such strivings. Conscious and unconscious concerns about the cost of emotional relationships and the price to be paid for involvement are often first expressed in the patient's attitude toward the fee. Each new meaning of the fee as it emerges in the transference will need to be analyzed along with any countertransference reactions concerning the meaning of the fee to the therapist. This exploration can best be conducted if the therapist pays close attention to the way in which he or she negotiates the initial fee, discusses any subsequent changes in the fee, handles third-party payments, and analyzes any resistances and defenses that may express themselves through the manner and timing of the payment.

SETTING A FEE

I believe the fee should not be fixed by the therapist at some arbitrary amount, but, whenever possible, during the initial sessions be the subject of full discussion in an attempt to understand the significance of the fee to the patient and its impact on his view of the therapist as treatment is being considered. Obviously, psychodynamic psychotherapy or analysis is a long-term endeavor for both patient and therapist. The monetary implications of undertaking such a treatment need to be fully understood if the necessary "atmosphere of safety" (12) is to be established for both patient and analyst. A fee is best arrived at when the financial circumstances of the patient are made explicit, sometimes through direct questioning by the therapist. Such questioning is sometimes difficult for therapists to do. The patient is suffering or in emotional turmoil and to talk of money may seem insensitive. Obviously, tact and timing are essential. However, talking directly and explicitly about money matters also indicates to the patient that the therapist does not flinch from practical matters and is prepared to deal with nitty-gritty matters of life, including money, in an open and honest way. In so doing, the therapist is trying with the patient to establish an atmosphere of financial safety for both of them which will allow the treatment to progress in an atmosphere that is mutually acceptable.

As one tries to do this, it quickly becomes apparent that some patients tend to underestimate or overestimate what they feel they can afford. A frank discussion of their income and how they apportion it, before a fee is determined, is often helpful not only in setting a reasonable fee, but in being able to begin the exploration of any neurotic distortions about money and the fee that may reveal themselves in the discussion. It is important, for instance, to discuss not only the amount of income, savings, and insurance a patient may have, but the role of these assets in the patient's thinking about himself and his treatment. Could the treatment, for instance, be undertaken without the benefit of health insurance, and what could or should be done were this third-party support unexpectedly withdrawn during the course of treatment? Is the patient willing to spend some of his savings on treatment? If he is, why is he? If not, why not? The patient's attitude toward the role of insurance payments or other assets in his treatment should provide the therapist important information about the way in which the patient organizes and views himself in relation to others, as well as to his own impulses. Almost every therapist has encountered the patient who announces his insurance or his money has run out and he can, therefore, no longer afford the treatment or, at best, can only come less often. Often the therapist, by not fully exploring at the beginning of and during treatment the patient's attitude toward payment, has unwittingly set the stage for the expression of resistance through the fee.

Many therapists tell the patient at the outset of treatment what their "usual fee" for therapy is and then discuss the patient's ability to pay it. If the therapist or analyst will not accept less than his or her "usual fee" and intends to refer elsewhere a patient who is unable to pay it, such an approach is reasonable. If, however, the therapist is willing to accept less than the "usual fee," there is no reason to mention the fee to which he or she is accustomed. To do so may result in the patient's feeling either special (singled out for unusual treatment) or not up to standard. While such feelings can, of course, be analyzed, the therapist's statement about what is usual or standard becomes a complicating element. When the fee for treatment is not predetermined and set by the therapist, but can be introduced, instead, as a topic for discussion in an open-ended way, it will invite further analysis of the patient's decision-making process. The patient will be encouraged to explore more fully what he or she is willing to give and expects to take. This approach to the setting of fees can and should be taken only when the therapist feels enough internal freedom and has enough external resources to be able to accept a range of fees and be able to tolerate, at times, the expression of narcissistic and neurotic needs in a fee structure that seems reasonable or essential to the patient but which may need to be the subject of further exploration as the analysis unfolds.

Therapists, of course, will vary from one to another, from time to time, and from case to case as to what fee they regard as acceptable. (How we go about making these decisions about acceptability needs careful scrutiny on our part.) In no way should the therapist's being open to discussion of the fee before it is established imply that he cannot take care of himself or that he will submit to a gross under- or overevaluation when expressed through the patient's wish to pay a particular fee. Nor is the fee, obviously, the only or the most important issue talked about at the beginning of treatment. If the discussion of how the fee is to be arrived at is an open one, however, the therapist is often able to start to understand the ways in which wish, defense, resistance, and transference begin to organize themselves in relation to the fee and how this way of organizing a response may relate to other areas of the patient's life. Is the patient, for instance, unnerved by having to take some responsibility in the discussion and setting of the fee, preferring that the therapist establish it? Is this part of a larger pattern of avoiding responsibility or submitting to authority? If the patient is tempted to underestimate his resources to reduce the fee, doesn't such an attempt provide valuable information about how he feels about his own needs, their legitimacy, and the ways in which he must try to fulfill them? How and in what way does the patient include other people in his or her thinking and decision making? A more open-ended approach avoids a situation in which the patient feels he submits (with either unrecognized gratification or resentment) to an imposed order but can, instead, become a participant in the formation of the reality of the fee and is invited to explore just how he would go about constructing that reality.

One may object that the patient's participation in decision making concerning the fee, rather than merely reacting to a decision made by the therapist, may encourage the patient to act out rather than analyze his feelings toward the therapist and gives him the tools with which to do it. Acceding to the demands of the patient for narcissistic gratification by allowing him a part in setting the fee might well only obscure resistances, diminish motivation to work, and make the analysis of transference all the more difficult. This would be true if the setting of the fee in the manner I have proposed were done out of some act of altruism, good will, or a misguided attempt at egalitarianism rather than as a method by which to further explore the patient's psychodynamics and to establish the optimal conditions under which that exploration can continue. Furthermore, patients often act out in any case. They miss appointments, come late, or engage in activities outside the therapy hour that reflect and deflect transference feelings. While we do not encourage it, most of the behavior is tolerated by the analyst as he attempts to understand with the patient the feelings and conflicts that underlie such behavior. The same should hold true for the fee. Just as some acting-out behaviors will put an end to treatment, there are some attempts to manipulate payment that cannot be tolerated. For the most part, however, my experience has been that acting out around a fuller discussion of the fee is minimal, and the benefit of asking the patient to take responsibility not only for paying, but for helping to set the fee and to explore how he goes about doing that with the therapist, is often invaluable.

There may be certain instances in which a certain fee is accepted by the therapist, not because of the patient's inability to pay more, but for psychodynamic reasons. Eissler (2), for instance, points out that with certain schizoid or depressed patients not charging any fee or a reduced one may be necessary to engage them in treatment. In my experience, this is also true for certain delinquents and their families. It is also true for certain patients who have subtle difficulties with ego boundaries and for whom paying less assures them of a comfortable separateness which they may need in order to enter an intensive treatment. At times, the wish to pay less may not only be a form of withholding that seems psychologically necessary to the patient, but may also represent a wish to protect the therapeutic relationship from the "slings and arrows of outrageous fortune" which might bring it to an end. Almost every patient at one time or another has wondered, "What will happen if I run out of money?" Those patients with significant separation anxiety or lack of confidence in their ability to sustain good fortune may try to answer the question by making the fee one they could afford under almost any circumstance. Such attitudes and resistances that arise around the fee can often neither be fully understood or analyzed at the onset of treatment. Thus, in some cases, the therapist must be able to tolerate temporary or even sustained reduction in the fee if the treatment is to be begun. The following case illustrates such a situation.

Case Example

A young man who made a good living as an insurance salesman was reluctant to pay me the same hourly fee for analysis that he had paid another analyst for therapy prior to seeing me. Although he could afford the fee, he was frightened that his resources would be drained and that he would be unable to buy a home or take the rather splendid vacations upon which he had counted. While these attitudes toward the fee and their payment reflected a narcissistic orientation and fear of involvement which had, in fact, led him to seek treatment, they could be understood in the light of his experience. The patient was a child of parents who, after great difficulty and suffering, managed to flee the Holocaust. They were often in serious danger, and only by a combination of luck, ingenuity, and financial resources had they been able to survive. Drawing on his knowledge of history and his parents' experiences, the patient relived in fantasies tailored to his own childhood conflicts the dangers and the threat of annihilation of those Holocaust years. He was convinced one had to be rich, powerful, uncommitted, and able to move at a moment's notice in order to survive. He was not about to put all his eggs in one basket.

To insist that he give up such ideas and pay the higher fee in order to enter analysis would be to ask for a cure or mere compliance before the therapeutic work had begun. Understanding this man's anxiety about surviving and allowing him to set the lower fee he suggested was the first step in treatment. The meaning of the fee to him would, of course, have to be explored further and the gratification he obtained from this piece of acting out understood and interpreted. As he began to understand the extent of his fears about survival and his mistrust of others, and as he grew able to better commit himself to the analytic process, it might be expected that his neurotic need for assurance through the accumulation of money could be successfully analyzed and a higher fee, if necessary, negotiated. The patient, in fact, volunteered after some months of analysis to raise the fee. The meaning of his wish to give me more, however, came in the wake of his revelations to me of how awful a person he felt himself to be. He felt the need to better compensate me for tolerating him. The proposed fee raise was initiated only after its transferential meanings had been fully explored.

CHANGING THE FEE

Any raising or lowering of the fee on the part of the therapist may be a form of acting out and should be fully explored before it is put into effect. Eissler (2) suggested that it may be preferable to stay with the fee originally agreed upon at the beginning of treatment so as to provide the patient with a sense of security regarding the treatment situation. But I think that not discussing a change in fee, at times, in the light of some real change in the patient's or therapist's financial situation, some significant change in the economy (inflation or recession), or some better understanding of the fee's psychic meaning may also contribute to difficulties. Not raising a fee may reflect an inhibition of assertiveness on the analyst's part. Not responding to a request to lower it might, at times, reflect a failure to appreciate the realities of the patient's life. Such a request may not only imply a wish to be cared for or a resistance to analytic work. It might, in fact, imply the opposite: a wish to continue the work despite realities that make it difficult to do so. Freedman (13) has suggested that there are certain situations in which deferral of payment, sometimes for years, is advisable. He cites case examples of medical students whose parents are no longer willing or able to pay for analytic treatment. These patients will be earning a good living upon graduation and, Freedman feels, can be asked to pay the agreed-upon fee once they are employed. Such an agreement can be reached, obviously, only after careful consideration of its implications. In what way is the deferred payment of the full fee preferable to inquiring whether the student can work while in school and pay a reduced fee that he and the analyst think is reasonable given his circumstances? Does one approach move analytic inquiry forward better than the other? What are the transference and countertransference implications of assuming that the patient will be successful in the future and willing and able to pay off his debt? Is the process of termination significantly changed when the patient leaves with a debt to be paid in installments which will necessarily keep him in contact with the analyst? These questions need to be carefully explored.

What seems most important to me is that any change in fee be subjected to careful scrutiny. The meaning of the current and proposed financial arrangement to the patient must be explored. We should, as much as possible, discuss with the patient how best to change the fee.

Case Example

When, for instance, I mentioned to a patient that a raise in fee might be in order (without suggesting an amount), and I wondered how she felt about it, she avoided the subject for the rest of the session. The next day she said, "Well, you know, I'm not about to leave the analysis now, so I'll have to submit." This attitude, I knew, was the repetition of an attitude toward her father under whose self-interested and uncaring behavior she felt she had labored as a child. When I pointed out to her that I had suggested we discuss the matter, as she might have reasons for feeling an increase was not a good idea, she again insisted that I was going to impose an increase anyway. I pointed to her insistence on seeing me as she had her father and to her own repetition of feeling uncared for by men. When she realized I was, in fact, truly interested in exploring her thoughts and feelings about a fee change and the amount of increase, if any, she felt would be reasonable, she began to cry. She admitted to being afraid of her love and longing for me, and for her father, and recounted how she tried to control and deny these feelings through angry renunciations. She was, in fact, afraid that she would give me anything I asked for. Several weeks passed in which she struggled with her fears that her admission of love would end in her humiliation and would go unreciprocated. She then remarked that since she had some decision-making power over the fee, she could choose to retaliate for her unrequited love by withholding the higher fee from me. My response was that I understood she might choose to act toward me as she had toward her father. She again cried. She realized she was keeping a careful balance sheet of what she gave and what she received emotionally, just as she had seen her father, a tax lawyer, do with finances. At the end of the month, she decided to pay a slightly higher fee, commensurate with what she knew was the usual fee paid for analysis in the community. Later, she was to say, "I perceived it as a shock, the sudden awareness that you cared how I felt about an important decision that affected you."

For this patient, so easily subject to feeling ignored and narcissistically injured, always balancing the books to maintain a precarious self-esteem, the perception that she could be listened to and participate in a process was extremely meaningful. For her, the concrete demonstration, through the fee, of my wish to include her in the analytic process was most helpful in allowing her to tolerate with less fear her positive feelings toward me and through them to better understand her relationship with her father. At the same time, she began to become aware that she protected her mother from criticism because she needed her so much. Once she could feel safer with a man (me, father), she could begin to explore her idealized view of mother which hid her aggression and rivalry toward her. Such an exploration as I have described could only be done in a setting in which my own interest in a fee increase, though clearly present, did not take precedence over the analysis of conflict and defense. The patient had to feel safe enough to be free to refuse, to withhold as she had with her father, without jeopardizing the treatment.

CONCLUDING REMARKS

Psychiatric and psychoanalytic training often does little to prepare residents and candidates for dealing with the practical and theoretical issues surrounding the setting and collection of fees (see Chapters 10 and 14). Supervisors often pay too little attention to how the supervisee arrived at the fee for analysis or therapy. When a therapist and supervisor make a tacit agreement to avoid a full discussion of fees and their meanings to the patient and the therapist, a significant factor in the treatment may be overlooked and may continue to be ignored in the supervisee's future work. The therapist, in these circumstances, may not be asked to explore in supervision how much he values his psychiatric or analytic training, what asking to be paid or not paid means to him, and what conflicts around fees and money he may experience. Yet significant transference and countertransference feelings may be expressed in the attitude toward the fee. The failure to explore fees and their significance fully in supervision may result in some residents or candidates, upon graduation, terminating rather quickly with their low-fee cases. In these instances of premature termination, it is often the therapist's inability to negotiate fees or to understand the role they have played in the treatment for both patient and therapist that leads to difficulties. It is, therefore, important that in our own work with patients and in our supervision of other therapists we devote some time and thought to how we negotiate fees with patients.

REFERENCES

1. Freud, S. On beginning the treatment. (Further recommendations on the technique of psychoanalysis) (1913). *Standard edition,* Vol. 12, (pp. 121–144). London: Hogarth Press, 1958.
2. Eissler, K. R. On some theoretical and technical problems regarding the payment of fees for psychoanalytical treatment. *Int. Rev. Psychoanal.,* 1:73–101, 1974.
3. Haak, N. Comments on the analytical situation. *Int. J. Psychoanal.,* 38:183–195, 1957.
4. Borneman, E. *The psychoanalysis of money.* New York: Urizen Books, 1976.
5. Freud, S. Preface to Max Eitingon's report on the Berlin Psychoanalytical Polyclinic. Standard Edition (1923, Vol. 19, p. 285). London: Hogarth Press, 1958.
6. Lorand, S., and Console, W. Therapeutic results in psychoanalytic treatment without a fee. *Int. J. Psychoanal.,* 39:59–65, 1958.
7. Favreau, J. Report on Paris Psychoanalytic Clinic. *IPA Newsletter,* XIV(3), 5–6, 1977.
8. Lievano, J. Observations about payment of psychotherapy fees. *Psychiatr. Q.,* 41:324–328, 1967.
9. Shonbar, R. The fee as a focus for transference and countertransference. *Am. J. Psychiatry,* 21:275–285, 1967.
10. Hilles, L. The clinical management of the nonpaying patient. A case study. *Bull. Menninger Clin.,* 16:98–104, 1971.
11. Gedo, J. A note on nonpayment of psychiatry fees. *Int. J. Psychoanal.,* 44: 368–371, 1963.
12. Shafer, R. *The analytic attitude.* New York: Basic Books, 1983.
13. Freedman, A. Special fee arrangements in psychoanalysis. Presented at Fall Meeting, American Psychoanalytic Association, December 17, 1983.

13

The Influence of Fee Assessment on Premature Therapy Termination

John F. McRae, Ph.D.

Recent studies in several community mental health centers (CMHCs) have revealed that 13–45% of adult outpatients drop out of treatment within the first three sessions (1–4). As these dropout rates have come to light, questions have been raised about the reasons for them. In response, three classes of variables have been conceptualized by Baekeland and Lundwall (5) as important in a client's prematurely terminating treatment: intraclient (demographic, clinical, social expectations), intracounselor (counselor's experience, prognosis, and liking for the client), and extratherapy (family attitudes toward treatment, babysitting, transportation, work schedule problems, and fees for treatment).

Although there have been numerous studies of intraclient and intracounselor variables, little systematic research has been conducted on extratherapy variables related to premature termination of treatment. Garfield (6) interviewed early terminators to determine their reasons for not returning for a second appointment. Six of the 11 terminators cited some external difficulty (e.g., lack of transportation, no babysitter, or inability to get away from work). Three thought that therapy was not helping them, or they did not like the therapist; two stated they had improved. Garfield's (6) retrospective study suggested that premature termination does not necessarily mean treatment failure. It also suggested that extratherapy factors associated with dropping out of treatment may be a fruitful area for further research. Fiester and Rudestam (7) suggested that early psycho-

This chapter is based on a doctoral dissertation completed at the University of Utah. I am grateful for the assistance of Addie Fuhriman, Ph.D. in the preparation of this work and to the Salt Lake Community Mental Health Center for assistance in sanctioning the research and helping in data collection.

132

therapy termination cannot be equated with treatment failure in all cases. In their study they found that many patients unilaterally terminated despite their perception of the initial session as being an overall positive experience. This further suggests that extratherapy factors may be important.

Pope, Geller, and Wilkinson (8) recently found that neither fee assessment (no fee, welfare, insurance, scaled payment, full payment) nor socioeconomic status (SES) for individual psychotherapy in a CMHC was significantly correlated with number of appointments. They did find, however, that clients diagnosed as psychotic and with transient situational disturbances had significantly fewer appointments than neurotics and clients with personality disorders. They suggested that because of the failure to find that fee assessment had a significant effect on therapeutic process, it was invalid to consider that fee assessment served a therapeutic purpose. Unfortunately, their research design combined both failed and kept appointments, so that an analysis of the impact of fee assessment on failing appointments or dropping out was not possible. In addition, the study looked at length of treatment as a dependent measure, with the mean number of appointments being 13.

Balch, Ireland, and Lewis (9) examined the relationship between source of payment and therapy process variables for 404 admissions to a CMHC. They divided their clients into self-payers and third party plus self-payers. Their analyses found that third party plus self-payers had more frequent and longer clinic contacts than self-payers, even when SES, age, and sex were taken into account. Their findings tended to refute the idea that absence of personal payment or financial sacrifice would have a deleterious effect on the frequency and length of treatment contacts and the type of client discharge. However, their study left unanswered the question of the impact of fee versus no fee on premature treatment termination.

Psychoanalytic points of view favoring fee assessment have stressed the symbolic commitment made by the client through fee payments. "The analysis will not go well if the patient is paying less than he can reasonably afford to pay. It should be a sacrifice for him" (10). Nonpsychoanalytic rationales for the therapeutic effects of fee payment have also developed. Davids (11) employed a cognitive dissonance theory to predict that a low fee assessment might lead a client to devalue counseling and, subsequently, drop out prematurely.

In addition to these rationales for assessing treatment fees, many CMHCs are increasingly dependent for survival on client and third-party reimbursement. The degree to which they can become self-supporting is the degree to which they can guarantee their survival. Morrison (12), in reviewing the barriers to self-sufficiency for CMHCs, questioned their ability to survive in their present form after termination of federal grant support. He suggested focusing attention on all sources of revenue, including patient fees.

Other authors (5,7,13) have suggested that fee assessment may be a potent extratherapy factor, but no further systematic research has been reported. This study randomly assigns clients without private insurance or welfare, regardless of their ability to pay the sliding scale fee, to a no fee group or to a sliding scale fee group. In this way, the relatively "pure" effect of fee assessment (no fee versus sliding scale fee) on premature termination could be investigated.

METHOD

Subjects

One hundred first admission adult clients (18 years of age or older) to the Downtown Outpatient Unit of Salt Lake Community Mental Health Center (SLMHC) from September 1977 to February 1978 comprised the sample for this study. As a group, they had the following characteristics: 48% were male and 52% were female; 42% were 18 to 24 years old, 53% were 25 to 44 years old, and 5% were 45+; 37% were married, 43% were single, and 20% were divorced or widowed; 47% were unemployed; 92% were white; 15% had completed high school, 26% had college/technical training, and 17% were college graduates; 48% were referred by self, family, or friend, and 52% were referred by another agency; 66% had no prior mental health care, while 34% had received prior outpatient and/or inpatient care; and 25% were diagnosed as psychotic and 75% as nonpsychotic.

Dependent Variable

Dropout. A dropout was operationally defined as a client who was interviewed in an intake appointment and who was scheduled for another appointment but, subsequently, broke or cancelled the appointment and did not reschedule the second or third one within 2 months after the intake session. As long as clients kept a rescheduled third therapy appointment, they were not considered dropouts for the purposes of this study. This was done in accordance with Brandt's (14) observation that previous inconclusive studies have confounded dropouts, typically defined on the basis of arbitrary session number cutoffs, with dropouts defined in terms of the therapist's wish or expectation that the client should return for further treatment. Even if the clients notified SLCMHC that they would not appear for future appointments, they were considered dropouts since they did not have their therapist's concurrence. Clients who were terminated by the intake worker or therapist or were referred elsewhere were not included in this study. Clients who reached a mutual agreement of termination with their therapist during sessions two or three were not considered dropouts.

Independent Variable

Fee assessment. There were two major fee assessment conditions or groups utilized in this study: 1) no fee—regardless of their ability to pay a sliding scale fee, the clients in this group were informed that there was no fee for their treatment; clients were assigned to this no fee group on a random basis; and 2) fee—clients were charged a weekly or monthly fee. Both were set on a sliding scale, taking into account household income and the number of dependents.

Diagnosis. The primary diagnosis was determined at an intake staffing by a team of psychiatrists, psychologists, social workers, and a nurse using the diagnostic scheme of the *Diagnostic and Statistical Manual of Mental Disorders* (15). For the purpose of statistical analysis, each patient's diagnosis was assigned (employing the major categorizing framework of the DSM-II) to either a psychotic or nonpsychotic category.

Socioeconomic status. SES was computed by Hollingshead and Redlich's (16) two-factor index, which differentially weighted occupation and education. Those scoring above the midpoint on the scale were defined as higher SES, and those scoring below the midpoint were defined as lower SES. Data on occupation and education were routinely gathered at the time of the intake appointment.

Procedure

All first-time adult outpatient admissions to SLCMHC during their intake appointment who did not have private insurance or Medicaid (welfare) were randomly assigned by the intake worker to either the no fee or the fee group. In order to standardize the fee assessment instructions given to clients, intake workers were trained to use standardized wording in assigning clients to groups. Clients were then staffed at an intake meeting and assigned to a therapist for treatment.

RESULTS

Fee Assessment and Dropping Out

The basic purpose of the study was to look at differences in the dropout rate in the fee group versus the no fee group. A chi-square analysis of the data was significant beyond the 0.05 level ($X^2 = 5.16$, $df = 1$), indicating that not assessing a fee for treatment was a significant influence in premature treatment dropouts.

Other Findings

In addition to fee assessment influencing clients to drop out of treatment, a chi-square test between psychotic-other and drop-stay was found significant at the 0.02 level ($X^2 = 5.48$, $df = 1$), indicating that nonpsychotics were significantly more likely than psychotics to prematurely drop from treatment if they had not been assessed a fee for treatment.

Only 2 out of 25 psychotics dropped from treatment. Psychotics seemed to remain in treatment regardless of their assignment to fee or no fee groups. This was not the case with nonpsychotic clients, as 25 out of these 75 clients prematurely dropped from treatment. In fact, a chi-square test on only the nonpsychotic (other) clients between fee-no fee and drop-stay was significant beyond the 0.01 level ($X^2 = 8.77$, $df = 1$). A phi coefficient of correlation of 0.35 for this data was significant at the 0.01 level, indicating that fee-no fee assignment accounted for 12% of the variance associated with a nonpsychotic client dropping out of treatment.

In order to rule out the influence of SES on dropping out of treatment, a chi-square utilizing drop-stay and high SES-low SES was run. $X^2 = 0.68$ was not significant ($\pi = .50$, $df = 1$), suggesting that whether clients are high or low SES does not significantly influence whether they drop or stay in treatment.

Additional Findings

The study took place in a CMHC that routinely sets fees for treatment according to a person's ability to pay. The operating procedure in the center was to reduce the sliding scale fee to zero if the person stated that he or she was unable to pay the minimum $1.25 fee for treatment. In the present study, 71 clients were randomly assigned originally to the fee group. However, 19 of the 71 clients stated that they were unable to afford the minimum fee. Consequently, they had their fee waived. This reduced the fee group to an *N* of 52 and introduced a source of internal invalidity: differential experimental mortality between the fee and no fee groups. It was not possible to circumvent or avoid this source of invalidity by: 1) requiring these 19 clients to pay fees when they stated they were unable to, 2) refusing them treatment because of their inability to pay, or 3) including them in the fee group when, in fact, their fee had been waived. The first two potential actions were judged to be unethical, and the third would have violated the basic hypothesis of the study (i.e., does paying a fee influence premature termination or outcome?). It was decided to analyze the characteristics of these 19 clients so that they might be compared to the characteristics of those in the fee group, but it was decided to exclude them from the analysis of the hypotheses of the study.

As might be expected, the group of clients who had their fee waived were significantly different from both the fee and the no fee groups in terms of their SES. The basis of their fee waiver was inability to pay because of unemployment. Therefore, 89% of this waived fee group were low SES in contrast to 52% of the fee group and 69% of the no fee group. A chi-square analysis of the SES of the fee group and waived fee clients revealed that the groups were significantly different in their SES ($X^2 = 6.80$, df $= 1$, $\pi = 0.01$). On the other hand, the waived fee clients were not significantly different from either the no fee group or the fee group in terms of their diagnoses. Twenty-six percent of the clients whose fees were waived were psychotic in comparison to 19% of the fee group (from which they were excluded) and 31% of the no fee group.

In terms of their respective dropout rates, the waived fee clients experienced a 37% dropout rate, as did the no fee group, while the fee group had a dropout rate of 17%. When the waived fee clients were combined with the fee group, their combined dropout rate was 23% versus 37% for the no fee group.

The results in Table 1 contrast the findings of the study with and without these 19 clients whose fees were waived. The rationale for including these results is that they provide some data that suggest that a psychological set or expectation that a client will have to pay a fee for treatment may be important. In the case of this study, this waived fee group initially expected that there would be a fee for their treatment. It was only at the point of setting a minimum fee that it was waived because of their inability to pay.

Table 1
Contrasts of Significant Differences Found With and Without
19 Waived Fee Clients

	100 Clients	119 Clients

Hypothesis #1: There is a significant difference in dropout rate in the Fee group versus the No Fee group.

Results: X^2 significant 0.05 level X^2 nonsignificant $p=0.10$

Additional findings:

1. Psychotic diagnosis influences clients to remain in treatment.

Results: X^2 significant 0.02 level X^2 nonsignificant $p=0.20$

2. Nonpsychotic diagnosis influences clients to prematurely drop out.

Results: X^2 significant 0.01 level X^2 significant 0.01 level

3. Socio-economic status influences clients to drop out.

Results: X^2 nonsignificant $p=0.50$ X^2 nonsignificant $p=0.20$

DISCUSSION

Fee Assessment and Dropping Out

This study aimed to provide data concerning the little-researched extratherapy variable of fee assessment and its impact on premature psychotherapy termination. As indicated earlier, several researchers have reported a 13–45% range of dropout rates within three visits to a CMHC. The overall dropout rate found in this study was 27% within the first three visits. However, the dropout rate for the no fee group was 37% as compared with the 17% rate for the fee group.

The hypothesis that fee assessment influences whether a client prematurely terminates treatment was confirmed. Perhaps the lack of a symbolic commitment expressed through the fee, as suggested by Menninger (10) and others, is an important factor. A related explanation may be that clients do not value or expect much from treatment for which there is no fee and, hence, break appointments and drop out quickly. This explanation would confirm Davids' (11) use of cognitive dissonance theory to predict that no fee for treatment would lead a client to expect little from treatment and consequently devalue it and drop out.

Pope et al. (8) found that no fee, scaled payment, and full payment were not correlated with the number of appointments a patient had. They concluded that it was invalid to consider that fee assessment served a therapeutic purpose. The conclusion of the present study is that fee assessment serves a therapeutic purpose, particularly for nonpsychotic clients, in that clients return for therapy appointments and do not prematurely terminate treatment, as do their no fee counterparts. The conflicting finding between the Pope et al. study (8) and this study are perhaps best explained by this study's focus on early psychotherapy termination (within the first three sessions). In the Pope et al. study (8) the dependent measure employed was the number of visits, and the mean was 13. In addition, this study's attempt at random assignment of clients to fee and no fee groups more clearly demonstrates the impact of no treatment fee than the Pope et al. study did, where clients were assigned strictly on the basis of their ability to pay a sliding scale fee.

Diagnosis and Dropping Out

It was of interest that only 2 out of 25 psychotics (8%) prematurely dropped from treatment in comparison to 25 out of 75 nonpsychotics (33%). When the data on fee-no fee and drop-stay were analyzed on only the nonpsychotic clients, it was clear that not assessing a fee affected the dropout of nonpsychotic clients before the third session. The present study's findings suggest that psychotics do not prematurely drop from treatment, regardless of whether they are or are not charged a fee for their treatment.

The mean fee assessed clients was $2.50, with a range of $1.25 to $14. The assessment and collection of these small fees will not insure the financial viability of CMHCs. In fact, the collection of individual fees may cost more in administrative overhead than it returns. However, the assessment of a fee may act as an expectation-setting phenomenon that may enable clients to value their treatment and invest themselves in it, or at least to continue to return to treatment until they can hopefully benefit from it.

This expectation may even be true for clients who were to have a minimum fee set but had it waived because of an inability to pay. It may be worthwhile giving clients the information that they are about to receive fee-for-treatment services (valuable services) even if the fee may be justifiably waived. The present study seemed to confirm that nonpsychotic clients were much more likely to remain in treatment if they were given this expectation.

Some interesting speculation is created by comparing the findings of the study with and without the 19 clients whose fees were waived (see Table 1). When these clients are included in the fee group it seems that their low SES (due to their unemployment) reduced the level of significance (from $\pi = 0.05$ to $\pi = 0.10$) between fee-no fee and drop-stay, since their inclusion increased the dropout percentage from 17–23% in the fee group. As noted in Table 1, there is a stronger, but still not significant, trend for SES to influence dropout when the 19 clients are included in the analysis (with 100 clients $\pi = 0.50$, with 119 clients $\pi = 0.20$). This suggests that SES does have some influence on early psychotherapy termination.

The influence of diagnosis is also seen. When the 19 clients are not included, there is a significant difference ($\pi = 0.20$) in favor of psychotics remaining in treatment. However, when the 19 clients are included, this finding becomes nonsignificant ($\pi = 0.20$) because 3 out of the 5 psychotics who had their fees waived dropped out in contrast to only 2 out of 25 psychotics in the fee and no fee groups combined who dropped out. However, as noted in Table 1, the one finding that remains highly significant ($\pi = 0.01$ level), regardless of whether 100 or 119 clients are compared, is that nonpsychotics who do not pay a fee are much more likely to drop out.

It seems, according to this study, that fee assessment (and perhaps the expectations set by it and the value given to treatment as a result of it), employment status, and diagnosis are influential factors in premature dropouts from treatment. These factors should be considered by clinicians and CMHC program directors as they establish and carry out fee policies.

REFERENCES

1. Fiester, A. R. Pretherapy expectations, perception of the initial interview and early psychotherapy terminations: A multivariate study. Unpublished doctoral dissertation, Miami University (Ohio), 1974.
2. Fiester, A., Silverman, W., and Beech, R. Ravenswood Hospital Community Mental Health Center emergency/outpatient internal analysis. Unpublished manuscript, University of Illinois Medical Center, 1974.
3. Murphy, M. Results from evaluating a Canadian regional mental health program. *Hosp. Commun. Psychiatry*, 24(8):533–538, 1973.
4. Sue, S., McKinney, H. I., and Allen, D. B. Predictors of the duration of therapy for clients in the Community Mental Health System. *Commun. Mental Health J.*, 12(4):365–376, 1976.
5. Baekeland, F., and Lundwall, I. Dropping out of treatment: A critical review. *Psychol. Bull.*, 82(5):738-783, 1975.
6. Garfield, S. L. A note on patients' reasons for leaving psychotherapy. *Psychol. Rep.*, 13:38, 1963.
7. Fiester, A., and Rudestam, K. A multivariate analysis of the early dropout process. *J. Consult. Clin. Psychol.*, 43(4):528–535, 1975.

8. Pope, K. S., Geller, J. D., and Wilkinson, I. Fee assessment and outpatient psychotherapy. *J. Consult. Clin. Psychol.*, 43:835, 841, 1975.
9. Balch, P., Ireland, J. F., and Lewis, S. B. Fees and therapy: Relation of source of payment to course of therapy at a community mental health center. *J. Consult. Clin. Psychol.*, 45:504, 1977.
10. Menninger, K. *Theory of psychoanalytic techniques.* New York: Science Editions, 1961.
11. Davids, A. The relation of cognitive dissonance theory to an aspect of psychotherapeutic practice. *Am. Psychologist*, 19:329–332, 1964.
12. Morrison, L. J. Barriers in self-sufficiency for mental health centers. *Hosp. Commun. Psychiatry*, 28(3):185–191, 1977.
13. Graziano, A. M., and Fink, R. I. Second-order effects in mental health treatment. *J. Consult. Clin. Psychol.*, 40(3):356–364, 1973.
14. Brandt, L. W. Studies of dropout patients in psychotherapy: A review of findings. *Psychotherapy: Theory, Research and Practice*, 2:2–13, 1965.
15. Committee on Nomenclature and Statistics. American Psychiatric Association. *DSM-II.* Washington, D.C.: American Psychiatric Association, 1968.
16. Hollingshead, A. B., and Redlich, F. C. *Social class and mental illness.* New York: John Wiley & Sons, 1958.

14

Psychotherapy Fees
and Therapist Training

Stefan A. Pasternack, M.D.

Training in psychotherapy must provide adequate education and clinical and administrative supervision in the management of fees and monetary issues. This chapter will outline a set of basic fee attitudes and a schema for teaching them to trainees in psychotherapy. American psychiatry and medicine are undergoing profound changes in the method of payment in psychiatric/psychotherapy services (1,2). However, patients must pay for the services they receive one way or another—directly in a fee-for-service arrangement or indirectly through prepaid payment plans. Patients in therapy, therefore, are concerned about the worth of the services they receive and how their therapists account for them financially.

BASIC ATTITUDES AND FEE POLICIES
FOR TRAINEES IN PSYCHOTHERAPY

Trainees in psychotherapy benefit when they are provided with a clearly defined set of fee policies. These policies must be consistent with basic psychodynamic concepts and fit clearly within the context of a therapeutic relationship. In psychotherapy the formation, maintenance, and utilization of a therapeutic attitude is a cornerstone of treatment. Understanding, empathy, and helpfulness are crucial aspects of the development of insight into basic human problems.

The fee for psychotherapy is an integral part of the treatment relationship (3,4). It is the one aspect to which the therapist is entitled. As trainees come to appreciate the integral nature of money in the treatment, they are better able to make use of clear guidelines. Clear guidelines foster and protect the treatment relationship. Thus, trainees are better able to understand the phenomenon when patients are being dishonest, obsessively withholding, hysterically complaining, narcissistically demanding, or self-ishly unable to appreciate their financial responsibility to the therapist or the clinic. Firm guidelines also provide counterbalances to trainees' conflicts about money and their doubts about the worth of their service.

Psychotherapy as a Compensable Service

Psychotherapy is a professional service provided by a trained person, or one in training, to a patient for which an appropriate fee is to be charged and collected (3,5). Beginning therapists often doubt the value of their work and encounter difficulty charging for it (6,7). A psychotherapy fee emphasizes not only to the patient, but to the trainee as well, that psychotherapy has value in "the coin of the realm." The fee also reflects the fact that the educational organization or service organization believes in the trainees' basic competence and in the practical value of the work. Emphasizing to trainees that psychotherapy is a compensable service furthermore helps them appreciate the value of the educational/supervisory support that the educational organization provides for them as they become psychotherapists. In general, helping trainees and patients to understand the importance in therapy of the fee provides an additional contribution to the development by the patient and the therapists of a complete object relationship.

When there is ambivalence within the training organization about fees for services, the trainee's belief in his work is seriously undermined. Treatment is usually compromised, and outcome of therapy suffers.

The Sliding Scale

Since psychotherapy training programs often receive governmental or community funding and often utilize trainees to provide direct service, the fees are usually well below rates charged by fully trained professionals working in the community. A lower range of fees is usually determined by the income needs of the clinic program for revenue. The sliding-fee scale concept has been developed in most programs in a way to adjust a patient's fee according to his income, number of dependents, and insurance coverage. Trainees in psychotherapy need assistance in understanding the philosophy behind the sliding-fee scale—a philosophy that often goes beyond simple statistical characteristics.

Focus is too often on the patients' income and insurance as fee determinants, overlooking other areas that affect the trainee's self-concept.

Training in psychotherapy is usually conceptualized along a developmental line: an inexperienced professional undertakes further education and begins to treat less difficult patients with maximal supervision. As the trainee progresses, he gradually is assigned more difficult cases, and, with further education, he gradually needs less and less supervision and has a greater number of treatment cases. Such a progression fosters autonomy, self-confidence, and self-education and is conceived as an ego-building experience. Concomitantly, trainees should be asked to start newer patients at higher levels on the sliding scale as their training progresses, a reflection of their developing technical skills and progressive educational background. This idea of connecting the sliding scale to level of trainee experience is frequently overlooked.

The uppermost fees in the sliding scale are usually set well below private practice rates for several important reasons. First, trainees lack the education and experience of fully trained practitioners. Second, most community training programs do not wish to be considered in direct competition with the private practice community. Trainees need to understand these simple facts and to recognize that they should not compare themselves negatively with fully trained professionals who may be charging appropriately higher fees.

The lowest limit of fees, however, should not simply be based on the clinic's minimal financial needs. In some instances, ridiculously low fees denigrate the therapists' skill and denigrate psychotherapy itself. One clinic had a lowest fee of 50 cents. This was found to be unbelievable by the patients, who spent more on a soda or a bus ride. When such ridiculously low fees are charged, patients and therapists suffer from the disturbing notion that an hour of their professional time is worth so little. In such situations trainee morale and self-confidence may be damaged irreparably. Similarly, most patients cannot take 50-cent therapy seriously.

The upper level of fees is sometimes allowed to escalate beyond common sense. If administrative policy encourages all trainees, regardless of year, to set the highest fees, the value of training is undermined and grandiosity may be encouraged. Similarly, if administrative policy obliges trainees to charge as much as the private practice community or as much as "the insurance pays," the therapist's self-concept may also be corrupted. It is important not to set upper fees in such a way as to foster overcharging or to neglect the message that training and education and experience makes one's work more valuable.

The middle range of fees provides other dilemmas when setting fees on sliding scales. Since trainees tend to doubt the value of their work, they unwittingly tend to charge lower fees than they might appropriately establish. Less than adequate fees often come about when a sliding-fee scale is set in large increments. It is advisable for fees to be adjusted within a dollar or two dollars, rather than at 5- or 10-dollar increments. This gives the psychotherapy trainee a better experience in modulating charges and the opportunity to gain more experience in adjusting fees. It also fosters more specific inquiry into the exact details of a clinic patient's financial background. Less than adequate fees also may convey variously perceived messages to patients. Some may feel special; some may fear hidden expectation, if they are given a less than proper fee; others may feel they are getting away with something. Deviation from the clinic fee schedule, therefore, sets off various troublesome reactions in patients. Trainees need encouragement to adhere carefully to a well-established fee scale.

Recognition of the Value of the Work

Many psychotherapy trainees have been so involved in educational pursuits that they may have had few opportunities to earn income. For many, the psychotherapy fee is often the first income they have ever generated by professional activities. It is important that the fees generated by trainees in psychotherapy be recognized and given proper attention by clinic and organizational leaders. This fosters the residents' or trainees' motivation to follow fee policies. Trainees need to be given credit for their contribution to the general revenue base of their sponsoring organization. Giving credit may also take concrete form. Since it is not possible to regulate the flow of patients to the point where all trainees receive patients paying exactly the same fees, there will be variations in the amount of billings that each trainee achieves. Credit may be given to the trainees who collect the highest percentage of their billings in the form of trips to educational programs, books, or even financial bonuses.

We are trying to establish in the trainees a conviction about the meaning of their work. A basic attitude has to be that psychotherapy has value, and the fee is part of this concept. In the course of training, many experience difficulty believing that what they do "is really therapeutic." All too often, insurance companies schedule payments in such a way as to devalue cognitive procedures and heavily reimburse technical ones. Trainees often doubt the healing power of words and underestimate the importance they hold for patients. It is only with the passage of time that trainees come to appreciate the importance of a meaningful therapeutic relationship to a troubled patient. Trainees, therefore, need time to see that their services produce results. One way to demonstrate that their services are worthy is in the form of the appropriate fee they are encouraged to charge. With time, trainees come to recognize not only the human value of their work but its important financial value as well.

Changes in Fees

Changes in fees often present special problems for trainees. Careful policies must be elucidated. It is generally best for the fee to be set during the intake process. It should then be confirmed by the trainee-therapist's supervisor. During the course of therapy many patients may request changes in their fee, usually seeking a lower one. One must seek meaning in this request beyond the external reality explanation offered. Trainees need to be taught to give careful consideration to the multiple psychodynamic meanings and the reasons that a request for fee changes comes about at a particular juncture in psychotherapy. Some patients may regress during therapy and may seek dependency gratification in the form of a lower fee. A policy about changes and fees must be flexible enough to meet realistic demands but also oriented so that underlying meanings are sought. Fees may also be increased during the course of psychotherapy. Patients often are able to improve their level of functioning to the point that they substantially increase their own earnings. While fees should not be escalated beyond reasonable limits, it is unrealistic to allow patients to increase their own earnings and continue to pay a low fee. Similarly, as residents or trainees are encouraged to boost their fees when patients' income increases, it fosters their own conviction about the value of their work.

Charges for Missed Appointments

Charging for missed appointments is a controversial subject. It is wise to have a clear policy, one that emphasizes that missed appointments will be charged for. It's clear that childhood patterns of behavior are often aroused during psychotherapy. Resistance to therapy, acting out of emotional conflicts, and regressive desires to avoid painful material at critical junctures often result in missed appointments.

Neurotic patients with healthier object relations have an easier time accepting the idea that they must pay for appointments they miss. More regressed patients are often unable to appreciate the reciprocal nature of the psychotherapy relationship and their responsibility for payment. Trainees need to be alerted to the diagnostic aspects of the patient's reaction to being charged for missed appointments. It is thus important that this idea be carefully communicated to patients ahead of time so that they understand they will be held responsible for appointments that are set aside for them. Why should trainees be encouraged to charge for missed appointments? It helps them to understand that psychotherapy is truly a unique undertaking, unlike any other. It trains them to understand that it is often not possible to make use of time that has been set aside for one patient even if that patient cancels that appointment 24 hours or so early. Trainees are usually encouraged to establish regular appointment times since these foster psychotherapy work. Trainees also have many demands on their time and can rarely grant requests by patients for sudden changes in their appointments. While it may be worthwhile for trainees to attempt to offer alternate appointments, so often this only results in complications in the psychotherapy. Patients often make irrational requests for different hours. If the trainee fails to understand the underlying meaning of such requests, the psychotherapy may be compromised. Similarly, when patients refuse to pay for hours they have missed, it is often a reflection of the patients' lack of capacity for concern for the needs of others and for their monetary responsibility to therapist and clinic.

Should trainees be encouraged to make use of missed appointments for other patients? This also is controversial. It may be practical to do so. But often the patient's sense of having a unique relationship with the therapist may be undermined if he thinks he is easily replaceable. Trainees may benefit from the belief that they have important relationships with their patients and that their hours should be preserved. Although patients may complain about the financial costs, they are spared the psychological cost of feeling replaceable. Ego building may be fostered as the patient is helped to understand the unique nature of the psychotherapy relationship. Trainees often resist the notion that they should charge for missed appointments. Even though this may be carefully explained to them from the standpoint of object relations and ego psychology, so often their resistances to dealing with patients come into play. All too often, a misalliance between the trainee therapist and patient may take the form of canceled appointments. If this becomes frequent, not only is the therapy compromised, but the clinic may be deprived of an important source of finances.

Whatever one's basic orientation toward this subject may be, it is important that it be carefully established and conceptualized and enforced. On the whole, regularly set appointments should be paid for, regardless of the reason for their being missed by the patient, the only exception being a possible health emergency for a patient or a member of his family. Once again, however, flexibility is a critical clinical responsibility, and trainees need to be encouraged to take each instance on its merits. However, a clearly defined policy will enable them to more carefully appreciate the underlying factors when a patient departs from the usual routine.

SCHEMA FOR EDUCATION OF MONETARY
ISSUES IN THE PSYCHOTHERAPY PROGRAM

Many of the basic fee policies can, of course, be communicated during orientation sessions of organizational policy. Fee policy can be included also in a manual of policy and procedures provided to trainees. A number of other approaches should also be employed.

A useful adjunct is the educational seminar for fee issues. A reading list consisting of classical and more contemporary articles on monetary issues should be provided (8–13). Didactic sessions focus on the readings as well as on case presentations in which fee problems have arisen. Trainees should be familiarized with the existing literature and taught to use it to increase their understanding of clinical experience (9,14).

Small-group discussions are an additional educational approach. One session should focus on the trainees' personal financial goals and personal attitudes about money. Under the guidance of a sensitive group leader, trainees may be encouraged to discover how their own monetary experiences (paying tuition, applying for loans, earning money themselves, receiving money from family) may have influenced them in the management of fee issues and clinical situations. Trainees often harbor negative attitudes toward institutions as a result of their long years of paying tuition and feeling regulated by institutional authorities. Trainees tend to overidentify with the "underdog" patient. They may experience difficulty taking up clinic concerns about money. Thus, trainees often set their fees too low, bill incorrectly, fail to collect bills charged, and improperly handle insurance claims. In a number of instances, trainees collude with patients. A second small-group educational session should deal with the finances of the training program. This enables trainees to understand their role in providing revenue to the general income base. Trainees need to understand that they provide valuable income support for the training programs from which they will benefit. Charging for their own psychotherapy also constitutes a major development step for the trainee from the passive dependent status of being a full-time student to the full financial autonomy of full-time employment. Being able to understand that they generate substantial fees for their services during psychotherapy training thus provides trainees with a stepwise developmental process which contains many learning opportunities. A third group discussion should focus on countertransference issues as they relate to the fee. Trainees often become involved in one type or another of misalliance with patients regarding fees. Because of their guilt feelings about their work, they tend to overidentify with patients. A few examples are necessary to illustrate this material.

Case 1

A second-year trainee was concerned about the way he was managing a request for a reduction of fee. He had initially lowered the fee without any supervision or clinic authorization. He now found that the psychotherapy work was not progressing. When this was carefully investigated, it became clear that he had become involved in a serious misalliance with a patient. According to her income and insurance coverage, she fell into the $12 range on the fee scale. As her insurance company had no yearly maximum, but would only pay 50% of the fee charged, she had asked the resident to "double the fee" to $24 and then to discount her portion of it. By doing so, "the clinic still got its money" and the patient would not have to pay anything. Without carefully investigating this, the trainee accepted this proposal. As therapy progressed, this blatant corruption made the patient increasingly uncomfortable. She began to withhold material that she had freely provided before. The trainee overlooked the fact that he had perjured himself by knowingly giving false information on insurance forms. This led the patient to doubt his professional ethics. When he was provided supervision regarding the dilemma that had arisen in the case, he was able to understand that it was related to his need to help this "frail old woman" and his difficulty in setting limits. When the fee was revised, the patient gained increasing insight into her own manipulations and her demandingness. The initial reason for this example of fee misbehavior coming to light was the resident's discomfort which caused him to seek supervision. It subsequently led to the patient's gaining additional insight into her own contribution to the alienation from her family, which had led to her depression.

Case 2

Another resident wished to offer a patient "two sessions for the price of one." He gave extensive rationalizations as to why this was possible. He did not bother to look beneath the surface, but had accepted the patient's statement that she was "a pauper." It was then subsequently discovered, as the supervisor insisted that the resident pursue the matter further, that the patient was, in fact, the recipient of a large annuity. She had somehow concealed this from the resident, and he had succumbed to her feminine wiles. He subsequently revealed that he harbored guilt feelings about his work because he was "learning on the patient." He felt that she was helping him become a therapist and doubted that he was being of any assistance to her. He acknowledged that he was making a kind of financial restitution by giving her "a bargain." As the case developed in further work, it emerged that her wealthy father had given freely of his money but not of his love. She felt emotionally bankrupt and was attempting desperately to obtain extra nourishment from her therapist. Again, the reason this instance became apparent was because of the progressive discomfort on the part of the trainee about his involvement with his patient. Collegial small-group discussions provide a comfortable forum in which trainees may pursue their reactions to patients and discover their countertransference involvement. Support then leads to improvement.

In today's rapidly changing marketplace, it is necessary to provide a seminar that reviews the remarkable economic reorganization of American medicine and psychiatry (2,13–15). It is necessary for trainees to be given accurate information about the bewildering variety of third-party payment plans. Fees for psychotherapy are now included in prepayment plans such as the HMO, PPO, IPA, and EAP. In addition, revisions of Medicaid and Medicare and the introduction of diagnostic related groups (DRGs) need to be carefully discussed (2,13,15). Trainees are thus encouraged to explore the rapid changes taking place in the economy into which they will one day enter. Didactic discussions help them see the entire spectrum of these systems from fee-for-service variety of health plans. Trainees then can better understand the advantages and disadvantages of each delivery care system and payment method.

It is also important, in this rapidly changing set of circumstances, for mental health professionals to be equipped with data about the costs of psychotherapy, the impact of psychotherapy fees on insurance plans, and a variety of methods of payment. In order to ensure that mental health care is adequately funded by corporations, service organizations, local governments, and insurance companies, trainees must become forceful advocates for mental health programs. We have to train them so that they will be able to speak out about the value of their services and seek proper compensation for them.

Training programs regarding psychotherapy and fees must also include instruction in basic accounting practices. Such information fosters a sense of reality about money and gives them practical information about keeping a set of books. When trainees are taught how to maintain ledgers for their patient accounts, they are better equipped for future private practice as well as for future administrative roles. There is simply no substitute for having a professional accountant provide instruction in basic accounting procedures and providing them with basic accounting equipment. Trainees usually appreciate this as they recognize it helps them organize their own personal finances as well.

Providing instruction by a trained accountant also fosters management awareness and increases administrative skills. All too often, mental health clinicians have simply ignored budget and financial issues. They have more recently been displaced by a new mental health management class, a group of executives who oversee cash flow in clinics, handle the insurance forms, and make policies about charges. Thus, the status of the psychotherapist has been undercut in too many situations. Mental health professionals can no longer afford to ignore financial matters. Just as psychotherapy trainees are encouraged to assist their patients to broaden their ego skills to acquire new knowledge and to undertake a widening scope of activities, so should psychotherapy trainees be encouraged to acquire new knowledge such as accounting information. As the next generation of mental health professionals is trained, they should be able to read a budget statement, follow a cash flow record, and make sense out of financial ledgers.

No training program about fees would be complete without a careful review of basic insurance forms. Trainees are often puzzled by code numbers and the methods of reporting services to insurance companies. Sometimes patients will try to manipulate the unknowing, to falsify data, to submit overcharges, or to falsify initial time of diagnostic evaluation. Trainees need to be assisted to complete insurance forms properly. A short discussion and review of basic insurance forms usually is all that is required.

PROVISION OF ADMINISTRATIVE AND CLINICAL SUPERVISION FOR THE TEACHING OF FEES AND MONETARY ISSUES

Periodic performance appraisals are a regular feature of a good psychotherapy training program. Along with evaluation of such additional categories as the trainees' empathy, their capacity to form a relationship, and their ability to master diverse clinical material must now be added fee-related factors. Is the resident or trainee able to perform the appropriate number of psychotherapy hours of treatment? Does the trainee keep accurate records? Are all appropriate fees billed and collected? These questions become important measurements of the resident's work productivity. Productivity and proper utilization of resources now become a further measurement of a trainee's level of clinical maturity, for in later work situations trainees productivity will determine not only job status, but income as well.

An administrative supervisor should be appointed in each clinic situation to review the psychotherapy trainees' overall work output. Furthermore, the administrative supervisor must pay attention to the percentage of bills that are or are not paid. One may speak of a coefficient of

$$\frac{\text{collections.}}{\text{billings}}$$

This coefficient should approach approximately 90%. Losses greater than 10–15% of billing are usually due to mismanagement of patient cases. Is the trainee allowing patients to run up excessively large balances? Are patients submitting payments several months late? These are the measurements of the trainees' efficiency in dealing with fee issues. High balances and late payments are early warning signs for the attentive administrative supervisor. Prompt detection of problems should lead to prompt administrative action.

The administrative supervisor should follow up on accounting education by overviewing the trainee's set of books and methods of record keeping. Each trainee should complete a monthly billing sheet which lists the names of all patients seen, the fees charged, the number of sessions held, and any payments made. While there are various types of record keeping and collection systems from which an administrator may choose, it is important that policies be clearly established and consistently followed. Whatever system is established must be firmly enforced. It is important to instill in the trainees respect for the billing, collection, and bookkeeping system that is established. Once the billing and collection system is allowed to be treated in neglectful fashion a negative attitude becomes established in the trainees' mind which can undermine the entire system. Whatever way it is done, monthly accounting must be made for the work, results tabulated, and administrative review completed. It is best if trainees can prepare and hand out their own bills. This fosters the understanding of the patient about the treatment relationship. It also emphasizes to the patients that they are paying for services received directly from the therapist. It fosters the development of healthy object relationships and brings the fee issue more squarely into focus.

In prepaid payment systems such as HMO, where direct fees are not involved, there often is either a service voucher or some type of record entry system. Thus, in one way or another patients are made aware of the fact that they have a limited number of sessions available to them and that some accounting of the sessions provided is being kept. Thus, any training provided for residents in the management of fees translates into additional sophistication in managing issues in other fee systems.

Administrative supervision becomes most difficult when the administrator has to intervene in the event that bills have not been paid for more than three months. It is important to establish a firm policy that therapy must be stopped if bills are not paid. Once a patient has fallen three months behind in payment, it is not likely that payment will be obtained without going to extraordinary measures, sometimes involving a collection agency. It is wisest, then, to insist that the trainees keep accurate records so that accumulating balances and delayed payments can promptly be detected. This fosters prompt intervention in the conduct of the psychotherapy itself. And when clinical supervisors and trainees are unable to manage the issue, firm administrative action often produces either payment results or an ending of the therapy. At the very least, the trainee is then able to pick up another case which may generate revenue for the clinic.

There are many issues regarding clinical supervision and the collection and billing of psychotherapy fees. Many clinical supervisors are uncomfortable addressing fee issues with trainees. Some clinical supervisors mistakenly believe that if they address issues, this will undermine the establishment of their working relationship with the trainee and feel that they are becoming involved "in administrative issues." It is important to provide some overview of the fee issues for clinical supervisors. Supervisors should also be selected who support the organizational policies and who are willing to be alert to instances of fee dilemmas. Meetings may be held to raise the awareness of supervisors about these matters. It is important to have clinical supervisors of sufficient maturity. Adequate experience in their own professional work is necessary, in order for a clinical supervisor to be comfortable dealing with a wide range of fee misconduct that may be encountered in the course of training programs in psychotherapy. More experienced supervisors are likely to detect the meanings behind patient fee behavior more promptly and more thoroughly. Mature supervisors who are well out of their own training programs are also better equipped to assist trainees with their anxiety about fees and with technical measures necessary and also to provide a more sobering reality influence. Skillful supervisors help trainees master the fee-related problems, especially the countertransference issues that arise.

In some instances, trainees experience realistic discontent with the quality of their supervision. Poor supervision undermines the entire educational experience that the trainee is receiving. In such circumstances, trainees often feel they are being cheated. When these feelings develop, trainees often covertly protest their feeling of being cheated by acting out via fees. Thus, when trainees abet nonpayment, do not assign proper fees, or become involved in unusual fee arrangements, it is wise to review the supervisory experiences.

Some supervisors have a concealed contempt for the work of trainees in psychotherapy and unwittingly undermine self-confidence that the education program is trying to develop. When this happens, these trainees will tend to charge lower fees than they might under the management of other supervisors. In addition, some supervisors themselves have conflicts about fees and will not support their trainees making appropriate fee schedule charges.

SOME SPECIAL PATTERNS OF BEHAVIOR

A number of patterns of patient and trainee behavior emerge as likely areas of fee misconduct as noted in previous studies (3,6,7). One common patient pattern is the request for a lower fee. Such requests are often found to be more inappropriate than realistic and seem to spring from the patient's effort to test a therapist's willingness to support dependency. Some trainees easily succumb to a patient's wish to be treated with special indulgence and are likely to overlook the dependency issues implicit in such demands. Schizophrenic patients and young attractive women often make such requests, and both seem to be adversely affected when their therapist comply with wishes for lower fees. It is usually necessary for trainees to be extremely alert to the complex fantasies which patients attach to variation in fee. There are certain basic principles regarding requests for reduced fees. It is important to be certain that the fee initially established is a realistic one. When a request for a reduced fee is made, exploration must be conducted on a number of levels. One should be alert to the possibility of concealed assets or income. Manipulations do occur and often undermine the credibility of the therapist, if the patient is able to get away with it. Patients have many fantasies and conflicts about any changes in fees even though they may request them. Reduction of the fee may be seen as seductive, may be seen as a lack of trust, or may be seen as a number of other possible things. There are many derivatives of this, and the therapist's task is always to understand them (3,7).

Some patients are patently sociopathic and manipulative in their fee considerations with trainee therapists. Patients may falsify the income information they give. In one case where this happened, the deception was only brought to light when the patient's wife inadvertently revealed the true family income. In this instance, the trainee's need to remain helpful instead of succumbing to moralistic and critical value judgments was highlighted. It was essential that the trainee deal with his own anger and not take it out on the patient. A therapeutic attitude prevailed during careful supervision and enabled the trainee to avoid castigating the patient for his pathological behavior. The trainee struggled to work toward a helpful and honest scrutiny of the problem with the patient. The patient rewarded the trainee's tolerance with hard work on his "instruction in dishonesty at the hands of parents who had encouraged him to lie and steal during his lifetime." Sociopathic traits had been ingrained in this patient as if they were essential for survival. Now, in his own capacity as an investment counselor, he was giving somewhat shady advice and harbored guilt feelings about his tendencies to exploit clients. The profound guilt had been in part responsible for his severe psychosomatic problems and further complicated his life.

Complications often arise in dealing with insurance companies and payment of fees by third-party carriers (3,9,14). In general, patients often try to remove themselves from responsibility for their fees. They may try to leave the issue of payment for the doctor to negotiate with the insurance company. This tendency to avoid direct responsibility for service being provided for them always requires careful clarification. It often will lead to the discovery of immaturity, reluctance to take up responsibility in other areas of life, and unfulfilled dependency yearning. Other patients may try to involve trainees in falsifying the dates in which they started therapy, if they obtained insurance coverage after the fact. Some patients may be conflicted when their insurance companies seek information regarding diagnosis and treatment issues. In some instances patients did not wish insurance companies to receive information.

One patient was indignant when his trainee therapist asked him about the request for information which the patient's insurance company sent to the therapist after the patient filed a claim for reimbursement for payment for treatment. Although the patient had sought payment from the insurance company, he did not wish to have required information released to the insurance company. He secretly and then openly resented the need for a report. This presented a crisis for the trainee therapist, who was confused by the patient's ambivalence. Supervision enabled the therapist to understand the coexistence in this patient of contradictory emotions and how they were expressing themselves in the handling of third-party payment. When the issue was then brought back into the treatment, the patient was able to accomplish a considerable amount of insight into his conflicts and other areas of ambivalence. It was clear that the working alliance, in this case, as in many others, can easily be interfered with when reports have to be submitted to insurance companies. It is sometimes useful to have patients actively participate in writing reports that are sent to insurance companies. Under no circumstances should reports be sent to insurance companies without the patient's approval of the report and reading of it. Although other clinicians may disagree with this approach, it minimizes the patient's opportunity to deny the validity of the information released and minimizes the patient's opportunity to sabotage the therapy.

Occasionally a patient may completely refuse to pay a bill. In one case, a young woman had ignored her bill for months. She refused to believe that therapy would be interrupted unless she made payments promptly. Even though she was given adequate warning that treatment was to be terminated, she did not really believe it. Once treatment was terminated, she continued to come for appointments. She had a significant difficulty in her reality testing. She had always been able to manipulate others to get what she wanted in the past. When she made payment on the bill, treatment resumed. It was clear that she had been overindulged by her family and had developed extremely manipulative ways to get what she wanted. In instances where people frustrated her wishes, she acted out with reckless driving, abusive drugs, promiscuity, and suicidal threats. She would literally stop at nothing in order to force someone to give her what she wanted. Termination of the therapy was the actual first time that someone had simply compelled her to live up to her part of the bargain in a working relationship. Although the following months were stormy with the venting of great rage and many episodes of acting out, therapy was able to continue. Gradually, her infantile behavior subsided, and insight allowed her to make significant developmental steps forward.

CONCLUSION

Training in psychotherapy must include careful education and clinical and administrative supervision on various aspects of fees and monetary issues. With firm guidelines and clearly developed fee policies to assist them, psychotherapy trainees are better able to deal, not only with fee issues, but also with all other aspects of the therapeutic relationship involving reciprocity, setting of limits, and assisting patients to live up to their responsibilities. When fee issues are carefully taught, trainees are able to gain self-esteem through the production of revenue as well as the treatment of psychotherapy cases. In times of dwindling support for educational programs in psychiatry and mental health, educational directors ought not to overlook the potential benefits of careful instruction in monetary issues regarding psychotherapy fees.

REFERENCES

1. Bittker, T. The industrialization of American psychiatry. *Am. J. Psychiatry*, 142:149–153, 1985.

2. Muszynski, S., Brady, J., and Sharfstein, S. Paying for psychiatric care. *Psychiatr. Ann.*, 14:861–869, 1985.
3. Langs, R. *Psychoanalytic psychotherapy.* New York: Jason Aronson, 1973.
4. McKinnon, B., and Michaels, K. *The psychiatric interview in clinical practice.* Philadelphia: W. B. Saunders, 1974.
5. Balint, M. *The doctor, patient, and the illness.* New York: International Universities Press, 1957.
6. Pasternack, S. A., and Treiger, P. Psychotherapy fees and residency training. *Am. J. Psychiatry*, 133:1064–1066, 1976.
7. Pasternack, S. The psychotherapy fee: An issue in residency training. *Dis. Nerv. Syst.*, 11:913–916, 1977.
8. Abraham, K. Contributions to the theory of anal character. In *Selected papers of Karl Abraham*, International Psychoanalytic Library, #13. London: Hogarth Press, 1927.
9 Chodoff, P. The effects of third party payment on the practice of psychotherapy. *Am. J. Psychiatry*, 129:540–545, 1972.
10. Ferenczi, S. *Contributions to psychoanalysis.* Boston: Richard C. Badger, 1916.
11. Fenichel, Y. *Psychoanalytic theory of neurosis.* New York: W. W. Norton, 1945.
12. Freud, S. Character and anal eroticism. *Standard edition*, Vol. IX (pp. 167–177). London: Hogarth Press, 1959.
13. Gibson, R. Strategic planning and marketing of mental health services. *Psychiatr. Ann.*, 14:846–851, 1985.
14. Halpert, E. The effect of insurance on psychoanalytic treatment. *J. Am. Psychoanal. Assoc.*, 20:122–133, 1972.
15. Vorwaller, C. Profit minded management in the non-profit sector. *Psychiatr. Ann.*, 14:851-857, 1985.

15

Transference, Countertransference, and Other Therapeutic Issues in a Health Maintenance Organization (HMO)

Sidney S. Goldensohn, M.D.

In the course of the treatment of mental illness, all therapists and patients become involved in transference and countertransference responses. In prepaid group practice, however, these reactions are modified by the effects of the third-party payment system. This chapter will explore some of these effects and compare them with transference and countertransference phenomena usually encountered in the fee-for-service market.

Much of this chapter is based on the author's experience with the Mental Health Service of the Health Insurance Plan of Greater New York (HIP). A detailed description of this service has been described in the literature (1-4). Approximately 340,000 HIP enrollees are now covered for psychiatric services in this program. This number represents a growth of 100% over the past five years, a growth that, in part, reflects the public's acceptance of the prepaid concept for mental health care.

A brief overview of the HIP program is noted. The basic psychotherapeutic orientation of the staff is that of psychodynamic psychotherapy. The primary goal is to return the patient to a functioning level as promptly as possible. A broad spectrum of outpatient and inhospital mental health services is available. Group therapy and family therapy are practiced when indicated. There is no upper limit to the number of services a patient can receive or to the period of time he can remain in treatment, although intensive psychotherapy is excluded.

Transference and countertransference phenomena arise from two anxiety sets: one is class related and the other personal. Class-related anxieties originate in the socioeconomic backgrounds of patients and therapists. Personal anxieties result from the unique interpersonal histories of both patients and therapists. Many transferential and countertransferential experiences demonstrate a merging of cultural and personal anxiety factors; personal anxiety sets may be intimately and intricately interwoven with socioeconomic antecedents and determinants. Nevertheless, manifestations of transference and countertransference in third-party payment systems tend to fall into one of these two categories.

TRANSFERENCE PHENOMENA

Transference in third-party payment systems is strongly influenced by socioeconomic factors. Three socioeconomic subdivisions are used for purposes of discussion: upper-middle to middle class; middle to lower-middle class; and the poor, including recipients of welfare. There is much overlap between these groups.

Transference issues will be discussed relating to fees, duration of treatment, treatment setting, authority problems, and the patient's self-image.

First, transferential phenomena relating to fees will be discussed. The fact that payment in an HMO system is by premium rather than fee for service affects the patient's attitudes toward his therapist and his treatment in a variety of ways. The patient may feel that he is a degraded and passive "charity" or "clinic" patient. This attitude is most common in poor welfare patients who were self-supporting at one time in their lives. Patients who have never earned an adequate income frequently demonstrate a different, expectant attitude. Discomfort about not paying a fee may be a projection of the patient's feelings of worthlessness and may not simply be related to the condition of poverty.

Some other views expressed by patients are that the clinic is for "second-class patients" who receive "second-class treatment." Middle-class patients, especially, tend to accept cultural myths related to "expensive is better." Cultural attitudes about fees will be reflected in the patients' relationships with their therapists. For example, a patient who equates a high fee with high-quality service may exhibit a derogatory attitude toward his therapist or toward the mental health service. Paul Chodoff (5) described concerns for the treatability of so-called nonpaying patients (so-called because many patients pay sizable premiums); he stressed the necessity for dealing with the patient's fantasies of being a "free, special child."

If a therapeutic endeavor is to be successful, the patient must assume some degree of responsibility for and personal commitment to the treatment. Borderline patients, especially, find this a difficult task. If their magical expectations that the therapist alone will make them well are encouraged, no change can be expected. Scanlon (6) believes that "benign neglect" on the therapists' part in dealing with issues such as nonpayment or missed appointments serves to collude with the patient's dependent, irresponsible stance with the world. Nash and Cavenar (7) suggest that the absence of direct payment of the fee by the patient may mobilize shame or guilt to a degree that precludes the patient's involvement in therapy. We have found, however, that some enrollees do not realize that they are indeed paying for their treatment through their premiums, and we find it is therapeutically useful to bring this to their attention.

Some patients are aware that the HMO plan has a finite treatment capacity and that others are entitled to share the services. Those patients who received parental attention only for selective needs that were thought worthy may feel guilt about receiving treatment and may question the validity and seriousness of their problems.

None of the attitudes relating to fees has proved a serious handicap to therapy. They can be worked through, assuming they are not manifestations of more deep-seated personality difficulties (8) and if the countertransferential responses from the therapist do not reinforce the patient's irrational attitudes.

Treatment of children in the HMO system tends to obviate or reduce a problem commonly encountered in the fee-for-service market. This is the problem of premature termination of treatment by a parent because of resistance to paying for treatment, especially when the expected results are not immediately forthcoming. This is less likely to happen in a third-party payment plan. In addition, the guilt that the child might feel for causing a financial burden is reduced or removed when payment is prepaid by premium.

Transferential behavior pertaining to duration of treatment will be the next focus of attention. The issue of duration of therapy is often raised by our patients. Most accept the explanation that there will be no definite cutoff, that the duration of treatment will depend on the time required to relieve their presenting symptoms or problems. We rarely begin treatment by telling the patient that his presenting symptoms are manifestations of deeper problems. Rather, we suggest that many problems are associated with interpersonal or communication difficulties and are subject to significant change within a brief period of treatment. Most of our patients appreciate this approach as compatible with their primary aim of symptom reduction.

An undue concern about the duration of treatment may be an expression of transference feelings regarding dependency. Long-term treatment may stimulate fears of dependency, and short-term treatment may arouse feelings of rejection or provoke envious comparisons with other patients.

Lower-class patients are frequently reluctant to commit themselves to any treatment beyond symptomatic relief. In early sessions the therapeutic emphasis is on providing concrete help for the reality problems confronting the lower-class patient in the here and now. The patient is primarily interested in what happened today or yesterday, and there tends to be little or no continuity between one session and the next. Poverty patients require a therapist to be giving in a concrete and demonstrable manner, especially in the early phase of treatment. For example, during a session the therapist might call the welfare office to straighten out a problem for the patient rather than promising to do so later. In this way the therapist gains the trust of the patient. Frustration may be aroused in the therapist who wants to work too quickly with history and psychodynamics. It is common sense, however, that concrete problems need to be alleviated before interpersonal difficulties can be approached (9).

Upper-middle-class patients, in contrast, tend to expect long-term treatment and may reject the short-term approaches offered. They tend to be sophisticated about psychiatry; many have been oversold on the curative value of psychotherapeutic modalities, although the public's evaluation of intensive therapy is now in a state of flux. Similar attitudes in upper-middle-class patients are encountered in private practice. In an HMO, however, they are likely to be manifested by resistances to the limited goals of treatment (return to function). A broad range of conflicts may be precipitated in regard to this issue.

The treatment setting is another source for transferential expression. Patients, particularly those from the welfare group, may equate the mental health center with "home." The transferential experience of the mental health center as home, usually an idealized home and family, fills an important need of these patients. The staff, including the office personnel, are seen as "good parents" who will make up for past deprivations. These patients appreciate the friendly atmosphere and welcome the proffered coffee and candy. The ambiance is a positive aspect of therapy for this group. It is worth noting that in our mental health center, black and white therapists treating patients of different races rarely encounter resistances that could be attributed to differences in color alone. The model of an interracial staff working together harmoniously apparently creates an atmosphere in which skin color does not frequently become an overriding transferential issue.

The transferential significance of the setting is less often positive for upper-middle and middle-class patients and may even be negative for them. Sometimes middle-class patients are disturbed by the bare simplicity of the clinic decor, the noisiness and disorder in the waiting room, and the inadequate soundproofing. These factors do not seem to distress lower-middle-class and poor patients. Noise and disorder are not usually considered nuisances by the young and, in fact, put children and young people at ease.

With the marked growth of our HMO population two new mental health centers were opened this year. They are spacious and tastefully decorated. The architectural design includes moderate-sized, clustered waiting areas with separate sections for children. The design offers the patients a sense of privacy and comfort. This modern-type setting has, in fact, reduced the mild dissent previously expressed by our more affluent subscribers, while the less affluent do not appear to be threatened. Furthermore, the soft pastel colors and coordinated furniture probably have a therapeutic effect on patients. Indeed, a professionally designed, functional office need not be restricted to the fee-for-service market.

The therapist and the organization are responded to as authority figures. HMO patients act out their authority problems with their therapists, as in private practice, with rebellion, compliance, ingratiation, or other transferential behavior. Fears of being rejected by the therapist because of unlikability, unworthiness, lack of productivity, or other negative qualities are common. The fears of rejection are aggravated in the poor patient, who feels he can neither "bribe" the therapist with financial payment nor "buy" a different therapist. He perceives his acceptance as tenuous and therefore is less free to risk criticizing the therapist than is a patient of higher economic status. Conversely, the middle-class patient who believes that "expensive is good" may regard the therapist as a cheap, and hence dispensable, article who can be discarded at whim for better goods.

The poor patient often reacts with hostility to new authority figures and institutions. He may have come to the HMO for help because of conflicts with other authorities. For example, a child may be brought to the center for behavior problems in school. Patients having difficulties with other authorities usually distrust the therapist initially and perceive the therapist as an arm of the institution with which they are in trouble. Many patients view us as the "soft" police and fantasize that we will manipulate them subtly to make them conform to social norms that they reject. This transferential expectation is not essentially different from what occurs in the private sector.

Poor patients often view the HMO as a remote, awesome bureaucratic organization in relation to which they feel alienated, insignificant, and powerless. Many of their authority problems are transferred to this depersonalized organ of the "system." Some of these patients try to handle the clinic with defensive ingratiation; other patients with inadequate impulse control may act out by becoming abusive. Middle-class and upper-middle-class patients are less likely than the poor to become intimidated by the establishment. They see the HMO as an instrument designed to serve them and realize that the mental health center is dependent on them for support.

Finally, becoming a patient at the mental health center affects the enrollee's self-image and self-esteem. For the upper-middle- and middle-class patient there is some experience of "comedown," concern about lack of choice in the treatment planning and therapist, feelings of superiority to the other patients, and, occasionally, contempt for the therapist. In spite of these attitudes, many upper-middle-class patients have been helped significantly. The self-esteem of the poor welfare-class patient is often enhanced by the personal attention given to his emotional needs in the simple, attractive, clean, comfortable, "homey" treatment center. By and large, the middle- and lower-middle-class patient is content that he is getting his money's worth. He recognizes that his premium is payment, and his self-esteem seems least affected by the concept of being a patient in a prepaid mental health clinic.

COUNTERTRANSFERENCE PHENOMENA

A mental health center tends to develop an individual and unique "character structure" (10), based on several factors. Chief among these factors are the staff (particularly the director), the patient population, and the bureaucratic organization in which the center functions. Whatever the character structure of the center, it is an important consideration in countertransference phenomena. The countertransference factors to be discussed are related to salary, authority problems, and the therapist's self-image.

Being salaried may permit the therapist to feel more comfortable in his work. An inappropriate desire to please or placate a patient, arising from fears of losing him and the income he represents, is removed. It can become easier to confront patients, to probe painful issues, and to behave spontaneously. Some psychiatrists in private practice likewise express the idea, perhaps self-deceptive, that they could be more therapeutically productive if they were not "driven" to deliver $75 worth of wisdom at every session. The HMO therapist may also welcome the freedom from having to personally bill the patient. He does not need to "dirty" himself by taking money for services rendered. Meyers (11) found, for example, that psychiatric residents preferred that the receptionist set and collect fees rather than assuming responsibility themselves. The impersonality of third-party payment has its drawbacks, however, in the loss of opportunities to analyze transference and countertransference attitudes associated with the direct exchange of money through the payment of fees (6–8).

Conscious or unconscious pressures to increase one's patient load until it becomes barely manageable, or to continue therapy beyond a point of small return, do not operate in an HMO as they do in private practice. Economic incentives encouraging unnecessary services are not present. However, removal of fee-for-service incentives may also produce a therapist who lacks ambition and gets by with a minimum of effort. It may allow the therapist to dehumanize his patient and to overuse modalities such as drugs and simple reassurance and thus to sidestep the difficult task of becoming emotionally involved in a psychotherapeutic relationship. The therapist may be tempted to ignore the needs of his patient, to act out with him, to shorten visits, or to discharge him prematurely.

Unlike the self-employed private practitioner, the therapist in the HMO is a member of a well-defined organization and has a boss (director or board of directors) to whom he is accountable. When the salaried therapist has unresolved problems with authority figures in his organization, the difficulties may become manifest in a variety of untherapeutic countertransference responses. These reactions are usually provoked by unresolved authority problems presented by the patient. The therapist may act out his own wishes through the patient by encouraging excessive compliance, detachment, or rebellion. In this way, the patient may be used as a scapegoat for the therapist's conflicts with clinic authorities.

In the HMO, organizational policy promotes the treatment of a maximum number of patients, with minimal time devoted to each patient. The director must encourage the staff to adhere to the goal of return to function in order to provide proper care for all enrollees. Under these circumstances some therapists manifest their need to please authority by an eagerness to terminate patients prematurely. Ironically, rebellious attitudes to authority may take the form of overinvolvement with patients and overextended duration of treatment.

The quality of the therapist's self-image is a factor of major importance in treatment. A poor self-image will interfere with therapeutic effectiveness by lowering the therapist's confidence in himself, by reducing his capacity to function as a rational authority, and by encouraging countertransferential feelings and attitudes that are not helpful to the patient. Working within an HMO alters the therapist's self-image and self-esteem in a direction and to a degree that will vary depending on the therapist's personal history, value systems, cultural milieu, and therapeutic orientation.

For therapists who highly value independence, individualism, private enterprise, and financial success, being salaried is "low status." Their self-image is further demeaned by the fact that they earn less than private practitioners. These therapists may consequently feel disdain for dependent, passive patients who mirror their own unacceptable qualities. They may reject patients who have not "made it" economically, especially poverty patients. On the other hand, therapists who prize cooperation, teamwork, and social service more than rugged individualism or monetary success will derive a sense of enhanced self-esteem from their association with an HMO. Their contributions to the community, their service to the underprivileged, and their collaboration with an interracial and integrated staff will yield significant satisfactions.

The therapist's value judgments about his patient population constitute another important variable influencing his self-image. He may view blue-collar workers, welfare recipients, and the underprivileged as second-rate people, or he may consider them worthwhile individuals who have been deprived of opportunities for development. Needless to say, a therapist's evaluation of his patient's worth will be perceived by the patient and incorporated into the patient's evaluation of himself.

SUMMARY

Therapists employed in an HMO are faced with a special set of circumstances; they belong to a closed system in which the system is both the provider and the insurer. Clinicians in an HMO, according to Budman et al. (12), function in three roles simultaneously: they represent the plan in allocating its finite mental health resources, they represent the patient's interest in "feeling better," and they represent their own perspective as clinicians with an interest in enhancing the patient's personality structure and coping style. The tension generated by these multiple perspectives is considerable. Transferential and countertransferential issues are, therefore, affected by the demands of the patient to get help and the requirements from oneself to be an effective therapist.

Specific transference and countertransference reactions characteristic of mental health services in a HMO or third-party payment plan have been described. Among the transference issues considered to be of greatest importance are responses to payment by premium rather than fees for service, attitudes toward the limited duration of treatment and related treatment goals, reactions to the HMO as an authority, and the effects of being treated in a clinic setting. The countertransference issues of major significance include reactions by the therapist to being salaried, responses to the authoritative, bureaucratic organization, and the reactions of the therapist as they reflect his or her self-image and value systems.

REFERENCES

1. Goldensohn, S. S. A pre-paid group practice mental health service as part of a health maintenance organization. *Am. J. Orthopsychiatry*, 42:154–158, 1972.
2. Goldensohn, S. S., Fink, R., and Shapiro, S. Referral, utilization, and staffing patterns of a mental health service in a prepaid group practice program in New York. *Am. J. Psychiatry*, 126:689–697, 1969.
3. Goldensohn, S. S., Fink, R., and Shapiro, S. The delivery of mental health services to children in a prepaid medical care program. *Am. J. Psychiatry*, 127:1357–1362, 1971.
4. Goldensohn, S. S., and Haar, E. Transference and countertransference in a third-party payment system (HMO). *Am. J. Psychiatry*, 131:256–260, 1974.
5. Chodoff, P. The effect of third-party payment on the practice of psychotherapy. *Am. J. Psychiatry*, 129:540–545, 1972.
6. Scanlon, P. Fee and missed appointments as transference issues. Social casework. *J. Contemp. Social Work*, 63:540–546, 1982.
7. Nash, J. L., and Cavenar, J. O. Free psychotherapy: An inquiry into resistance. *Am. J. Psychiatry*, 133:1066–1069, 1976.
8. Halpert, E. The effect of insurance on psychoanalytic treatment. *J. Am. Psychoanal. Assoc.*, 20:122–132, 1972.
9. Goldensohn, S. S. Psychotherapy for the economically disadvantaged: Contributions from the social sciences. *J. Amer. Acad. Psychoanal.*, 9:291–302, 1981.
10. Gittelman, M., and Goldensohn, S. S. Applying community psychiatric principles to child treatment. *Am. J. Orthopsychiatry*, 45:295–296, 1975.
11. Meyers, B. S. Attitudes of psychiatric residents toward payment of psychotherapy fees. *Am. J. Psychiatry*, 133:1460–1462, 1976.
12. Budman, S. H., Feldman, J., and Bennett, M. J. Adult mental health services in a health maintenance organization. *Am. J. Psychiatry*, 136:392–396, 1979.

III

PAYMENT STRUCTURES AND MANAGEMENT ISSUES

16

The Meanings and Effects of Insurance in Psychotherapy and Psychoanalysis

Eugene Halpert, M.D.

Over the past two decades the use of medical insurance coverage to help defray the cost of psychotherapy and psychoanalysis has increased spectacularly. Two decades ago such coverage was a relatively rare phenomenon. Today, more often than not, the patient will have insurance coverage of some kind. Most commonly the insurance company will pay a specified percent of the cost of each session with a set limit on the total amount of overall reimbursement. The patient may have this insurance coverage as a fringe benefit from his own, his spouse's, or his parent's employment. The complexity of the insurance forms that must be filled out by the therapist varies from the most simple, requiring only name, dates of treatment, and diagnosis, to those asking for detailed, personal information about the patient.

All these variations in the amounts paid per session, the total coverage, whose coverage it is, and what specifically has to be put down on paper by the therapist have psychological as well as practical significance for the patient. Depending on the unconscious conflicts of the individual patient, the psychological significance and emotional ramifications of the insurance may assume major importance in the therapy and may even compromise the patient's treatability. The patient's ability to work effectively within the treatment situation will be more certainly impaired by insurance coverage if the therapist is not alert and responsive to the possible meanings of the insurance coverage to his or her patients.

The early psychiatric literature—for example, Auster (1), Avnet (2), Glasser and Duggan (3), Goldensohn et al. (4), Green (5), and Kennedy (6)—was almost exclusively focused on administrative problems, questions

169

of financial feasibility, and related statistical matters. In general, this same focus on external practicalities related to insurance coverage, often with the purpose of seeking to justify the inclusion of the treatment of psychiatric disorders in various insurance coverages, has continued to dominate general psychiatric writings and concerns in regard to insurance coverage. Despite the ever-increasing frequency of the phenomenon of insurance coverage for analysis and psychotherapy, there are relatively few contributions in the psychoanalytic literature dealing with the meanings of payment by insurance and the effects of those meanings on the treatment.

Halpert (7) found that the need for control as well as protection against castration and the depletion of body contents were major themes in the unconscious fantasies that accompany the use of insurance to pay for analysis. Halpert also felt that if the *entire* fee was paid by insurance, and obsessive anal characteristics were prominent in the analysand's psychology, then resistance might intensify to the point of rendering the patient unanalyzable. In another paper Halpert (8) reported on a man who in psychotherapy developed a transference to the anonymous third-party payer, the insurance company. He noted that ''the insurance company, unlike the therapist, gratifies transference wishes, it takes care of and protects the patient'' (p. 67).

Gray (9) noted that some patients were conflicted about whether or not they should use their insurance coverage and stressed the importance of analyzing the patient's conflict and decision whether they elected to use their insurance or not. Gray was of the opinion that insurance coverage ''has little adverse effect on the conduct of otherwise adequate analyses in a situation in which the contract remains exclusively between doctor and patient'' (p. 110). Langs (10) was of the opposite opinion. He felt that the violation of confidentiality inherent in third-party payment was too disruptive of the bipersonal field to allow analysis to proceed adequately. Halpert (11), in a more recent paper, expressed an opinion somewhat between that of Gray and Langs. He felt that

> in the *usual* case, though fantasies of all kinds may be attached to it, the insurance does not attain central importance. While usually not of central importance, the analysis of the feelings and fantasies connected to the use of insurance coverage for analysis does always provide another avenue for attaining insight into conflict, transference and resistance.

However, Halpert also felt that there

> seem to be some patients . . . who because of a particular fit between

the unconscious gratifications and fantasies connected with insurance and their particular psychopathology and defensive structure are not analyzable with insurance coverage.

In light of this diversity of opinion regarding the effect of insurance coverage on insight-oriented treatment, it is particularly important to state that insurance, the protection against loss, has important dynamic and affective meanings. The uncovering and interpretation of these meanings are of the same importance in the treatment of patients as the understanding of their thoughts and feelings about money and payment for treatment in cases where there is no insurance coverage.

While there are individual variations in the meanings of insurance to patients, there are certain common concerns and fantasies which deserve discussion. Before doing so it is important to note that there are also common patient responses to the use of insurance coverage for payment of treatment and common technical problems and issues that arise in relation to its use. The most common conscious patient response aside from the relief and pleasure due to the feeling that someone else is defraying the cost is a greater distancing or isolation of feeling and thought in relation to money and payment. Since it is an anonymous amorphous "someone else" who has assumed at least part of the financial burden, feelings and fantasies about the financial transactions involved are more easily isolated and denied than when the patients pay the bill themselves. For this reason it is essential that the analyst or therapist not accept assignment of fees. Patients should pay the fee and collect direct reimbursement from the insurance company themselves.

Another technical problem inherent in the use of insurance is that it calls for the analyst or therapist to act rather than to speak. The fact that the analyst or therapist puts something into action rather than speaking for the purpose of helping the patient gain insight contributes to the formation of two of the most common kinds of fantasies: those of collusion, fraud, and robbery and those of intrusion and exposure.

The use of insurance in other areas of life is often connected not only with fantasies of theft but with actual fraud. For example, with auto insurance it is common practice for individuals who have sustained damage to their cars to collude with a mechanic to submit an inflated claim or estimate so that they can collect more from the insurance company than that to which they are entitled. Patients in analysis or psychotherapy not infrequently have the same conscious expectations when they come for treatment. One adult patient who did not have insurance coverage herself, but whose parent did, asked the analyst to make out the bill and the form in her father's name so that she could be fraudulently reimbursed. Others have asked to have the fee per session inflated on the form or extra sessions added to the bill so that the amount of their reimbursement would be increased. These maneuvers are all overdetermined, often involving identification with corrupt parents, attempts to prove that the analyst or therapist is corrupt and dishonest so that they need not trust him or her or be honest, and symbolic acting out of deep-seated, unconscious fantasies of incestuous illicit intercourse and theft of the parental (or maternal fecal) penis.

Even though the therapist obviously would not go along with these corrupt requests, there are other factors inherent in the filling out of insurance forms which form a kernel around which the patient can elaborate fantasies of collusion and deception. Chief among these is the need to report a diagnosis to the company. In reporting a diagnosis the therapist is often torn between the need to be honest and the wish to protect the patient's right to confidentiality as much as is possible. This conflict is intensified if the most truthful diagnosis touches on the more personal issues of a patient's life. For example, if the patient is in treatment for a perversion or some other sexual symptom, most therapists will enter a diagnosis which evades the basic truth but which validly reflects some part of the clinical picture. Even though the therapist may be correct in doing so, there is nonetheless a certain participation in a collusion. Since the question of diagnosis also touches on some of the more basic concerns of the patient—"What is wrong with me? Am I crazy? Will I lose control?"— even when the therapist or analyst enters the most correct diagnosis, there may be a feeling of not entering the correct diagnosis.

Also allied to the question of diagnosis are fantasies and fears of exposure and intrusion. Often derivatives of these concerns appear in the form of the patient denying any feelings or thoughts about a diagnosis. Other patients will initially betray their concerns about exposure by forgetting the form or otherwise delaying bringing it in. Still others will directly ask the analyst to put down the most general nonrevealing diagnosis possible while simultaneously wondering what the analyst really thinks. As I have stated elsewhere (11),

> As in any situation the patient's varying ways of dealing with a problem, in this instance the fears of exposure, are dictated by reality factors, the ego's defensive style, the superego's structure and the particular pressures emanating from the id. When it can be analyzed, the fear of exposure may be found to relate via the principle of multiple functioning and overdetermination to the whole range of possi-

ble narcissistic mortifications ie. everyone will know I'm crazy, everyone will know I'm castrated, etc. and every possible guilt: everyone will know my secret sexual crimes and I'll be mocked and punished.

That the patient's fantasies of intrusion and exposure are supported by certain external reality factors is attested to by the current federal administration's attempts to gain authority for access to hitherto private records such as bank, medical, telephone, and insurance records. These attempts have been reported in the press, *The New York Times* of October 6, 1981, as well as in *The Newsletter* of the American Psychoanalytic Association (September 1981).

Primal-scene fantasies are also commonly stimulated by and associated with insurance coverage. The company may be unconsciously seen as the excited child trying to peer into the parental bedroom, here equated with the therapeutic consultation room. In some instances the patient may identify with the company in this regard and be excited by the idea of secrets being obtained or forced out of the analyst. The insurance form itself is in some instances sexualized, being equated unconsciously with the patient's and/or the analyst's body, and the filling in of the form being equated with intercourse and impregnation. Patients sometimes fill in spaces on the form that the therapist is supposed to fill in. They rationalize that they want to make it easier for the therapist to fill out the form. Patients who do this are often defending against fantasied sexual submission, and are therefore plugging up all possible openings. In addition, they are identifying with the therapist in doing what he should be doing as well as exploring and filling his openings.

SUMMARY

The use of insurance coverage for payment of psychoanalysis or psychotherapy has unconscious meanings which can be of great significance to the patient and can adversely affect the progress of treatment unless the therapist is alert to this possibility. Because the payment with insurance tends to lend emotional distance from the payment of money to the therapist, it is easier for patients to isolate themselves from all the issues surrounding money in the transference.

In addition to all the usual unconscious equations of money, as well as defenses and resistances to insight in this area, insurance poses an additional set of problems, as outlined above. If, however, the treating person listens for the derivative manifestations of the meanings of insurance for the patient, the exploration and interpretation of various aspects of insurance can enhance insight and working through. There are, however, some people whose dynamic constellations are such that the use of insurance so fits in with their own defensive modes and simultaneously offers them such instinctual gratification that analytic and psychotherapeutic work becomes much more difficult or impossible.

REFERENCES

1. Auster, S. L. Insurance coverage for mental and nervous conditions: Development and problems. *Am. J. Psychiatry*, 126:698–705, 1969.
2. Avnet, H. H. Psychiatric insurance—Ten years later. *Am. J. Psychiatry*, 126: 667–674, 1969.
3. Glasser, M. A., and Duggan, T. Prepaid psychiatric care experience with UAW members. *Am. J. Psychiatry*, 126:675–681, 1969.
4. Goldensohn, S. S., Fink, R., & Shapiro, S. Referral, utilization and staffing patterns of a mental health service in a prepaid group practice program in N.Y. *Am. J. Psychiatry*, 126:689–697, 1969.
5. Green, E. L. Psychiatric services in a California group health plan. *Am. J. Psychiatry*, 126:681–688, 1969.
6. Kennedy, J. F. Message from the President of the U.S. related to mental illness and mental retardation. *Am. J. Psychiatry*, 120:729–737, 1964.
7. Halpert, E. The effect of insurance on psychoanalytic treatment. *J. Am. Psychoanal. Assoc.*, 20:122–133, 1972.
8. Halpert, E. A meaning of insurance in psychotherapy. *Int. J. Psychoanal. Psychother.*, 1:62–68, 1973.
9. Gray, S. H. Does insurance affect psychoanalytic practice? *Bull. Phila. Assoc. Psychoanal.*, 23:101–110, 1973.
10. Langs, R. *The bipersonal field.* New York: Jason Aronson, 1976.
11. Halpert, E. Insurance. *J. Am. Psychoanal. Assoc.*, 1985 (in press).

17

Fees in Beginning Private Practice

Thomas G. Gutheil, M.D.

INTRODUCTION

As the substance of this book makes clear, there are many aspects to money in the transactions and practice of psychotherapy and psychoanalysis. Rarely, however, are these issues as laden with tension and conflict as at the beginning of private practice. Thus, the developmental step of becoming a private practitioner serves us as a magnifying glass through which to observe, in intensely detailed fashion, the basic clinical issues around money: not so much newly discovered as writ with a broader brush.

This chapter addresses some features of this developmental phase, a phase usually recalled with pain by the trainee. The relative paucity of data on this specific subtopic (1) suggests that—perhaps because of remembered distress and discomfort—this phase is probably quite conflicted and likely to be quickly forgotten; similarly, it may remain a focus of ambivalence for the clinician.

Following an illustrative case example, the topic of fees in beginning private practice will be addressed under a series of rubrics; regrettably, a significant overlap among these inevitably arbitrary headings must occur. A generally analytic or dynamic viewpoint will be assumed throughout.

CASE EXAMPLE

A case report of remarkable interest and heuristic utility has recently been published by Chessick (2). In it this renowned theoretician, clinician, and teacher of clinicians reveals with remarkable candor a complex case which he describes in the title as "a failure in psychoanalytic psychotherapy." Chessick's frankness in describing, among other factors, his own countertransference reactions to this difficult and demanding patient makes the case a truly valuable one for the student.

Surely it would be an enormous disservice to the candor thus shown to quote Chessick out of context, but, unfortunately, no other approach will serve, since I am interested only in highlighting the financial issues, which were only a part of a multifactorial piece of clinical work. I thus urge a caveat on the reader: that it not be assumed that I have done any justice to the richness of the clinical vignette.

Chessick describes a 22-year-old college student with complex clinical difficulties in the context of attempting to finish college. She had gone to a large number of therapists and, importantly, was heavily in debt to the local school, because her arbitrary and unreliable father had failed to pay the tuition after promising to do so. The arrangements for the fees in therapy were that the patient would pay for each session individually, but that her father, a businessman, "would be willing to help her pay for the treatment."

On this arrangement, therapy was begun on a twice-weekly regimen. The patient revealed among other details that her father originally filled out an application for her to go to college but then reneged on his promise to pay the tuition. Early in the treatment, the patient reported that "it was hard to get the money from [the father] for the payment for the treatment, although he was grudgingly giving [her] the required checks."

About five months into the treatment, the father abruptly indicated his refusal to pay for any more therapy sessions, claiming that he had no money. Chessick notes that the patient and he himself were confronted with a "financial crisis." He relates:

> The patient and I spent the months of November and December in a colossal effort to mobilize this family and try to get them to help support the treatment. . . . I talked to the mother who promised faithfully that she would pay for the therapy—but never gave the patient any money toward it. The father simply stated he had financial debts and could not support the treatment at this time but vaguely promised the patient at some future date he would pay for the treatment again. To my rather desperate suggestion that the patient go to work full-time and pay for the therapy, she responded with outright rage, because the whole aim of the six months had been for her to get back to college. . . . As a last resort, I wrote a millionaire who sits on the Board of Directors of a charity clinic for which I was a consulting psychiatrist and asked if he would possibly support this patient's therapy. . . . At this point, the patient reported that she owed money to several of the other therapists she had previously

seen, also because the father had promised to pay and then neglected to do so and they had not—like me—requested payment at each session. (2, p. 141)

In an interesting demonstration of self-sufficiency, the patient subsequently independently negotiated two years of free therapy with the support of the millionaire mentioned earlier, whose name the patient had obtained indirectly. Her forthright description of her difficulties apparently got the millionaire to agree, whereas he had previously refused Chessick. Chessick then notes in his report:

When I remarked happily on what a kind and charitable act this was, she snapped, "He can't buy my friendship." I believe that the therapy never recovered from this December episode because the patient felt an empathic lapse on my part due to my preoccupation with the problem of payment for the treatment. (p. 142)

Later in therapy Chessick states:

The patient mentioned: "I am thinking of the story of the man that I read about in a magazine recently. He was seeking a wife and owed a very large hotel bill." This was the last communication the patient ever made to me and I never saw her again after this session. (p. 144)

Because of the extreme and narrow specificity of my selection of these materials, I must reiterate again my caveat about the distortions inevitably introduced by quoting a therapist out of context. However, these excerpts may serve to demonstrate the enormous complexity and interweaving of financial issues into the perceived or misperceived therapeutic and clinical contract; the interaction of transference and countertransference around monetary issues; the role of interesting reality surprises (such as the concession of the millionaire to fund two years of a stranger's therapy); rescue fantasies in various forms; shared anxieties and even "despair" about the fee; and similar issues familiar to all clinicians. This interweaving of themes in the work of a very experienced and senior therapist merely points out the ubiquity and pervasiveness of monetary issues in the therapeutic work.

THE FLEDGLING THERAPIST

Few roles in life are as difficult to play as that of the beginner or tyro. In therapy—which occurs under the constant exposure and scrutiny of one or more other persons—the difficulties of this task are immense. As will be discussed in the remainder of this chapter, many different themes and currents enter into the difficulty, but the role of beginner serves as a prime mover in these problems.

One of the ways in which the role of beginner may impinge on problems around fees in early private practice relates to problems of technique. For more experienced practitioners, fee setting is a piece of their work under the general rubric of clinical administration (3). Typically, the therapist has made some contact with the patient in the first interview, such that the patient feels somewhat understood and—not uncommonly—optimistic about the therapist from an infusion of hope. Mehlman (4) has described this in terms of the therapist making contact with that issue of narcissistic vulnerability or injury which triggered the arrival of the patient in therapy. This capacity to reach the key issue— after which the patient can turn with some relief and optimism to the negotiation of administrative details like fees, even in the very first session—is not always accessible to the beginning clinician because of inexperience.

This question is, of course, related to the fact that early alliance formation by the beginning therapist in general is less effective and supportive than with the more experienced therapist. This not only reflects actual technical skill on the therapist's side but also speaks to the significant role of powerful distractions that enter into the context of the first meeting. Beginning therapists often describe becoming distracted and preoccupied by concerns about what the patient thinks about the office decor; about the comfort and support of the chair in which patient or therapist is sitting; about the patient's views of the new stationery they have recently ordered; and so on—all of which concerns may communicate themselves in various ways to the patient who, not inaccurately, feels that he or she is not the subject of the therapist's undivided attention. The extreme form of this problem is the therapist being, or being perceived as, obsessed with the fee to the exclusion of all else, out of anxiety about the issue.

One of the areas in which the distractability of the beginning practitioner may make itself most evident is the difficulty in recognizing indirect allusions or associations to the fee. For example, when a patient, upon being presented with the bill, associates to exploitative, withholding, sadistic, or unsympathetic objects, or when a patient who is aware of a large unpaid balance associates to various indebtednesses, debtors, creditors, and the like, the inhibition in the area of this subject may be sufficient to deter the clinician from openly and candidly exploring the topic as it might relate to the fee for the therapy.

EXPERIENCES FROM THE CLINIC

Although it is regrettably common for trainees to have had no experience at all in fee setting—as when all of these negotiations are handled by a separate, often remote, billing office in the training center clinic—clinic experience in fee setting, even when present, is not always aimed in the direction of optimum interaction between the patient and therapist. A predominant theme is the way in which clinic fee setting allows the therapist in a certain sense to stand aside from the process, as Pasternack and Treiger have so precisely pointed out (5). The clinician is able to maintain the position that the money "isn't really for me; only for the administration," thus permitting the trainee to view him or herself as a kind of pipeline through which the patient transacts business with the hospital or clinic—the latter seen somewhat in the abstract. This clear avoidance allows the novice not to come to any direct grips with the psychological experience of fee charging for him or herself.

In its worst transformation, a "misalliance" is formed between the clinician and the patient. In this misalliance the patient's nonconstructive feelings of victimization and entitlement resonate inappropriately with the resident's similar feelings (such as feeling underpaid or undervalued by the hospital or institution), such that patient and clinician engage in an unconscious conspiracy to deprive, defraud, shortchange, or punish the "common enemy," the institution. The resident's failure to charge an adequate fee; failure to charge any fee; or tendency rigidly to charge according to certain rules, such as those for missed appointments, may all be clear examples of this process.

An extremely valuable contribution to this subject has been made by Allen (6) in his article describing a seminar for residents entering private practice. The matter of fees is discussed by Allen under the heading "Being Liked as Opposed to Being Effective"—an interesting juxtaposition, capturing one level of the fee conflict in young therapists. Allen's contribution merits quoting at some length:

> The discussion of directness and aggression was then used as a point of departure for a discussion of fees [!] . . . . The residents tended to ignore the importance of the fee as a part of the therapeutic interaction. . . . It was a source of considerable anxiety to many in the resident group. There was also considerable guilt about the prospect of asking fees approaching what their teachers asked of patients. (p. 417)

In addition, Allen underscored a point that represents a very powerful focus of potential misunderstanding, both among clinicians and among outsiders attempting to make sense of the clinical interaction and fees. This section of Allen's discussion is provocatively titled "Self Interest as Opposed to the Patient's Interest." Allen notes:

> . . . there was some feeling that collecting a fee, learning from a patient, or benefiting in any way from the practice of psychotherapy must of necessity be to the patient's disadvantage. As is evident from this material there was a strong tendency for many of the residents in the group to dichotomize issues, seeing benefits as flowing to only one of the parties in any given relationship. They had difficulty in accepting the fact that many—perhaps most—of the facets of human interaction can be of mutual benefit. (p. 417)

Notice that Allen's resident seminar seemed to be portraying the transaction of psychotherapy as a version of a "zero-sum game," whereby there is one winner and one loser. The idea of an exchange of fees and services to the mutual benefit of the parties appears unavailable to beginners in their conceptualizations.

REALITY ISSUES

The title for this section might well be considered something of a euphemism since, from a dynamic viewpoint, all reality is somewhat filtered by the selectivity of the patient's perceptions, transference, biases, and similar factors; needless to say, the same filtering effect must appear in countertransference. Be this as it may, however, there is inevitably a reality component to fee setting which did not escape the awareness of Freud in his 1913 paper "On Beginning the Treatment" (7). Freud comments:

> In my opinion it is more dignified and ethically less open to objection to acknowledge one's actual claims and needs rather than, as the practice is now among medical men, to act the part of the disinterested philanthropist, while that enviable situation is denied to one and one grumbles in secret. . . . (pp. 131–132)

Freud here, of course, addresses the "actual claims and needs" as referring to the clinician's need to earn his living and make his way in life.

A highly pragmatic description of fee setting occurs in an article by Fox (8), a practice management consultant from California, who—as part of a series of articles on how to establish a private practice—offers one on "How to Set Your Fees." Fox points out:

Fees are not figures that are simply drawn from the air. There are sound business reasons for setting specific fees for each procedure. . . . Fees are based upon several factors. Besides being commensurate with the community, they are determined by basic business rules. (p. 74)

In fairness to Fox, she also points out that, despite these seemingly objective touchstones, "since you have never charged for your services before it is hard for you to appraise your value in the market place" (p. 74). This subtlety takes us to our next topic.

NARCISSISTIC ISSUES AND QUESTIONS OF IDENTITY

A resident, beginning to see private patients, commented that he had no difficulty deciding on a fee, since he was quite convinced that his clinical skills were at least equal to those of his least competent senior instructors, who charged "full fee"; he therefore felt fully entitled to charge "full fee" despite being only in his third year of residency. (1, pp. 38–39)

In this vignette the interactions among issues of self-esteem, narcissism, entitlement, and perhaps even competitive strivings, are clearly interwoven around the question of setting a fee; the point could also be made that the response is somewhat counterphobic to possible anxieties about issues of self-worth due to the transition into the marketplace.

In an excellent discussion of the topic of fees, Schonbar (9) has commented: "In our culture money is also a symbol of worth, prestige, competence, masculinity, freedom, control and security, focal conflicts in many people." Describing the trainee in the clinic she comments:

Left to his own devices, [the trainee] characteristically undercharges and experiences much conflict about the issue of missed or cancelled sessions. A fixed system [of payment by fixed rules] would relieve him of the anxiety and guilt aroused by his low self esteem and his devaluation of the service he has to offer. To me this is reminiscent of the statement that, without financial sacrifice, the therapy would become a matter of indifference to the patient; to what degree might this be a reflection of the fee on the part of the therapist that what he has to offer is not really much after all? (p. 278)

An interesting dimension of this point was provided by a psychologist/nun under my supervision, who works as a clinical therapist; I will refer to her as Susan Smith. Because of her dual identity, she is aware of the meaningfulness of whether a patient refers to her as ''Sister Susan'' or ''Dr. Smith.'' The manifest dynamics of this nomenclature revealed themselves to be the issues of a professional who unequivocally merits a fee (the doctor) versus the altruistic, self-impoverishing ''sister'' whose reward will doubtless come from heaven and who would see a fee as a gross intrusion on the spirituality of the helping relationship.

This example clearly illustrates how questions of role identity may enter into negotiations. In this regard Randolph (10) describes some of the difficulties in private practice nursing in terms of fees, and Levin (11) illuminates some of the issues and conflicts in private social work practice in analogous ways. Both authors allude indirectly to the notions of the philanthropic origins of all helping professions (including medicine) which may be viewed as conflicting with the notion of collecting fees for the work.

ANXIETY AND GUILT

These affects can intrude upon many aspects of therapeutic work as Schonbar alluded to above, but it is perhaps around fee setting that the multiplicity of conflicts may become most intense, yet, at the same time, most clearly illuminated. One beginning therapist commented, ''When I gave the patient the first bill, I suddenly felt like a charlatan!'' (1) This does suggest that the focus on the ex-resident's helping role, identity capacities, skills, and value to the patient become intensely focused at that moment of transaction. In these areas, the therapist's guilt about receiving money from the patient for doing what he or she likes or wants to do may stir up strange feelings of unentitlement, which many patients—especially entitled ones—may mobilize. Since the stance of victimization is extremely common for many clinical entities, such as the borderline syndrome, tension in the therapy may readily focus in these loci:

> A borderline patient spent a great deal of time negotiating with the therapist for fee payment from a legal case that was at that time still in litigation without an explicit endpoint. Reluctantly, the therapist agreed to embark on this trial of treatment. During the course of the therapy the patient then revealed that it was her characteristic approach to life to attempt to extract maximum benefit from all possible sources of help and to use every opportunity, policy, or entitlement to its full limit.

LOVE AND MONEY

Schonbar (9) makes the pungent comment:

Some therapists feel guilty about "selling" a human relationship, seeing it as a kind of prostitution. Similarly there are those who, despite Freud's admonition [about reality needs], cannot admit of the crass, business-like aspects of the treatment situation in terms of satisfying their own needs for status and security. The professional role this type of therapist needs to assume is somehow denigrated by the symbols of being "in trade." (pp. 278–279)

Schwartz and Wolff (12) extend this metaphor as follows:

The psychotherapist has often been likened to a prostitute because he accepts a fee for his services. In [a contemporary text] the suggestion is made that what the therapist sells is very much like what the whore sells; namely, a human relationship, pseudo- or counterfeit-love. The therapist is supposed to be "friends" with, is supposed to "love" the patient. In our opinion, this is a distortion of the therapeutic relationship; such a view is commonly held by those who vulgarize what they fear. (p. 5)

In my own supervision of residents, I suggest that, although the psychotherapeutic relationship may in fact be a form of loving, that practitioner who treats therapy as more closely resembling love is more prone to enter into serious difficulties than the practitioner who keeps clearly before his/her eyes that therapy is a specific form of work, undertaken with a contract. In this regard, it is noteworthy that one of my teachers, usually perceived (correctly) as the most empathic of interviewers, tended to refer to the therapist as a "serviceman" to emphasize, as I understood it, this very feature of the therapeutic interaction.

Somewhat in caricature of the above issues, the beginning private practitioner may vacillate among a series of positions, the endpoints of which might be defined as altruism and masochism. On one hand, the wish to be helpful to all patients at all times reflects the therapist's commitment to serious clinical work. On the other, the clinical guilt earlier addressed about collecting money from needy or low/middle-class patients may express itself in masochistic surrender. An example of this latter occurred in connection with a gift: not the usual one from patient to therapist, but in this case from therapist to patient.

A borderline patient was seeing a clinical social worker who had just begun private practice. The patient was clearly struggling with much repressed anger and the social worker was experiencing some hesitation in confronting this directly. At one point when the patient was in tears about a particular interaction she had had with a boyfriend, she asked the therapist for a tissue. The therapist indicated her usual tissue supply—a "pocket pack" of tissues in a florentine leather case located at the side of the desk—and impulsively said to the patient, "Why don't you keep the box [i.e., the case]?" In subsequent supervision, the therapist realized that this was, at the unconscious level, a bribe to the patient to avert the anger which the therapist intuitively sensed was present, so that the patient would no longer feel anger toward the therapist but gratitude for the gift.

These issues of love versus money, and related themes of givingness as earlier demonstrated, are brought forward sometimes with great intensity in relation to the subject of fees for missed appointments. Cancellations serve as an interesting example of this heightened focus, in regard to which Schonbar (9) advocates an open and flexible approach. The common questions involve the validity of the reason for the canceled appointment, the role of physical illness, patient vacations as distinct from therapist vacations, and the like. One therapist known to the author has such negative feelings about New England snowstorms that snowstorms are an "automatic excuse no matter when they occur"! Again, the cancellation appears to mobilize issues with the greatest complexity because it represents, in a certain sense, "something for nothing" in a highly literal sort of way.

Along the same lines, DiBella (13) makes the following comment:

In our society, "true love" is not supposed to be "contaminated" by monetary considerations. People harbor great ambivalence toward money; it is worshipped yet condemned. . . . The puritan ethic still abounds; to self-indulge is sinful; to covet anything of value is wrong. Our punishment for wanting such is guilt, mortification and other distressing feelings. (p. 512)

DiBella further makes the point:

A large percentage of physicians refuse direct dealings with patients about money by using an intermediary; namely, the United States Post Office or a secretary. Avoiding this responsibility these physicians seem to more easily see themselves as concerned, charitable and purified of the sordid stuff called money. Similar distancing is achieved by the physician who feels compelled to hand the bill to the patient disguised in an envelope. (p. 515)

An extreme form of this approach occurs with one private practitioner who gives no bills at all, out of an expressed concern that they are potentially distracting and intrusive transitional objects, to which the patient may relate at the cost of important dynamic issues. This therapist has advised (personal communication) that the patient take full responsibility for remembering on his or her own to bring the check in at the beginning of the month. Failure to do so is explored in the characteristic way.

ANGER, ENVY, AND RESENTMENT

Among many other roles the fee for the beginning private practitioner may be used to express certain feelings that go along with the wealth of issues stirred up by "hanging up one's own shingle," especially in the treatment of wealthy patients, particularly successful patients or patients with other virtues and capacities. Therapist envy may be stirred up together with various kinds of resentments that interfere with the objectivity necessary to clinical work. In tension with the anger that occurs toward those who make us feel guilty, other forms of resentment may emerge. Stone gives one example (14):

If a therapist comes to feel he is "worth" $35.00 a session, his then taking on a patient at $30.00 a session in no way tarnishes his self image, because he considers his time worth all of that and a little besides. The therapist can even regard himself as being respectful, a bit charitable even, toward his patient, without having to resent him as a burden (as he might if the patient were paying only a slight amount). This state of affairs is rather the norm among those in the earlier part of their careers. (pp. 24–25)

Stone here captures the complex ways in which subtle resentments of the patient may express themselves around the issue of payment or even be mobilized by it.

Another subtle resentment may emerge around the length of time that it takes for skill and efficacy to be demonstrated in a psychiatric (as opposed to, say, the surgical) field, as Stone (14) points out. The therapist may experience resentment around the patient's clear perception of the therapist's youth and, by implication, inexperience and may attempt to use the setting of the fee as a means of correcting this tension.

TEMPTATIONS AND CORRUPTIONS

Perhaps more than in many other areas of the work, the role of the fee in serving as a temptation and possible source of corruption is more prominent than are other elements of the therapeutic work. The misalliance earlier described in clinic work may find its counterparts in private therapeutic work. The classical example is work with the children in a family where the parents are paying. The clinician is always in danger of having the objectivity of his/her role and its autonomy-enhancing features corrupted by pressure—overt or implicit, either from the reality family or from the countertransference—to advocate "the family line" in contrast to the actual needs of the therapeutic task. Stone (14) addresses this dilemma:

> [In dealing with families of the wealthy who seek a high-priced expert] it sometimes happens that a therapist would be passed up unless he charges substantially more than he is accustomed to receiving. Otherwise he would be regarded as a "nobody." If the therapist insists on only his usual fee, he is passed up; if he acquiesces, he finds himself in the faintly meretricious position of not quite feeling he is worth what he is getting and of having capitulated to some power maneuver, albeit monetarily tempting, on the part of the family. (p. 25)

Another version of this difficulty occurs when the therapist overidentifies with the autonomous strivings of the child and participates unconsciously with the child in using a larger-than-usual fee to "stick it to the parents," in a manner that transparently may fail to advance the aims of the therapeutic work.

Perhaps the most common corruption of the therapeutic process occurs when the therapist accedes to a request for a lowered fee without exploration and simply accepts the fact that the patient's wishes must determine the action. Often fear of confrontation, earlier-mentioned anxiety about being liked versus being respected, and the like may enter into the process (15). Once again, misalliances around entitlement and victimization may become the dominant factors in this essentially corrupting transaction.

CONCLUSION

A borderline woman came into treatment with a known history of being a "deadbeat" with previous clinicians. An example was her $400 dental debt, which she rationalized by saying: "What is the dentist going to do, repossess my teeth?" Mindful of this historical element, the therapist and patient negotiated that the fee would be paid on the spot at the end of every session to prevent difficulties such as the foregoing. At a certain point in the treatment, when the patient began to be seriously committed to the work, she handed the therapist the check, glanced at it for a moment, and suggested, "This really is worth more than I'm giving you." The significant movement in the therapeutic work dated from that self-reflective insight.

This case example perhaps comes full circle with the case that began our discussion. The setting of fees in private practice mobilized all the issues alluded to elsewhere in this text about the feelings toward money, intensified by the novelty of independent and autonomous private practice by the young practitioner. It is clearly the role of instructors in this area to approach with full candor the challenges in this area, mindful of the trainee's often exquisite sensitivity to "money matters."

REFERENCES

1. Adler, J. S., and Gutheil, T. G. Fees in beginning private practice. *Psychiatr. Ann.*, 7:35–46, 1977.
2. Chessick, R. D. A failure in psychoanalytic psychotherapy of a schizophrenic patient. *Dynamic Psychother.*, 2:136–149, 1984.
3. Gutheil, T. G. On the therapy in clinical administration, Parts I, II & III. *Psychiatr. Q.*, 54:3–25, 1982.
4. Mehlman, R. D. Transference mobilization, transference resolution and the narcissistic alliance. Presented at the Boston Psychoanalytic Society and Institute, February 25, 1976.
5. Pasternack, S. A., and Treiger, P. Psychotherapy fees and residency training. *Am. J. Psychiatry*, 133:1064–1066, 1976.
6. Allen, A. A note on the making of a psychiatrist: The transition from resident to private practice. *Psychiatry*, 34:410–418, 1971.
7. Freud, S. On beginning the treatment. *Standard edition*, Vol. XII (pp. 121–144). London: Hogarth Press, 1958.
8. Fox, Y. M. How to set your fees. *Resident Staff Physician*, 31:74–78, 1985.
9. Schonbar, R. A. The fee as a focus for transference and countertransference. *Am. J. Psychother.*, 21:275–285, 1967.

10. Randolph, G. T. Experiences in private practice. *J. Psychiatr. Nurs.*, 13:16–19, 1975.
11. Levin, A. M. Private practice is alive and well. *Social Work*, 21:356–362, 1976.
12. Schwartz, E. K., and Wolff, A. Money matters. *Int. Mental Health Res. News*, 11:1, 4–7, 1969.
13. DiBella, G. A. W. Mastering money issues that complicate treatment: The last taboo. *Am. J. Psychother.*, 24:510–522, 1980.
14. Stone, M. Treating the wealthy and their children. *Int. J. Child Psychother.*, 6:15–46, 1972.
15. Buckley, P., Karasu, T., and Charles, E. Common mistakes in psychotherapy. *Am. J. Psychiatry*, 135:1578–1581, 1979.

18

The Clinical Management of the Nonpaying Patient

Arthur E. Reider, M.D.

INTRODUCTION

There are nonpaying patients and nonpaying patients. I will discuss those patients who have the ability to pay, whose financial situation isn't truly desperate, yet who do not pay their bills.

To some extent preventive efforts can be effective. A patient may make it clear that there are money troubles and be concerned about being able to continue in therapy. Although this could have elements of resistance (often fear of deepening feelings in the relationship), it is best to take such statements at face value. A discussion of a general time range of the duration of treatment, of the specific fee, and of payment arrangements is beneficial—even if, in certain instances, payment may need to continue after termination. Some patients refuse this, voicing an anticipation of feeling dependent or entwined after stopping. While this may prove impossible to work out with some, it can be evident to others that emotional growth, including an appropriate sense of autonomy, can be a presumed outcome of psychotherapy. For the latter group the therapist may clarify that the forecast of sustained dependency due to debt is perhaps a rationalization for an incomplete commitment to the goal of autonomy. If an individual is self-reliant, there are no fears of the emotional constraints of a debt to the therapist. The decision to defer payment can be accompanied by the suggestion, "You will end therapy feeling that I'm basically no different from anyone else—that we're separate people and that a degree of aloneness is unavoidable in being human." I have received agreed-upon deferred payments from several patients two to three years after treatment ended.

When overdue fees become an issue, it may be indicated to distinguish

189

this from transference phenomenon. The therapist may need to suggest that the fee can be approached as a reality apart from its transference and other symbolic meanings.

In contrast, what follows is the study of a single case in which the tension and therapeutic work were heightened with respect to money. If we distinguish deep, warded-off, emotional pain from superficial, symptomatic dysphoria, we observe how assimilation of the former is correlated with the maturation of adaptive traits. Money is frequently tied to deeply painful issues; hence, confrontation with nonpayment can be utilized in the process of "desensitizing" a person to previously unbearable pain.

CASE STUDY

Monica, age 33, is a part-time professional, the mother of two daughters, and a wife for five years. Her therapy lasted two years, with once-weekly sessions for the first year and then twice-weekly sessions. Her nonpayment of fees represents specific, unresolved emotional conflicts which will be described with vignettes which illustrate this facet of her therapy as central.

The only mention of money had been at the beginning of therapy, when the patient explained that she could not afford to pay the fee on the basis of the family income but that her husband's company would reimburse them substantially for medical expenses over and above the 50% covered by the insurance company. She explained that the company would not reimburse them until the end of the year and asked whether the therapist could wait until then for part of the payment. He agreed. There was a large unpaid balance at the time of the session under discussion, and the therapist had not yet said anything about it. The patient had said several times that she felt guilty about not paying the bill and that she was compulsive about not being in debt.

Monica came for therapy in the midst of an extramarital affair that had been going on for several months. She was angry at her husband for his devotion to a needy adolescent orphan boy whom he had befriended and insisted on having as a house guest. The early phase of treatment predominantly dealt with her love affair. She was ecstatic about her paramour's sexual prowess but despondent after their motel encounters. In therapy she referred to her need for sex with him as an "addiction."

Exploration of this "addiction" led to her painful feelings of isolation as a child with her parents and older sister. A welcome relief was her Uncle Clarence, an exciting and ostentatious visitor who brought her gifts and took her to restaurants alone for treats. He seemed to be patient, understanding, and warm. By the time of junior high school, she had a romantic interest in him; once, while they were alone in the car, she kissed him playfully on the ear—an action not typical of her. Coincidentally, she had an intense crush on her junior-high-school teacher. She had fantasies of herself and the teacher alone together after an atomic explosion, but her fantasies always faded out when the two of them walked toward each other.

She kept in touch with her Uncle Clarence, who was a well-known public figure, during high school and college. When she graduated from college, he wrote to her strongly implying interest in having an affair with her. Safe in the knowledge that he was far away, she could write a provocative letter and sign it, "With lust and wickedness." The affair never materialized; however, the yearning for an Uncle Clarence remained strong and, at times, dominated the sessions in therapy.

After six months of treatment, the marriage stabilized and the orphan was sent away. The patient recognized that she loved her husband and enjoyed their family life. At an intellectual level she scorned her fruitless "addiction." She saw, at least in words, that her "ordinary" life offered more. However, until the last six months of therapy—when the issue of the unpaid bill came up—she lacked confidence in being able to keep her ship on course. She was uncertain how much she could count on herself, especially in the face of disappointment, frustration, and the inequities she saw in comparing herself to others.

Until the final six months of therapy, the transference feelings toward the therapist were largely positive and idealized. The patient was open, saying what came to mind, but her expression of discontent about many painful memories had a note of qualification. It was as if she were saying, "Maybe I got gypped as a child, but now I've got you, and that makes it all better."

The issue of her unpaid bill brought with it an undeniably real affective experience that lay beyond interpretation, avoidance, or soft-pedaling of one kind or another. With this experience came a noticeable change in her everyday life and an ability to cope with previously intolerable situations. In the approximately 15 sessions dealing with the unpaid bill, a shift in the therapeutic relationship occurred. For the first time she perceived the therapist as both understanding her and yet definitely separate from her. She terminated treatment by her own choice about three months later. A year after termination of treatment, she spontaneously wrote a letter describing in detail her continued progress.

At the beginning of the series of interviews to be described, the patient began to bring up material about her father; heretofore she had recalled him as an ineffectual man who was bitter about his low-ly job, yet disinclined to risk achieving more. She had remembered his awkward compliments to her as an adolescent, but little else. The therapist had just been away on vacation for a week. Upon his return she greeted him with the report of a dream in which he [the therapist] had gone away to deal with an explosion. A friend had then told her [in the dream] that the patient's marriage could be annulled on a technicality. There was a pretty girl in the dream; the patient's ex-lover ran off with her.

We might expect that the patient's interpretation would be that she wanted to be with her vacationing therapist but could not, possibly because of her explosive anger. She might further have said that the second part of the dream gave her a way out of being angry about the vacation interruption; after all, if the marriage bonds do not hold, she, like the pretty girl in the dream, could be with the man of her desires. However, the patient did not interpret the dream that way. What she did say was more revealing of the direction the therapist would take. She said that if she paid the therapist money or if she were prettier, he would not have gone away.

In the next session the patient reported a dream of being teased by the therapist, which led to the question of whether she had felt teased by her father. She explained that she had but that it went both ways. She felt teased, but also she could get her father to do what she wanted. It emerged in the next session that her father had largely ignored her but that she had also perceived an implicit message from him that he felt that he should *make up* for his ignoring and depriving her. She realized that she had come to feel that she *deserved* something because her father had ignored her. She recalled that as a girl she had wished that her father were different—in fact, that he were Uncle Clarence. As these realizations occurred, she became much more overtly demanding in sessions, especially at the end as she was about to leave. It was clear that she now felt that her father/the therapist owed her something if he was going to end the session.

In the next session the patient began talking about her anger at someone who had been reviewing her work; it seemed that this was a hidden anger at the therapist. She then told the therapist that she had been cooperative and had trusted him with dreams and other intimate material but that he was being too confrontational and that this was not according to the "deal" or "bargain." "Deal?" the therapist repeated. "Bargain? The only deal I know of is that you pay your bill." She immediately said that she felt guilty. The therapist said that she felt her father had let her get away with things, and he suggested that they be on the lookout for a repetition of her feeling that way in therapy. The therapist queried, "What is going on with the payment?"

She said she was waiting for money from her husband's company. The therapist did not comment. Quietly, she then added that she had used some of the money that the company had sent her during the previous year (as reimbursement for psychiatric expenses) to pay their other bills.

It was clear that she was making private "bargains" with the therapist, about which he had known nothing. She believed that if she "cooperated," was "good," and "gave" dreams, she deserved to get away with things. The therapist had no business confronting her with facts that she did not want to know. In reality, she had run off with the therapist's money. This "deal" was now revealed.

The patient was quite unaware that the money had any meaning in therapy at the time. For the following six sessions, she kept unclear the question of just how much money she owed her therapist. She also avoided making any critical judgments concerning her father's treatment of her. Her dreams, however, were quite revealing.

The next time she came, she was clearly angry, although she did not say so. She told of a dream she had had the night before. The time was junior high school. She had lived with a man, and he had died. She went back to her apartment and found a man there. He tried to rape her. She fought him but could not kill him. She pushed her fingers into his eyeballs. The dream closed as follows: She had to stop therapy because she did not have the money.

We can now see that she could practically *kill* the therapist for asking her about the unpaid bill but would settle for destruction of vital orbs. Dreams have a way of furnishing immediate convenient solutions; what better excuse for putting his eyes out than that he was trying to rape her. Of course, *she* had no sexual feelings at all—lust was all on the part of the therapist, the lascivious father, crudely and provocatively complimenting her in her junior-high-school days. She would have to stop therapy, not because of her violence but because she had no money. It was as if her money problem were solved and beyond discussion. She can quit therapy and get away from the infuriating psychiatrist, who does not respond to her "cooperation." He will not make a "deal."

At the outset of the following interview, the patient gave the therapist a small check that had come from the insurance company. She said she was unclear about how much was due from the insurance company, how much was from her husband's company, and how much was due from her. In the next session she was still confused about how much money she owed, and the therapist asked whether she wanted to keep the matter confused. She did not answer. Then he asked whether her father was stingy with her. She said, with much hesitation, that she could not say he was stingy. The therapist suggested that calling her father stingy would take away the pleasurable deal with him. We can see that if she were good—and exempted her father from her usual judgment of him— she deserved something special. She was silent for a while and recalled a childhood memory: When the family went to the movies, her mother would prod her father for money for candy and then tell the children to thank him. "But," said the patient, "it wasn't his idea."

"Was he stingy?" The patient did not answer. The theme of vagueness persisted in the next session, when she reported a dream of receiving a check that was not clearly a check and the amount of which was also uncertain. She asked a woman in the dream for an explanation, and the woman was "vague." She recalled then how her father had not paid for anything at her wedding, even though he had done so for her sister, married several years previously. She pointed out that she did not complain about this at the time, nor was she complaining now. The therapist reminded her of the costs of therapy, and she said that it cost too much and that others complained about their fees but she did not. The therapist pointed out that she did not complain about the fee in therapy, nor had she complained about her father's not giving her money at her wedding, but that perhaps she did have resentment that was hidden by keeping the facts vague.

In the following session, the patient explained that she owed her father $2,000 as the result of a loan he had given her several years earlier. She told of the fantasy, still present, that somehow her father would change into someone wonderful—that the question of the loan would somehow disappear. She explained that, on one hand, she would not feel right until she repaid *all* the money she owed her father and, on the other hand, there persisted a feeling that she could not afford to pay him anything. The therapist said that by approaching her father in an all-or-nothing way, she kept alive the fond hope that her father would change from a frog to a prince. At this point, she had another memory about her father. When she graduated from high school, he promised her a typewriter (he had bought her sister one three years before for her high-school graduation). At the patient's graduation, however, her parents said they did not have the money and asked her to pay for the typewriter until they could pay her back; then they "forgot." The patient was silent. The therapist asked, "What are you feeling?" The patient replied, "I don't feel I deserve the money."

She began the next session by saying, "Whoops, I forgot to write out a check. I forgot to put checks in my checkbook." The therapist asked her what her decision was about paying him. Reluctantly and in a low voice, she said that she and her husband had finally discussed their finances and had decided to pay him $500. She said that she was not aware of not wanting to pay; in fact, she wanted to pay *more.* The therapist said that the incident with the typewriter seemed unfair to her, that—in reality—her father had said it would be a present. He asked what the understanding had been about paying for therapy. She said the understanding was that it was okay to postpone payment until the company reimbursement came through. And there she stopped. The fact that she did not continue and go on to explain how she intended to pay the therapist was evidence that she was continuing to misperceive him—seeing him as the father who should allow her a special deal. She did not want to acknowledge that an agreement had been made and that *she had her part to keep.* Because of this misperception, pointing out to her that she had used the medical reimbursement to pay other bills would have been as useless as talking to a sleepwalker. So the therapist set the kind of limit her father had never set. He said, "We cannot have the balance be more than $1,000." There was a long pause filled with tension. She finally said, "I feel reprimanded. I feel you're saying you're not going to make up for what my father didn't do."

For several sessions she had not let enter into her consciousness the reality that she would actually be required to pay the bill. At the beginning of the next session, she handed the therapist a check for $550, which met the limit. Then she explained, "I felt after last time like I'd broken up with a boyfriend. Of course, you were being realistic—I shouldn't go over $1,000." She then said that when the therapist had set the limit, she felt it was being mean—that she deserved something. Part of her, she said, felt that if the therapist liked her or found her interesting, he should not charge. "But," she went on, "if you didn't, then I'd wonder what you were getting. I'd feel you were in control of me—that you owned me." The therapist added, "Then you wouldn't have to worry, because you wouldn't be held responsible for anything."

In the following session, she thought of a magazine article on skin cancer that had brought to her mind recurrent thoughts about something being wrong with her body. She then put into words for the first time in therapy a memory of her mother's being admiring of her. Specifically, she recalled that her mother had said she was a very beautiful child. She smiled with pleasure as she recalled this and said, "I really like my mother. She enjoyed me."

In the next session she said she had written her parents that she would pay them $25 a month to pay off the $2,000 loan. At a restaurant, she had given her daughters 25 cents each to buy apple turnovers. She was pleased with her daughters' independence, just as she was pleased with the letter she had written her parents. Her husband had just left on a business trip, and she was feeling differently about his being away. She realized that she could be competent on her own and recalled a previous conviction that if she were competent—for example, in driving—she would not be cared for.

At the next session, she reported a dream that she was on a commercial airliner. "It seems I didn't have enough money. There was a cafeteria. It was a huge plane. I didn't get anything to eat. I was thinking I couldn't get any of the main dishes because I didn't have enough money." She saw a magazine and wanted to take it without paying but did not. She said the magazine reminded her of the one she read in the waiting room. "The whole business about 'Do I have to pay?' I really wanted to read the magazine. It seemed very attractive. The big thing in my mind was whether I should pay or end up owing you $10,000 or whatever the bill would have come to."

Later in this session she thought that she was contradicting a statement of the therapist's and became anxious. She thought of another recent dream in which she was screaming hatefully. "I was surprised. I was like a firehose with water pouring out." She went on to talk about how she had never allowed herself to have differences of opinion with her sister-in-law and recalled a time when the latter had minimized the patient's accomplishments by saying they were "a dime a dozen." Now she said she could have retorted that she, herself, was not a dime a dozen. As she said this she reported that her heart was pounding.

The patient was becoming more assertive. Her wish to get something for nothing and her devalued view of herself were undergoing change. This took place as painful memories of her father entered into the therapeutic work and became undeniably clear because they were reexperienced as a present reality with the therapist. It is interesting that we do not hear about the father in the material after that reported above. What followed in the subsequent two months dealt more with siblings, peers, and her husband. Of course, the intrapsychic struggle went on. In a Labor Day dream the patient depicted herself with railroad workers in 1900, deciding not to throw stones because it was useless and running off with a cashbox instead. Now the patient had, as it were, joined a union, a brotherhood or sisterhood, and that is what her real-life activity reflected.

There was a change in the patient's use of her aggressive energies. The fuss at the end of the session did not recur. She approached everyday decisions about her children's schooling, her role in an organization of women, and her part-time career more realistically, less grandiosely, and less fearfully. She tolerated her husband's trips away from home without excessive anxiety.

She recognized a new sense of freedom of choice. At a country club dance she realized that she did not have to play tennis with an overly competitive man and instead was free to dance. (A year earlier she had felt such a fierce compulsion to "prove herself" every time she played tennis, which she hated, yet could not say "No.") She noticed her pleasure in the jams and bread she made herself. After a particularly enjoyable episode of sexual intercourse with her husband, she jokingly told him that sex was like "money in the bank." She began to notice that she could "take pleasure"—a significant phrase because it combines the active, aggressive word "take" with "pleasure." Her aggression, one could speculate, had been detoured in a sexualized childhood game of "You owe me and I hate you" with her father. And as long as she remained bound to her father in this manner, her libidinous yearnings remained checked and stunted, bound up with the filmy and insubstantial substitutes for the father she had wanted. She had been bound to her Uncle Clarence, her lover, and an image of the therapist. These substitutes made her feel at times aroused and powerful but did not permit her freedom.

DISCUSSION

There is universal agreement in the literature that questions of money produce considerable emotional reaction in psychotherapy and psychoanalysis. Freud (1), Ferenczi (2), and Fenichel (3) attributed the heightened charge in the concept of money to its tendency to be invested with strong basic instinctual energies.

In his early paper on technique, Freud (1) stated that it is preferable for the therapist to be frank and realistic about fees rather than to grumble in secret or make complaints about patients' ingratitude. His belief that financial sacrifice on the part of the patient can be an incentive for successful treatment is well known. He held that when the treatment is free, "the whole relationship is removed from the real world."

It is less widely recognized that Freud also said he had found exceptions when free treatment was very successful and that he was an advocate of free psychiatric treatment for the poor (4). Freud even took on an American psychiatrist as an analysand, with payment made by a third party (5). The few discussions of money in the brief analysis included Freud's interpretation of a dream about truancy as indicating the analysand's wish to skip sessions and keep the third-party payment for himself. In that case, in contrast to the present case, the patient had no awareness of such a motive.

Haak (6), a Stockholm psychoanalyst, wrote about the important role of firmness on fees in enabling the patient to work out maladaptive passive, self-sacrificing tendencies. The patient feels that "he has entrusted himself to a strong person who knows what he wants, who will not allow himself to be directed or frightened, who will stand up to various kinds of provocations and testing attempts . . . who lives as he teaches," he said. "All this also counteracts the patient's illusion of being in a privileged position—the favourite child" (p. 193). Haak warns against excessive "kindness" about fees, which may inhibit the patient's aggression. Being "kind" may mean that the analyst "has guilt feelings, that he is masochistic, that he is in love with the patient, that he wants to bribe the patient to love him, that he is afraid of the patient and that he is afraid of being considered greedy" (p. 194). Covert aggression and playing the all-giving mother can also be involved.

Wiener and Raths (7) describe the cultural conflict caused by the coexistence of private and public services. They assert that the cultural inconsistency over fees can negatively influence therapeutic outcome.

Gedo (8) reviewed 242 of his consecutive cases in the previous six years and discussed the 7% of nonpayers. To explain the pathological common denominator of this group of "deadbeats," he referred to Ruben's concept of delinquency in children as a defense against object loss (9) and to Winnicott's concept of the transitional object and transitional phenomena (10). The nonpaying patients were compared with deprived young children with anaclitic depression; their distress was relieved by the therapist's external presence. "But the maintenance of the internalized representation of this object depended on the illusion of symbiosis. When disillusioned by reality, these patients used the transitional phenomenon of withholding payment to deny their separateness" (p. 370).

Gedo (8) distinguished between those of his "deadbeats" who "did not deny their indebtedness but maintained an unpaid debt as a way of ensuring regular communication with me after formal therapy came to an end" and those "who used paranoid defenses to justify their retaliative withholding . . . " (p. 370). He suggests realistic management of delinquent fees but adds that collection can be carried out with therapeutic concern rather than with vindictiveness. In cases where nonpayment is a new symptom, arising from therapeutic regression in the transference, Gedo says, it is the therapist's responsibility to help the patient become aware of the underlying impulse. He believes that for the patients of his more primitive "deadbeat" category, "the price for not having some difficulties in collecting one's fees is failure to deal with the core problems of these patients" (p. 370).

In 1967 Lievano (11) published the results of his study of 20 patients in a state outpatient clinic. Some paid their bills completely, others in part, the rest not at all. Lievano admitted his bias in favor of being lenient with clinic patients about payments, but he was unable to find any clear relationship between outcome of therapy—as measured by a rating scale—and payment or nonpayment.

Schwartz and Wolff (12) and Chessick (13) criticize the depiction of therapy as a form of counterfeit love or friendship. The former refer to failure to collect a fee as "a way of inappropriately loving the patient, being responsible for the patient in a way the therapist should in fact be responsible only to his family and perhaps some friends." Both articles find a correlation between mismanagement of money matters by the therapist and neglect of other aspects of therapy. Chessick sees the integrity of the therapist as the key variable in the therapy, not any "right answers," and provides examples of his own straightforward approach to money matters.

Schonbar (14) described a relatively "flexible" approach to money along the lines of Fromm-Reichmann. Two case histories illustrate patients' feelings of victimization and distrustfulness about money issues.

Hilles' case study (15) of a clinic patient offers the most detailed description in the available literature of the meaning of money in therapy. Her patient stopped payment when the treatment began to mean something to her. She saw paying as a sign of commitment. She had never completed a single plan or followed through on any relationship in her life. Paying, the patient felt, was tantamount to giving up her negative relationship with her mother, whom she had consistently pushed away. She feared further intimacy because she was afraid that "total surrender" would be demanded by the therapist. When the patient did begin paying again—after an interlude of nine months—she developed visual symptoms, which she viewed as an expression of "protest" against her progress toward health. The therapy of this "borderline" patient was interrupted by the therapist's move to another city.

Allen (16) points out how management of the fee can function for limit setting, constructive permissiveness, and other helpful therapeutic effects. He gives brief summaries of several cases, most of which demonstrate limit setting. In one of the "permissive" examples, as did Schonbar with one of her cases, he decided not to charge so that a negative distortion of the therapist would be undercut. Regrettably, neither Schonbar nor Allen discusses possible complications of deliberate noncharging for purely therapeutic purposes.

Balsam and Balsam (17) provide the most comprehensive coverage of the subject. In addition to brief cases (one of which resembles Hilles' case), a balanced overall therapeutic approach concerning money is presented.

On the basis of experience in the British National Health System, R. M. Balsam states that the "savior fantasy" is to some extent promoted by the British system, in which the therapist can avoid confronting, and thus working out, his own conflicts about money.

SUMMARY

Money has a particularly strong investment of irrational meaning and thus, as a reality factor, can be a potent catalyst (or obstacle) to the therapeutic process. Frequently, the transference cannot be seen clearly, by either patient or therapist, until vagueness about payment is cleared up.

In the case described in the first part of this article, the patient intellectually recognized early in therapy that reality could be more substantially satisfying than her "addiction." It was not until the work on the unpaid bill occurred, however, that she could part with the rewards of a distant, fantasied relationship.

It should be clear that confrontation with money matters cannot always bear therapeutic fruit. Much depends on the development of an alliance with the patient, the patient's conscience, and the therapist's sense of timing. Sadness and rage were mobilized in the sessions reported. When the patient accepted the reality of the financial arrangement of her therapy, she felt as if she had broken up with a boyfriend, and her rage, although contained, was of violent intensity. The unpaid bill was like a seed crystal in the precipitation of these components of "emotional pain." In the words of another patient, the therapy gave this patient "a cup to put her bitterness in"; as the late Elvin Semrad was fond of saying, she could then "leave the bad behind and take the good with her."

REFERENCES

1. Freud, S. On beginning the treatment (1913). In *Standard edition*, Vol. 12 (pp. 121–144). London: Hogarth Press, 1958.
2. Ferenczi, S. *Sex in psychoanalysis* (pp. 319–331). Boston: Gorham Press, 1916.
3. Fenichel, O. *The psychoanalytic theory of neurosis.* New York: W. W. Norton, 1945.
4. Freud, S. Lines of advance in psychoanalytic therapy (1919 [1918]), *Standard edition*, Vol. 17 (pp. 157–168), 1958.
5. Pulver, S. Freud and third-party payment: A historical note. *Am. J. Psychiatry,* 131:1400–1402, 1974.
6. Haak, N. Comments on the analytical situation. *Int. J. Psychoanal.,* 38:183–195, 1957.
7. Wiener, D., and Raths, O. Cultural factors in payment for psychoanalytic therapy. *Am. J. Psychoanal.,* 20:66–72, 1960.

8. Gedo, J. A note on non-payment of psychiatric fees. *Int. J. Psychoanal.*, 44:368–371, 1963.

9. Ruben, M. Delinquency—A defense against loss of objects and reality. *Psychoanal. Study Child*, 12:335–355, 1957.

10. Winnicott, D. Transitional objects and transitional phenomena. *Int. J. Psychoanal.*, 34:89–97, 1953.

11 Lievano, J. Observations about payment of psychotherapy fees. *Psychiatr. Q.*, 41:324–338, 1967.

12. Schwartz, E., and Wolff, A. Money matters. *Int. Ment. Health Res. Newsl.*, 11(2):1–7, 1969.

13. Chessick, R. Ethical and psychodynamic aspects of payment for psychotherapy. *Voices*, 3(4):26–31, 1968.

14. Schonbar, R. The fee as a focus for transference and countertransference. *Am. J. Psychother.*, 21:275–285, 1967.

15. Hilles, L. The clinical management of the nonpaying patient: A case study. *Bull. Menninger Clin.*, 35:98–112, 1971.

16. Allen, A. The fee as a therapeutic tool. *Psychoanal. Q.*, 40:132–140, 1971.

17. Balsam, R. M., and Balsam, A. Thinking about money. In *Becoming a psychotherapist: A clinical primer* (pp. 113–132). Boston: Little, Brown, 1974.

19

The Extension of Credit to Patients in Psychoanalysis and Psychotherapy

Charles K. Hofling, M.D., and Milton Rosenbaum, M.D.

The financial aspects of the transactions between patients and physicians in general, and between patients and long-term psychotherapists in particular, quite properly have been increasingly scrutinized in recent years. The image of the physician has, in this respect, become somewhat tarnished. While his scientific reputation remains generally high, he is often perceived as being excessively concerned with the monetary rewards of his profession. The position of the medical psychotherapist (including the psychoanalyst) in this respect is somewhat special. It is not, generally speaking, that his earnings are particularly high, but that his attitude toward the payment of fees has seemed unusual, both to the general public and to many of his colleagues.

Beginning with Freud, the classic stance of the analyst has been that he *leases* his time to the patient on a contractual basis. The patient is expected to pay promptly and regularly for his assigned four or five hours per week, regardless of whether or not there is any apparent benefit or even whether or not the patient appears for his appointed hours. (Some analysts will, and others will not, accept cancellations in dire emergencies, and many—perhaps most— psychotherapists will accept cancellations made for legitimate reasons at least 24 hours in advance.) There is, of course, the obvious and very practical point that intensive psychotherapy (including analysis) requires spending very large amounts of time with each patient and thus limits the number of patients making up the psychiatrist's practice, with the result that he is typically dependent for his livelihood (to an unusual degree for physicians) upon the patient's fulfillment of his side of the bargain. Alongside these practical considerations,

another set of considerations develops, having both a clinical and a theoretical basis, which tends to impart a rigidity to the handling of the financial aspect of the interaction between patient and therapist. These considerations have to do with the realization of the central significance of
the transference and countertransference (in a sense, the unrealistic) elements of the interaction. For the sake of seeing clearly the nuances of
transference and countertransference, of understanding the latter, and of
effectively interpreting the former, it is deemed of cardinal importance to
minimize the intrusion of reality factors into the therapeutic process. The
following comment by Haak (1), while literally true, exemplifies the extreme caution promoted by this point of view:

> To succeed in talking the analyst into granting certain favors in
> respect of the fee can be and, by certain patients, has been experi-
> enced as having fooled the analyst. . . . Too low a fee or too great
> generosity (of the analyst) may easily give cause for aggression
> against the patients which reduces the analyst's possibilities of an-
> alysing them. (p. 194)

In a similar vein, Gedo (2) reported an instance in which he extended
credit to a patient after the latter had experienced a financial crisis. Subsequently, the patient created a crisis that led to nonpayment and the analyst
stopped treatment.

During the past 20 years or so there has developed a fuller study and
a greater appreciation of the role played in the therapeutic process by the
realistic aspects of the relationship between patient and therapist—and
thus a greater flexibility of technique—but the old image lingers among
dynamic psychiatrists, their colleagues, and sophisticated elements of the
general public.

The present study, an investigation of the extension of credit to patients
in psychoanalysis and long-term dynamic psychotherapy and the effects
of credit on the course of therapy, is offered as a contribution to the
understanding of the degree of flexibility which actually obtains in such
practice today. Our interest in this subject developed spontaneously out
of our practices and a broader interest in those aspects of practice which
represent a departure from conventional modes and thus are seldom
presented in the literature or even openly discussed. As it happened, we
had both extended credit to patients (in analysis or analytic therapy) on
a more-or-less formal basis instead of merely allowing them to become
delinquent in the payment of fees.

CASE EXAMPLE 1

The patient, a 21-year-old single woman, entered psychoanalytic treatment after dropping out of college during the middle of her third year. The diagnosis "schizophrenic reaction" was based mainly on her withdrawal from social contacts, loss of interest and poor performance in academic work, mild paranoid ideation, overt hostility to her parents, and extreme personal isolation. She was an only child, her father's favorite, extremely bright, with obvious potential for intellectual and personal development. The fee was paid by the father, a successful corporation executive.

By the beginning of the third year of treatment, the patient had progressed considerably (graduated from college, held a job as a laboratory technician) and was gradually emancipating herself from her family, especially her father. At this time, the patient reported that her father told her he did not believe she needed further treatment and that unless she returned home (about 50 miles from the city in which she worked and the therapy was being conducted) he would refuse to continue to pay for her treatment. Although I was aware of the transference as well as countertransference aspects of the situation, I told the patient I would continue to see her, regardless of whether the father carried out his threat to discontinue payment. She agreed to repay me when she was in a position to do so.

For four months I continued to send monthly statements to the father and finally (to my great relief) the father paid and continued to do so until the conclusion of the analysis. I believe, despite the obvious transference and countertransference and acting out on the part of the patient because of her father's refusal to pay, that the reality factor—namely, my willingness to continue to treat her—strengthened the therapeutic alliance and had a beneficial effect on the outcome of therapy.*[M.R.]

CASE EXAMPLE 2

The patient, when first seen, was 30 years old, the mother of four children, and the wife of a capable but very junior executive of a large corporation. The original diagnosis was "hysterical personality with episodes of hysterical psychosis." (In the light of present understanding, the pa-

---

*Despite the diagnosis of schizophrenic reaction, the patient was admitted to a first-rate medical school, graduated with honors, and is now actively and successfully engaged in the practice of medicine.

tient would probably have been diagnosed as a borderline personality.) She had previously undergone two unfavorable experiences in psychiatric treatment, one had included prolonged hospitalization with a course of electroconvulsive therapy. Nevertheless, the patient had a number of significant assets, including high intelligence, good physical health, and a loving husband.

We embarked upon a course of expressive psychotherapy, with the patient being seen three times a week and with the bill being paid by the patient's wealthy mother. As expected, results were slowly achieved, but, by the end of the second year of therapy, the patient was in somewhat better condition; this improvement was manifested by certain alterations in behavior, which were gratefully accepted by the husband but displeasing to the mother. The latter made several efforts to control the therapy; when these failed, she responded by discontinuing her financial support.

Several options were discussed in the therapeutic hours, and the one finally adopted was one rather timidly suggested by the patient herself in consultation with her husband. The arrangement—formally made, though never written—was that the husband would assume eventual payment of all fees dating from the mother's discontinuance of assistance. There would be no reduction in fees or in the frequency of sessions. For the ensuing year and one-half, the husband would pay one-half of each month's bill; for the next year, he would pay each month's (current) bill in full; thereafter he would pay all current bills while undertaking repayment of the debt at the same rate as that at which it had been incurred. As is apparent, the assumptions were several: that treatment would be prolonged, that the patient and her husband were acting in complete good faith, and that the latter's financial situation would steadily improve. All assumptions eventually were borne out and the debt was paid in full and on time.

The patient remained in psychotherapy for about 10 years, the therapeutic outcome being quite satisfactory. The short-term effects of the financial arrangements were favorable, involving a diminished dependence upon the mother and a transfer of this dependence to the husband and the therapist. The intermediate effects were unfavorable, involving an increased difficulty in the patient's expression of angry feelings toward the therapist in the transference. By the end of the transaction (i.e., the start of the seventh year of the psychotherapy), all detectable effects had subsided; the material being relived and considered was quite basic, and the therapy was proceeding along conventional lines.

As would be assumed from this glimpse of the situation, the countertransference was predominantly positive. The realistic aspects of the situation were, of course, favorable, depending largely upon the therapist's appraisal of the husband (whom he had interviewed at the outset of treatment). [C.K.H.]

After sharing these experiences with one another, we decided to institute an inquiry among colleagues with the idea of ascertaining the frequency of such departures from tradition and their effects upon the course of therapy.

METHODOLOGY OF THE STUDY

Our subjects were 157 psychoanalysts and psychotherapists, not representative of all American psychiatrists but representative of a sizeable segment of that larger group. We wanted subjects who (a) were primarily engaged in intensive long-term therapy (so that the opportunity for extending credit on a formal basis would have arisen), (b) were thoroughly trained in dynamic psychiatry (so that they would give special attention to subtle changes in transference and countertransference phenomena), and (c) were known to us personally (so that we could depend on a high percentage of answers to the questionnaire).

Two hundred and fifty questionnaires were mailed; two hundred and

Table 1
Demographic Description of Subjects

Persons receiving questionnaire	Identifiable respondents
Mean age: 52.9 years	Mean age: 53.7 years
Age range: 32–74 years	Age range: 32–74 years
Sex distribution: 15 (6.0%) women; 233 (94.0%) men	Sex distribution: 6 (5.9%) women; 96 (94.1%) men
Geographical distribution: 128 (51.6%) east of Mississippi; 120 (48.4%) west; 22 states and D.C. represented	Geographical distribution: 53 (52%) east of Mississippi; 49 (48%) west; 20 states and D.C. represented
149 (60.1%) psychoanalysts; 99 (39.9%) nonanalysts	62 (60.8%) psychoanalysts; 40 (39.2%) nonanalysts
228 (91.9%) American Board of Psychiatry and Neurology Diplomates	94 (92.2%) American Board of Psychiatry and Neurology Diplomates

forty-eight reached their destination. To maximize the response rate, we did not ask our respondents to identify themselves. Nevertheless, a good many of them (102) did so spontaneously. This circumstance enabled us to ascertain whether or not the actual respondents were typical of the group to which we had sent the questionnaire. As can be seen from Table 1, the subgroup of identifiable respondents is representative of the entire group to whom questionnaires were sent.

The following explanatory letter and questionnaire were mailed:

Dear_____:

In a recent conversation, deriving from studies we had individually undertaken on unconventional forms of psychotherapy, we found ourselves talking about various transactions between therapist and patient which are seldom (or never) discussed in the literature. Among such features was the matter of the therapist's extending credit to the patient; i.e., of offering a remission of fees for a given period, either in whole or in part, with a definite understanding of repayment later. Although both of us have done this, we found that we had no clear idea as to the extent to which this experience might have been shared by our colleagues. We decided to undertake a study of the question.

Enclosed with this letter is a brief questionnaire, which we should greatly appreciate your filling out and returning in the enclosed envelope.

Yours cordially,

QUESTIONNAIRE

1) Have you ever extended credit to a patient in psychoanalysis or extended psychotherapy? Yes _____ No _____

2) If "Yes," on how many occasions? (Please check one)
    Only 1 _____ 1 to 3 _____ Over 3 _____
   If on more than one occasion, please indicate the data individually in your replies to the following questions (up to four cases).

3) Was (were) the patient(s) in ("classical") psychoanalysis or in psychotherapy?

	Case 1	Case 2	Case 3	Case 4
Psychoanalysis	_____	_____	_____	_____
Psychotherapy	_____	_____	_____	_____

4) Was the remission of the fees partial or complete (during the time involved)?

	Case 1	Case 2	Case 3	Case 4
Partial	_____	_____	_____	_____
Complete	_____	_____	_____	_____

5) Was (were) the amount(s) owed you by the patient(s) eventually (check one)

	Case 1	Case 2	Case 3	Case 4
Paid in full	_____	_____	_____	_____
In part	_____	_____	_____	_____
Not at all	_____	_____	_____	_____

6) Over what period of time was the credit extended?

	Case 1	Case 2	Case 3	Case 4
0–6 months	_____	_____	_____	_____
6–12 months	_____	_____	_____	_____
1 to 2 years	_____	_____	_____	_____
Over 2 years	_____	_____	_____	_____

7) Did this procedure exert an observable effect on the therapy?

	Case 1	Case 2	Case 3	Case 4
Yes	_____	_____	_____	_____
No	_____	_____	_____	_____
Do not know	_____	_____	_____	_____

8) If it did, was the overall effect (check one)

	Case 1	Case 2	Case 3	Case 4
Helpful	_____	_____	_____	_____
Deleterious	_____	_____	_____	_____
Not clearly either	_____	_____	_____	_____

9) If there was an observable effect, was it primarily

	Case 1	Case 2	Case 3	Case 4
In the transference	_____	_____	_____	_____
The countertransference	_____	_____	_____	_____
Both	_____	_____	_____	_____
Neither	_____	_____	_____	_____

10) Was (were) the patient(s) male or female?

	Case 1	Case 2	Case 3	Case 4
Man	_____	_____	_____	_____
Woman	_____	_____	_____	_____

11) Was (were) the patient(s) of the same or the opposite sex (to your own)?

	Case 1	Case 2	Case 3	Case 4
Same sex	____	____	____	____
Opposite sex	____	____	____	____

12) What was your age at the time of your decision about extending credit?

	Case 1	Case 2	Case 3	Case 4
	____	____	____	____

13) What was the age of the patient at the time of your decision about extending credit?

	Case 1	Case 2	Case 3	Case 4
Age	____	____	____	____

14) What was the clinical diagnosis?

	Case 1	Case 2	Case 3	Case 4
	____	____	____	____

15) Who paid the fees before credit was extended? (Check one)

	Case 1	Case 2	Case 3	Case 4
Patient	____	____	____	____
Spouse	____	____	____	____
Parent	____	____	____	____
Other (specify)	____	____	____	____

16) Any comments which you would care to make about the area under consideration would be deeply appreciated.

RESULTS OF THE QUESTIONNAIRE

1. Of the 248 questionnaires, 157 (63.3%) were returned by an arbitrarily selected cutoff date, two months after our last mailing.*
2. To the first question, 123 (78.3%) responded Yes; 31 (19.7%) responded No; 3 (1.9%) responded equivocally.
3. The 123 Yes responders indicated they had extended credit (in the sense of the questionnaire) to 362 specific patients. Some of

*Ultimately 67.3% of the questionnaires were returned.

the responders indicated they had extended credit to more than 4 patients. Thus the total number of patients to whom credit had been extended was something in excess of 362 and the average number of patients per Yes responder was over 2.94.

4. Four (4) Yes responders, accounting for 8 patients, answered only the first two questions of the questionnaire. Thus 354 patients (credit-instances) were more-or-less fully described. Of these, full credit had been extended to 130 (36.7%) and partial credit had been extended to 224 (63.3%).

5. Of the 354 patients, 220 (62.1%) eventually paid in full, 94 (26.6%) paid in part, and 40 (11.3%) did not pay at all.

6. Respondents judged 133 (37.6%) to have shown a favorable effect to the credit-extending experience per se; 58 patients (16.4%) were judged to have experienced an unfavorable effect; in 101 instances (28.53%) the respondent indicated that there had been an effect but that this effect could not be clearly perceived as either favorable or unfavorable; 62 (17.5%) responded "No" or "Do not know" to the question "Did this procedure exert an observable effect on the therapy?" In the attempt to evaluate the correlation, if any, between observable effects and transference and countertransference manifestations, the last mentioned group has been subtracted from the 354 total, leaving an *n* of 292.

7. In relation to the credit experience, 69 (23.6%) of 292 patients showed transference but not countertransference phenomena; in 12 instances (4.11%) there was evidence of countertransference but not of transference phenomena; in 110 instances (37.7%) there was evidence of both transference and countertransference phenomena; and in 101 instances (34.6%) there was evidence of neither transference nor countertransference phenomena.

8. Of the 133 favorable effects, 43 (32.3%) took place with related transference phenomena only; 5 (3.8%) took place with countertransference phenomena only; 42 (31.6%) took place with both transference and countertransference phenomena; and 43 (32.3%) took place with neither transference nor countertransference phenomena being observed.

9. Of the 58 unfavorable effects, 15 (25.9%) took place with related transference phenomena only; 1 (1.7%) took place with countertransference phenomena only; 39 (67.2%) took place with both transference and countertransference phenomena; and 3 (5.2%) took place with neither transference nor countertransference phenomena.

10. Of the 101 instances in which respondents perceived effects of the credit experience but could not describe them as either favorable or unfavorable, there were only 43 instances in which the question on transference and countertransference was answered. Of these, 2 (4.7%) took place with transference phenomena only being observed, 1 (2.3%) took place with countertransference phenomena only, 15 (34.9%) took place with both transference and countertransference phenomena, and 25 (58.1%) took place with neither transference nor countertransference phenomena.

11. Of the entire series of 354 patients, 73 (20.6%) were in psychoanalysis and 281 (79.4%) in psychotherapy.

12. Of the 73 patients in psychoanalysis, 28 (38.4%) showed a favorable effect of the credit experience, 11 (15.1%) showed an unfavorable effect, and in 34 instances (46.6%) neither a favorable nor an unfavorable effect was noted.

13. Of the 281 patients in psychotherapy, 106 (37.7%) showed a favorable effect of the credit experience, 43 (15.3%) showed an unfavorable effect, and in 130 instances (46.3%) neither a favorable nor an unfavorable effect was noted.

14. Marked differences exist between specific respondents with respect to the effects they noted of the credit-extending experience. For example, one group of 16 respondents reported a total of 47 instances with the effects favorable in 100% of the cases. Another group of 16 respondents reported a total of 45 instances with the effects favorable in no cases, unfavorable in 28 cases (62.2%), and neither favorable nor unfavorable in 17 cases (37.8%).

15. The most common diagnostic entities reported (using the nomenclature of the respondents) were: depression (all kinds), 61; anxiety reactions, 32; hysterical reactions and personalities, 23; neuroses and neurotic personalities (not otherwise specified), 30; borderline states and personalities, 27; obsessive-compulsive neuroses and personalities, 24; schizophrenias, 15. Among the wide variety of other diagnoses made with lesser frequency was that of narcissistic character, of which there were 7. (In a number of instances the question on clinical diagnosis was not answered.)

16. In Table 2 we have listed those diagnostic categories where the proportions of the various effects of the credit experience differed appreciably from the overall averages.

17. The correlation of repayment efforts with the (other) effects of the credit experience is shown in Table 3.

Table 2

Diagnosis	Number of cases	Number of favorable effects	Number of unfavorable effects	Number of uncertain effects or no effects	Percent favorable of all cases	Percent favorable of (favorable + unfavorable)
Anxiety reactions	32	16	4	12	50.0%	80.0%
Depressions (all kinds)	61	31	10	20	50.8%	75.6%
Obsessive-compulsive neuroses and personalities	24	14	1	9	58.3%	93.3%
Narcissistic characters	7	0	3	4	(0%)	(0%)
All cases	354	133	58	163	37.6%	69.6%

18. Of the 102 respondents who identified themselves, 62 were analysts, 40 were nonanalysts.
19. The 62 identified analysts had extended credit to 42 analytic patients and 88 psychotherapy patients.
20. Of the respondents who identified themselves (102), 20 were in full-time (or geographical full-time) academic positions; 82 were primarily in private practice. The 20 in full-time positions reported data on repayment in 50 instances; the 82 primarily in private practice reported data on repayment in 223 instances.
21. Of the 50 instances (academic), 40 patients (80.0%) repaid in full, 10 patients (20.0%) repaid in part, and no patients failed to repay at all.
22. Of the 223 instances (private practice), 134 patients (60.1%) repaid in full, 62 patients (27.8%) repaid in part, and 27 patients (12.1%) made no effort to repay.

Table 3

	Whole population (354)	Patients repaying in full (220)	Patients repaying in part (94)	Patients making no effort at repayment (40)
Favorable effects	133 (37.6%)	110 (50.0%)	18 (19.2%)	7 (17.5%)
Unfavorable effects	58 (16.4%)	20 (9.1%)	31 (33.0%)	10 (25.0%)
Uncertain neither or none	163 (46.0%)	90 (40.9%)	45 (47.8%)	23 (57.5%)

23. In the subgroup of 50 instances, 27 patients (54.0%) showed favorable effects, 5 patients (10.0%) showed unfavorable effects, and 18 patients (36.0%) showed neither favorable nor unfavorable effects (or no effects).

24. In the subgroup of 223 instances, 78 patients (35.0%) showed favorable effects, 40 patients (17.9%) showed unfavorable effects, and 105 patients (47.1%) showed neither favorable nor unfavorable effects (or no effects).

25. The mean age of all respondents (as contrasted with all identifiable respondents) was 54.1 years; the mean age of all Yes respondents was 54.4 years; the mean age of all No respondents was 53.8 years; and the mean age of therapists at the time of extension of credit was 44.3 years.

26. Of the 354 credit-instances reported, the questions about gender of patients and therapists were answered in 324 instances. In 174 of these instances (53.7%), the patients were of the opposite sex to the therapists; in 150 instances (46.3%) they were of the same sex.

DISCUSSION

Despite a good bit of cautionary material in the literature on treatment technique, a great majority of the psychiatrists in our sample had, in the course of psychoanalysis or intensive psychotherapy, remitted patients' fees, in whole or in part, with the definite understanding of subsequent payment. Those who did so usually did so more than once, the average being about three times (2,3,4).* Nearly two-thirds of the patients involved in such experiences eventually paid in full; only a small minority made no effort at repayment (5).

Nearly one-half of the patients did not show either a favorable or an unfavorable response to the credit experience per se (except, of course, that the arrangement permitted them to continue with the original therapist). Of those evincing one or the other, the great majority showed a favorable effect (6).

The precise role played by transference and countertransference phenomena in producing such effects of the credit experience as were noted is not entirely clear (7,8,9,10). That such phenomena were at times only minimally involved is evident. This finding suggests a greater ability on

---

*The numbers in parentheses refer to the items in Results upon which the immediately preceding statements are based.

the part of many patients (and therapists) to distinguish between reality elements of the therapeutic situation and purely subjective elements than has sometimes been supposed.

On the other hand, it seems equally clear that transference and counter-transference elements were sometimes of critical importance in our study. Of particular interest is the finding that both transference and counter-transference phenomena were noted in only 31.6% of cases showing favorable effects, whereas they were noted in 67.2% of cases showing un-favorable effects. This finding suggests that when patient and therapist fail to distinguish (emotionally) between realistic and subjective aspects of their transaction in the introduction of such a parameter as credit ex-tension, the procedure is likely to be associated with adverse effects.

Essentially no difference as to the relative frequency of the effects of the credit experience (favorable, unfavorable, neither or none) was noted between patients in psychoanalysis and patients in intensive psychother-apy (11,12,13). The finding that credit was extended to 42 analytic patients and to 88 psychotherapy patients by the identified analysts probably reflects that fact that analysts today see more patients in psychotherapy than in classical analysis or that patients selected for analysis are likely to be better financial risks. It is well known that the decision to recom-mend or accept patients for psychoanalysis rather than psychotherapy is influenced by many factors, not least important of which is the financial one.

The diagnostic breakdown of the patients seen by our respondents is, in general, not very informative since (a) differing nomenclatures were used, (b) many patients were given more than one diagnosis, (c) there was no way of being certain of the diagnostic criteria being used, and (d) a number of respondents did not fill out the question on diagnoses. How-ever, the roster of patients appear to represent a fairly average distribu-tion of psychiatric patients who are likely to be accepted for intensive psychotherapy or psychoanalysis (15). It is of interest that the number of favorable effects of the credit experience exceeded that of the unfavorable effects in all of the major diagnostic categories. In fact, the only category where the reverse was true was that of narcissistic character (16).

The correlation of repayment efforts on the part of the patients with the quality of their experience of the credit extension were, in general, what we expected. Patients repaying the full amount had, for example, nearly three times the proportion of favorable effects as did those patients making no effort at repayment (17).

While statistically not very unusual in a series such as the one in our study, it is nevertheless of interest that some respondents seemed always to observe favorable effects of the credit-extending experience while others seemed never to observe such effects. Since about one-third of our respondents remained anonymous, it is not, at the moment, possible to probe extensively into differences in the therapists that might have come into play here, but a follow-up could be of interest (14). However, we do know that 20 of the 102 respondents who identified themselves by signing the comments required in item 16 of the questionnaire were in full-time (or geographical full-time) academic positions and the 82 were primarily in private practice. The patients of the former group differed from those of the latter group with respect to two parameters examined in our questionnaire: they made a greater effort at repayment, and they had a higher ratio of favorable to unfavorable experiences (18,19,20,21,22). We speculate that these differences may have two explanations: (a) the patients of the former group had greater ego and superego strength, and/or (b) the psychiatrists in the former group, being less dependent upon practice income, were more relaxed about the whole transaction and thus handled it more effectively.

Data on the age of respondents are inconclusive, except that they do not support the idea that extension of credit, if it occurs at all, occurs largely out of the tharapist's necessity, i.e., to a much greater extent in his earlier rather than his later years of practice (25). Data on the gender of patients and therapists are also inconclusive. There was, however, a preponderance of opposite sex to like sex instances (26).

COMMENTS FROM RESPONDENTS

One hundred three respondents (65.6%) were sufficiently interested in the subject of the study to offer comments, which ranged from a few sentences to a few pages in length. Of the respondents who said they did not believe in or had not extended credit on a formal basis, almost all said that in most instances they delayed payment from two to four months and lowered fees if the patients could not afford to pay. Several respondents said they had extended credit early in their practice, but when they had gained more experience (and perhaps a better selection of cases) they did not extend credit since they were able to handle the situation as part of the therapeutic process. Others said that while they did not recommend credit extension, they did it frequently.

A few experienced and well-known respondents said flatly that extending credit is a mistake—the potential for disrupting the treatment is enormous—while a few others (equally experienced and well known) said that it is helpful. Several analysts stated that they had extended credit after therapy was well established and productive, since interruption would then have been deleterious. The dollar loss to them ranged from four hundred to fifteen hundred dollars, but they "would do it again." As one colleague put it, "I consider it as a challenge to my therapeutic skills and perhaps as a surreptitious form of gambling on my therapeutic ability (since I do not go to Las Vegas or play the stock market)."

Our respondents indicated that the most common clue given that extension of credit is significant in the transference is increased reference on the patient's part to being either special or worthless. One well-known analyst has always extended credit to those who have needed it and has never been cheated. The issue is always brought into the analytic work by him or the patient. He said, "I believe that therapists who claim that motivation for treatment can be judged primarily on the basis of money, fees, credit, who pays, etc., misunderstand the ideas of motivation and resistance to treatment."

Some respondents specifically mentioned that the extension of credit to psychiatric residents (all of whom repaid in full) was considered to be a positive factor in the outcome. One respondent stated: "I have been reluctant to extend credit, having frequently heard admonitions against allowing patients to 'get into your debt.' It presents, however, an important possibility where one sees a number of young people in training, as I do." Another respondent said: "I think that, whatever the procedure, it affects both the transference and countertransference, but certainly no more than charging fees that the patient cannot afford and which may appreciably distort his or her life-style."

All these responses indicate how important it is to pool data since, by and large, most psychotherapists (especially analysts) see relatively few patients and are likely to base judgments and come to conclusions about a variety of issues with far too little data. Obviously, in extending credit many factors are involved, but certainly the particular personality of the therapist plays a role. Therefore, the fact that there is a difference in opinion does not mean that some therapists are right and others wrong. (One case can be a gratifying experience, while in another the therapist feels trapped.) To sum it up, if the therapist, regardless of reasons, does not feel comfortable in extending credit, he should not do so. Yet one of the results of this study might be to encourage a more flexible attitude with respect to the financial aspect of therapy, especially among those psychiatrists who have held rather fixed opinions.

REFERENCES

1. Haak, N. Comments on the psychoanalytic situation. *Int. J. Psychoanal.*, 38(3/4): 183–195, 1957.
2. Gedo, J. A note on non-payment of psychiatric fees. *Int. J. Psychoanal.*, 44(3): 368–371, 1963.

20

Purchasing a Practice: A Personal Account

Ann E. Carlisle, Ph.D.

Why would anyone want to purchase a private practice in psycho-therapy? I am often asked this when people learn that this is how I began my practice as a licensed clinical psychologist in Houston in 1981. This brief chapter will describe my experience in taking over another psychologist's practice, provide some information about the business transaction itself, and assess how well the process worked for me.

As the end of my final year of postdoctoral training approached, I was earnestly exploring different options available to me in the field of clinical psychology. While thinking over the advantages and disadvantages of going into private practice, I met a young woman psychologist who was leaving Houston and wanted to sell her practice. I didn't expect to be seriously interested, but this woman intrigued me enough that I decided to investigate further.

This psychologist and I talked together several times during the next two weeks. My preliminary questions concerned the numbers and type of clients in her practice, the nature of her referral sources, how long she had been in practice, her annual income for the duration of the practice, and her style as a therapist. She, in turn, was assessing me, deciding whether or not I was an appropriate person to take over her practice. She indicated to me that she based her decision on the attitudes and judgement I expressed in our numerous informal case discussions, and on my professional qualifications and experience. By this time we had developed a mutual professional respect and warm personal feelings.

Our negotiations then began in earnest. My colleague, whom I shall refer to as the "seller," was quick to inform me that she had one or two other interested buyers, but I never really believed the others were as serious as I was.

She gave me a written formal offer to sell the business. She established her asking price by consulting other therapists who had either bought or sold a practice. As it happened, there were very few such therapists for either of us to ask, since buying and selling psychotherapy practices is not yet very common. There wasn't much basis for determining the market value of a practice. Her asking price was approximately 50% of her 1981 gross income for the previous 12 months.

After extensive investigation into the workings of her practice, I countered with an offer to buy at approximately 20% of her average annual gross for the previous four years that she had been in practice. I made it clear that this was the top amount I was willing to pay, even though her practice might well be worth more to someone else. My colleague accepted this offer without much further negotiation, except to determine the terms. She agreed to hold the entire note, payable in four annual installments at a low interest rate, with the first payment due nine months from the date of sale. This provided advantages to both of us, in that I would not need to borrow money from another source, and she could distribute this income over four years for tax purposes.

The amount I offered for the practice was based primarily on how much I might otherwise have had to borrow for business and living expenses for the initial months of building a practice. I consulted a certified public accountant to work out projections of how much I would be likely to earn if, in the worst case, only 30–50% of her current clientele agreed to consult me as their new therapist. (About 70% actually transferred over.) I was fortunate to find a CPA who had experience in selling other types of professional practices. He proved to be quite helpful to me in verifying the seller's financial statements and making educated guesses about the worth of such a practice to me.

An attorney who had some experience with professional practice transactions also assisted me in evaluating the worth of this practice. He reviewed the CPA's analysis and the information I had gathered about the seller's practice and provided further guidelines for finalizing the purchase. He prepared the legal documents necessary to formalize the transaction and to protect me from any liability the seller may have incurred during the time the practice was hers (for example, her accounts payable and receivable were to be kept completely separate from mine). A clause was written into our contract that the seller agreed not to go into practice in the Houston area for a period of six years. The seller also engaged an attorney to advise her on legal procedures. She and I agreed to share equally the cost of drawing up the legal documents.

There were other considerations which influenced my decision to purchase this practice. My professional respect for this individual was paramount. I would have dropped the matter entirely had I not found her to be competent and ethical and somewhat similar to me in her style of working with her clients. She also seemed trustworthy and likeable, and she clearly enjoyed working with people. I checked with psychologists and other mental health professionals in Houston to ensure that my impressions of this psychologist's integrity were valid. I later learned she had also inquired of my reputation with some of her former clients who were acquainted with me, and with some of my professional colleagues. In retrospect, I appreciate that she took seriously her responsibility to transfer her clients to a trustworthy therapist.

We discovered a few expectable differences in our respective styles of working with clients, but these did not seem problematic. Our general approaches were similar in that we both preferred to be somewhat informal and to approach clients in a warm and fairly supportive manner most of the time. We both seemed to value an empathic listening perspective, accompanied by psychodynamic interpretations.

I did not actually observe this psychologist's clinical work with her private clients until after I had agreed to purchase the practice, but I did have the opportunity to watch her teach one session of a self-assertion training group for men and women. This helped to establish my confidence in the quality of her work.

Once our legal papers, the purchase of business and the promissory note, were signed, we began the actual transfer of the practice. We took three weeks to accomplish the individual introductory sessions with the clients who expressed interest in meeting the person who would be taking over the practice. These were extremely interesting sessions. The clients as well as the therapists were all somewhat anxious in each initial session. My colleague's role was to assist the clients in summarizing their therapeutic work and to help them make a comfortable connection with me. But, as we proceeded, we realized we had another crucial task to accomplish in these introductory sessions: helping our clients complete their farewells to their old therapist. As separation issues became apparent, I began to function in these sessions as a consultant to aid the client in terminating with the original therapist.

I feel sure that the transfer of the practice would not have gone as well as it did if we had failed to address the termination issue. Fortunately (and as so often happens in the fascinating world of psychotherapy), the clients taught the therapists what was needed to make the process work. The affect and grief expressed by most of the clients was an undeniably potent factor. How could these people begin working with a completely new therapist without properly acknowledging their deep attachment to the therapist with whom they had shared so much of their innermost selves?

Termination work was the primary theme of our transfer process. It seems to me that my rapport with the clients was most clearly being established when I resonated with and discussed their difficulty in ending with their former therapist, and when I was able to help them express their range of emotions including grief, fear, and anger. I suspect that it was easier for these clients to develop confidence in me when they saw that I did not expect them to transfer their trust to me immediately.

In most cases, the joint meeting between the client and the two therapists was the last session the client had with the therapist who was leaving. In two instances, however, clients requested another session alone with my colleague to finish the farewells. One person was so upset by the termination that the other psychologist asked me to sit in on a second session with her and the client to help them complete the process. This particular client did not consult with me again for several weeks, but later entered into therapy with me for a few months, revealing only at the end that it had taken her a long time to ''like'' me, because she continued to miss her first therapist. Some clients declined to attend the introductory meeting with me, indicating that they felt their work was nearly completed or that they were not motivated to continue at this time. One woman said that she had her own methods of choosing therapists and that she didn't want any help finding someone else. Some clients transferred to me and stayed with me fewer than six sessions, and several became clients for one to two years. The most common situation was to continue for several months, but less than a year.

In assessing how much I was willing to offer for this practice, I had taken into consideration the seller's candid information that several of her clients approached their therapy as a short-term project. Her estimate of which ones would want to continue with me was accurate in all but two cases.

Another important part of our business agreement was that the selling therapist would write a general letter to all current and former clients, telling them about me, sending my résumé and card, and expressly recommending that they contact me for any consultations they would have brought to her. This was accomplished a few weeks after we finished the transfer of the current clients. It was not long before I began receiving calls from former clients who wanted appointments. As of this writing, four years after I took over the practice, there are still occasional calls for appointments from persons who received this letter in the summer of 1981. I can only conclude that many clients consider it helpful for the therapist who leaves to provide them with some help in finding a new therapist. Further verification of that comes from clients who transferred immediately to work with me. Several commented that they were relieved that they didn't have to go through the painful process of searching for another psychologist.

The attorney who assisted with the practice transaction clarified for me that what I was purchasing was "good will," both in legal terms as well as in actuality. The seller could in no way guarantee which, if any, clients would agree to transfer to the new therapist. The seller, furthermore, was not willing to sell at a price based on the results of the transfer of clients. Such a formula would have been complicated, at best, considering all the intangibles involved in a practice takeover.

Whose good will did I purchase? It went further than the actual clients who were in ongoing therapy at the time. It was apparent to me that they relied a great deal on what their therapist told them about me. Their trust in her helped them to trust me, at least initially. But another significant aspect requires some discussion: the challenging problem of gaining the good will of the seller's referral sources.

Every successful practice is dependent on good referral sources. Satisfied clients often refer their friends, family members, and co-workers, but there is no substitute, especially while a practice is getting established, for professional referral sources such as medical doctors, employee assistance counselors, and supervisors of personnel in high-stress occupations. If these people know a therapist personally, and know her or him to be reliable and competent, they are more likely to make referrals to that person than to someone they don't know. This is the other half of the good will one purchases as an essential part of the private practice.

We used different approaches to connect with referral sources. In the case of the seller's major referral persons, she telephoned all of them directly to let them know that I was taking over her practice. Each of them was invited to join us for coffee or lunch, or to meet at their office, if more convenient for them, so that introductions might be made. This provided me with a valuable opportunity to describe how I work and the kinds of clients with whom I work best, and it gave us enough time to get acquainted with each other. These efforts also associated my name with the seller's to the referral sources. As a follow-up, the selling therapist sent a letter of recommendation, my résumé, and professional cards to all of her current and previous referral sources.

Of these several and varied sources, some bore no fruit at all except for the pleasantries of the initial meeting. Two sources proved very strong, however, and continued to make frequent referrals throughout the first two years of my practice. Most other sources were rather sporadic. In retrospect, I would say that the most valuable support, besides the two strong sources mentioned above, was the letter sent to all former clients and referral sources. Otherwise, my purchase of good will in the referral source area was mildly disappointing, but it was adequate to get my practice off to a solid start four years ago.

FINAL COMMENTS

I have no regrets about my decision to purchase the particular practice that I took over. I doubt if I would have done it had all the circumstances not come together in terms of the right kind of person selling the practice, clientele with whom I thought I could work well, a reasonable purchase price with no immediate payment required, and the right timing, as I was just completing postdoctoral training. Another major factor was my readiness to make what was for me a quantum leap from being a team player in an institution, with the security of having someone else pay my salary, to assuming total responsibility for my own income by starting my own business. I am pleased I made the decision to go on my own.

21

Money: The Medium and the Message

Daniel V. Voiss, M.D.

THE FRAME

The traditional relationship between a patient and psychotherapist, or psychoanalyst as a professional consultant, is usually initiated by referral through the health care system or directly requested consultation paid for by the person seeking assistance. This results in a contractual relationship between the patient and the consultant, a contract that provides the opportunity for development of a framework within which the two parties may negotiate and function for the mutual benefit of each. Fees for services of the professional consultant are an integral part of the framework within which this relationship operates. The meaning and the messages arising from issues provoked through necessary payment of a fee create a fertile field for analysis and subsequent resolution of a wide range of disturbing fantasies and affects, which probably cannot be addressed without such a contractual framework.

The significance of the direct fee for service, in this context, cannot be underestimated; it is the sine qua non of a comprehensive and successful resolution of the competitive, narcissistic, libidinal, aggressive, destructive, and other psychological issues which will come to focus upon the exchange of money in any thoroughly conducted psychotherapy or analysis. It is the responsibility of the "consultant" to assist the "consultee" in arriving at an understanding of these issues, primarily through analysis of the transference. This consultative framework provides a unique opportunity for both the "consultant" and "consultee" to explore motivating inner processes. It is an uncommon and unique situation; the very conflicts that erupt around money matters on the consulting chair or on the couch are enacted and reenacted daily in the world of commerce and industry at tremendous cost to all involved without any opportunity for analysis and understanding. Decisions about money in commerce and industry are made without awareness of the unconscious impact of such decisions on the goals that prompt those decisions; as a consequence, the objectives of those goals are distorted. The analytic consulting chair or couch provides the laboratory for development of comprehensive understanding of this aspect of financial decisions. However, the information out of this laboratory seems never to reach beyond the boundaries of those who work within the laboratory.

WHO GETS PAID

The battle for the health care insurance dollar has been increasingly acute over the last several years. Mental health benefits are at the forefront of reductions by third-party payers, an observation that provokes concern from social workers, psychologists, psychiatrists, and psychoanalysts. Reduced benefits in this area occur in spite of the fact that repeated studies of insurance programs which provide mental health benefits reveal a significant reduction in overall medical costs (1,2). Psychotherapists and psychoanalysts have been aware of the inverse relationship between psychotherapy and medical care for decades. Nevertheless, funding, in the form of mental health fees from third-party payers, has been progressively slashed or deflected to medical or medically based interventions. Most of the health care expenditures for so-called medical problems are actually being utilized to subsidize the somatic psychological defenses of the 15–20% of the population who absorb 80% of the health care dollar. Health insurors are in a highly risky and competitive market for their product. Decisions regarding benefits are made on the basis of spreading the risk, minimizing the cost, and maximizing the coverage in terms of the number of people who can be profitably insured by a given insurance dollar. These are actuarially based business decisions. Most prospective insurance clients, individuals and businesses, do not believe they have or will have so-called mental health needs until that situation is personally experienced; medical and surgical disorders are still more acceptable. Therefore, within the health care industry, extensive subsidization of professional mental health consultation will become progressively taboo!

Although there will be fewer financial resources for psychotherapy and psychoanalysis, there will continue to be billions of dollars spent each year by the public and private commercial/industrial complex for psychological problems resulting in civil litigation and worker compensation claims. It is likely that these claims, in all areas of the country, will increase while the health care insurance dollars diminish. This has already begun in some sectors of the country. So-called "stress" claims already account for 10% of all industrial injury claims filed. There are approximately three million industrial injury claims each year in the United States. Of those claims which involve any extended disability, 90% are for neuromuscular complaints or "pain." The industrial compensation system was constructed as a no-fault system, but it has not worked out that way. This is a very different system than the health care system with which most of us are familiar; it is legally mandated, highly regulated, excessively political and litigious, and provides wage loss benefits as well as first-dollar coverage for medical expenses evolving out of alleged industrially related injuries or illnesses. Forty percent of the benefits paid under this system are for psychological symptoms not recognized or acknowledged as such. This money, as with the general health care system, will be spent to support the somatically expressed psychological defenses of individuals who can no longer effectively cope and who attribute their dysfunction to their employment. The public or private organizations that provide these benefits are not concerned as long as the cost-to-benefit ratio stays within acceptable parameters, which it often does not do.

There have been a number of in-house studies by industrial insurance carriers, as well as individual state agencies, which clearly but indirectly document the magnitude of psychological factors in the cost of claims. Nevertheless, the psychological factors are ignored, denied, or not recognized as such, and this information leads to no further or more appropriate intervention by regulation or legislation. In fact, some states indicate they do not pay for psychiatric claims. This, of course, is as much of a self-deception as that of the private health insurance which pays nothing for psychiatric benefits and thousands of dollars for hypertension, headache, anorexia, ulcerative colitis, or other disorders with a predominantly psychological etiology. The relationship of the unconscious to medical symptoms is well documented by many authors but most effectively, in my opinion, by Silverman (3).

In 1977, a physician consultant to the Department of Labor and Industries of the state of Washington undertook an extensive study which further documented and emphasized the extent of psychological factors involved in industrial claims. In summary, it was discovered that 4.5% of compensable claims accounted for 36% of the costs of industrial claims in the years studied; this 36% amounted to 63.5 million dollars. More to the point, however, was the finding that in 90% of those claims, there were absolutely no objective medical findings. In other words, 57 million dollars was spent on claims for described medical disability which were, to use the legal jargon, in all medical probability, psychiatric claims unrelated to the described industrial injury. This study was done eight years ago (ref. 4 and A. Dean Johnson, personal communication, 1983).

THE PROBLEM

Many of those who fall into the psychosomatic groups described above will be referred for psychiatric or psychological evaluation and sometimes treatment by legal counsel or the agency administering the claim. These referrals, for the most part, are requests for assistance in understanding the complexities presented by the claimant. In addition, they are requests for recommendations to guide decision makers, including the court. The usual question of these evaluations, if early in the claim, is a question of financial responsibility; who is responsible for this person's musculo-skeletal/pain/psychological distress—the employer or the patient? As with all medicolegal conflicts, there is much ambiguity and uncertainty. For instance, back pain, as a sympton, can either be an expression of an acute traumatic injury arising out of or in the scope of employment, or it can be an expression of psychological disturbance related to intense, repressed affects, particularly rage or depression, unrelated to employment. If the claimant states the disabling pain arose from bending or twisting on the job, this cannot be disputed if the only way of understanding such complaints is that they arise only from a physically traumatic event. Psychoanalytic investigation of these cases is obviously not possible, and evaluation by clinical interviews in an adversary context presents significant obstacles, even with the availability of sophisticated projective testing.

The prevailing wisdom among most of those who administer, litigate, and adjudicate these disability claims is that the claimant's disability is primarily motivated by the wish to receive money; there is a presumption that the claimant is greedy and that this is what precipitates the claim or causes the claimant to remain off work. There is undoubtedly an element of projection in this attitude! Psychiatrists and psychologists collude in this misperception with repeated references to a phenomenon called "secondary gain." There is never mention, let alone discussion, of "primary gain," which is the psychological sine qua non of the entire process. It is the responsibility of the clinical consultant in this arena to elucidate, insofar as possible, the "primary gain"—those mechanisms which are responsible for the presenting symptom complex and its unrelenting continuation. Failure to address this aspect of the issue is not only costly to the insuror but destructive to the individual. As Freud

pointed out, money does not bring happiness; "money is not an infantile wish." Money indeed is not an infantile wish, and it is not the motivation for the costly, continuing disabilities mentioned above. Money, in this
system, is a necessary artifact which comes to prominence because it provides, in part, an opportunity for the solidification of a particular mode
of psychological adaptation to non-industrially related psychological trauma. The disability in these cases is a symptom of the psychological trauma,
and not a symptom of a physical event. In the approximately 300 cases
that I have extensively analyzed, the major underlying issues are narcissistic. By that I mean these are symptoms which function to maintain
the "structural cohesion, temporal stability, and positive affective color-
ing of the self-representation." They are symptoms which hold the individual together, psychologically (5).

The primary issues in these cases can only be determined by the ex-
amining clinician's insistence on the opportunity for extensive clinical interviews and sophisticated projective psychological testing in addition to
a review and analysis of every available document associated with the
claim.

"Pain" and neuromusculoskeletal dysfunction are the two major complaints which lead to costly claims for disability not associated with objective medical findings.

Over 30 years ago, a well-documented study of patients with chronic
back pain graphically demonstrated that the emotional state of the individual—disturbing affects, wishes, fantasies, and recollections—provoked
pain complaints and electrical activity in the muscles about which the subject complained. The electrical activity and discomfort were clearly associated with ideas and affects; no neuromusculoskeletal anatomical pathol-
ogy was ever identified. All socioeconomic groups were represented in
this study, and only 15% of the cases studied were compensation cases (6).

In every situation in which expression of affects is inhibited, by either
external reality or inner standards, or a combination of the two, symptoms may be experienced and expressed as musculoskeletal or pain complaints brought about by a regressive solution to such a conflict. These
conflicts, their depth and scope, cannot be resolved by behavioral and
neurophysiological approaches to these symptoms as though "pain" or
"musculoskeletal complaints" were concrete, readily identifiable entities.
There is very little written in the psychoanalytic literature about the "pain"
phenomenon (7,8,9). However, during the past 15 years or so, a body of
literature has developed which supports the concept of "pain" centers
in which individuals are allegedly taught to live with their "pain."

These centers for the treatment of "pain" are equivalent to the spas of Freud's time and equally ineffective in regard to modifying and subsequently enhancing the psychological adaptation of the individual. The success rate of these programs is estimated at approximately 20%, which is equal to the success rate of no intervention at all. The usual cost of these three- or four-week programs is from $5,000 to $10,000 and many of those referred return for second and third admissions. Public and private industrial insurance carriers and self-insured corporations utilize these resources with little objection. These programs focus on the manifest complaints of the individual with efforts directed toward controlling the expression of symptoms. There is no attention to the dynamic, communicative, and adaptive aspects of the presenting symptoms. In this respect, these programs cannot provide effective consultation to either the individual being evaluated or the referring individual or organization because symptoms are elevated to the position of a discrete diagnostic entity and the etiology is not pursued! Effective consultation requires the understanding of a thoughtful, psychoanalytically trained clinician who is able to pursue *all* the relevant issues in a given situation.

The following clinical vignettes are offered as representative of the several hundred cases I have evaluated, "analyzed," and reported on over the past few years.

CASE STUDIES

An attractive 25-year-old woman, mother of a seven-year-old son, was referred for evaluation three years after she had filed a claim for an alleged on-the-job injury, a muscle strain in her upper back. This kept her from working for her employer or at home. There had never been any objective medical findings, and each of the physicians involved in her care had become discouraged and referred her elsewhere. The last physician threatened referral to a psychologist. That threat prompted the company, which had been paying two-thirds of her salary while she was off work, to make a psychiatric referral. In addition to medical expenses, this young woman had received approximately $25,000 in wage loss benefits for time loss from work.

The described "injury" was preceded by increasing anger with her employer, on whom she felt financially dependent and by whom she also felt cheated and betrayed. Immediately following the described "injury," which occurred at closing time, the claimant asked her employer to drive her to an emergency medical clinic across the street. He declined on the basis of obligations to his wife and new baby. This further "injured" and enraged the claimant. During the evaluation, thematic analysis of the TAT suggested sexual conflicts and other non-work-related difficulties which were subsequently disclosed. The claimant had become aware several weeks prior to the described industrial injury that her husband was involved with another woman; she was indeed feeling cheated, betrayed, and narcissistically injured. This young woman adamantly refused an offer of psychiatric treatment because this would deprive her of symptomatic revenge on the betraying husband as that was displaced onto the employer. It was apparent that the on-the-job "injury" represented and became the focus of a severe narcissistic injury incurred in the marriage and not etiologically related to her employment.

It was my understanding that the anger in response to the marital, narcissistic injury became somatically expressed and displaced from the marital situation to the employment. A minor physical event, stretching muscles already tense from psychological conflict, occurred in the context of a painful psychological state. This provided a somatic rationalization for her disturbed inner state. This all-too-common and transient bodily experience became the barrier to conscious awareness of the extent of the woman's rage toward her husband and fear of further abandonment by him. The "inability" to work was an expression of aggressive retaliatory wishes against the husband and a demand she be provided for by him, symbolically through the employer. However, the receipt of payment for not working validated the claimant's position that she could not work because she was injured as a result of her employment and unconsciously because she was crippled by her husband's betrayal. The ongoing payments served to reinforce the denial of her anger but, paradoxically, intensified unconscious guilt over her hostile wishes toward the husband-employer. This unwarranted payment provoked recurrent complaints of pain. It is more than coincidence that the word "pain" is derived from the Greek word for penalty or punishment. The money this young woman received gratified her hostile wishes, thereby intensifying her need for "pain" as a means of punishing herself for such wishes. The complaints of "pain" also communicated her experience of the humiliation and fall in self-esteem that she experienced as a consequence of her husband's actions. Compensation was not compensation at all but, at an unconscious level, served to perpetuate her complaints. Awarding money under these circumstances gratifies the hostile wish, both punishing the object (employer-husband) and punishing the subject (claimant) for her aggressiveness by increased suffering expressed as "pain." Monetary reward keeps the cycle going. The "primary gain" for this claimant, in regard to her injury, was the opportunity to psychopathologically process intense, angry affect. The "secondary gain," money, was truly a secondary issue.

A 54-year-old woman was referred by her treating physician for evaluation of back pain complaints. She had been "injured" seven years previously, had not worked since, and was involved in litigation against the
industrial insuror with the assertion that she was permanently and totally disabled by pain as a consequence of her injury. Exclusive of medical
expenses, the subject had received approximately $60,000 in time loss
benefits and had been through three pain centers for another $18,000 to
$24,000. She had been the "beneficiary" of continuing medical care which
consisted of all popular back treatment modalities including surgery. There
were never any objective medical findings either before or after the surgery, except for a scar.

During the clinical interview, this woman could talk only about her injury and her "pain." She felt treated badly by everyone involved in her
situation, except her attorney. When the discussion shifted away from her
back and onto her personal life, the claimant became increasingly uncomfortable, agitated, and somewhat hostile. With caution and discretion, I
was able to proceed further and inquired about her two children. Her son
was in all kinds of trouble, occupationally, maritally, and legally, yet the
claimant could comfortably discuss her son's difficulties without any evidence that she was disturbed by them. She then proceeded to describe,
with a peculiar affect, her 33-year-old daughter who had a very successful
career and lived and worked in the same town as the claimant. The description of the daughter sounded extremely idealized and unreal! I was
struck by the change in tone of voice as the claimant elaborated on her
daughter's activities and accomplishments. I inquired as to when the
claimant had last seen her daughter. "I haven't seen her in 10 years. She
won't see me because I've had a drinking problem! She is a very firm
Christian! I respect her!" I commented that the daughter's refusal to see
her did not sound terribly Christian to me and that it must be very painful for her to be so near and yet so far from her daughter. At that point,
she exploded, "This doesn't have a damn thing to do with my back injury." Whereupon she stood up and terminated the interview. There was
obviously an affirmation in this woman's denial (10)!

No one would doubt this woman was in a great deal of "pain." She
maintained her defensive pain complaints through an unconscious collusion with her attorney and the industrial insurance system which provides the opportunity for this kind of regressive resolution to a complex
and painful intrapsychic problem if that problem is expressed somatically. This woman's symptoms are conversion symptoms which serve to
keep intolerably disturbing affects out of awareness. Through the "accident on the job," a back strain, the subject can symptomatically express

her emotional pain and assign responsibility for its expression to external forces beyond her control. The idealization of the daughter masked her rage at this youngster for her abandonment. The relationship between loss, attachment behavior, and pain complaints is well described (11). The disability associated with continuing pain complaints is not only a punishment for the mother, it provides the possibility of a reconnection with the lost object through the fantasy of evoking painful feelings in the daughter (12). If this woman can prevail in her assertion that she is permanently and totally disabled, as a result of the described injury, personal responsibility and the narcissistic humiliation of a personal failure can forever be ascribed to forces over which she has no control. Unconsciously, she also says to her daughter, "You have permanently injured me." The symptoms and pain complaints reflect a change in the self-representation from abandoned mother to physically injured mother. Any monetary award in this situation supports the psychopathological process. Monetary reward becomes the evidence for the conversion of a narcissistic injury to "physical" injury inflicted, not by the daughter, but by the employer. Idealization of the daughter can be maintained through psychological separation of the daughter's hurtfulness by attribution of the "pain" to the employer. The future of this illusion depends on continuing disavowal of the significance of the daughter as a cause of the symptoms, and this disavowal is further reinforced by the monetary reward!

A 37-year-old man was seen for evaluation upon referral from an insurance company. This individual had had four back surgeries for excruciating "pain" and classical conversion symptoms. He had received time loss payments of over $50,000 during a seven-year span. Direct medical expenses exceeded $30,000. For several years prior to the industrial injury, this individual had had symptoms identical to those which precipitated the multiple surgeries. He had had two marriages, both unsuccessful, no children of his own, and psychiatric hospitalizations prior to the described industrial injury. The claimant was a tall, slender, rather aesthetic-looking man, soft and effeminate in his mannerisms. He was the youngest of five children and had been reared in a lumber mill town where his father was a foreman. The claimant was closest to his mother and sister. He had wanted to be a dancer since he was a small child. To say that his father discouraged his ambition would be an understatement. During his early adult years, the patient took dancing lessons and was briefly employed as a dance instructor. He subsequently left this occupation to take other employment and also to marry. His first marriage precipitated a progressive regression and withdrawal from work and school, which was followed by hospitalization for "depression." Medical records at that time noted chronic back pain complaints.

Following his hospitalization and subsequent divorce, the claimant was successfully employed for over three years. During the last year of that employment, he lived with a woman friend and her two children. He changed occupations, married his girlfriend, and moved to a new community. Almost immediately, he had an accident on the job to which he now attributed back pain complaints identical to those he had experienced previously. Increasing complaints of "pain" and episodes of falling eventually provoked surgical excursions into the back on four separate occasions. No definitive objective findings were ever established. The claimant never returned to work. He divorced, moved in with a male roommate, and entered the "gay" world. At the time of my evaluation, he was wearing a leg brace, walked with a limp, and had failed three separate efforts at "retraining" always in the last week of the programs and always due to "falling" and "severe pain." This man insisted that he was completely crippled. He experienced himself as a castrated, defective, victimized male as he dramatically demonstrated the brace that supported a right leg that was mildly atrophied due to disuse.

When I attempted to explore personal and historical aspects of the claimant's life, he became increasingly agitated and resistive. When I indicated that in all of his medical records, there were no findings that could account for his weak leg or pain, he was outraged. He pointed out, with emphasis punctuated by dramatic gesticulations, that he had been unable to work for years because of his industrial injury. With equal emphasis, he reminded me that he had been declared permanently disabled. He insisted on talking to his attorney at that point and stormed out of the office without any noticeable limp.

A comprehensive evaluation was never completed, but the clinical interview and medical records provided ample opportunity for an understanding of the major dynamics. This individual dealt with his fear of his father through an identification with his mother. His display of the "injured leg" was a somatic communication: "Look at my big but defective penis. I can't be a man." His outrage at my suggestion that he might not be defective was an obvious transference reaction; I was the father who insisted he "act like a man." His feminine passive orientation toward men was clearly expressed in his repeated provocation of intrusions into his body by other men, physicians who were to correct the defect to which he attributed his pain. He turns to his attorney who will support his psychopathology and help him obtain monetary verification that he indeed is defective as a man, because of his injury. The "primary gain" for this individual is that he can objectify his psychological sense of being defective and keep out of awareness the conflicts that give rise to that self-representation. "Secondary gain" is achieved through reliance on an attorney who unconsciously colludes with the claimant in the search for affirmation that his "defect" is a consequence of a situation in which he was a passive victim and for which he was not responsible. Much more could be said, but clearly the disability of this individual is a symptom of his psychological conflicts, not his described industrial injury.

CONCLUSION

Resistance to exploration and understanding of the unconscious meaning of communications through somatic symptoms is an expensive individual matter when confined to transference in the laboratory of the analytic relationship! When this resistance is institutionalized in the structure of the commercial/industrial compensation system, it is, monetarily, infinitely more expensive. This system is repeatedly confronted with the costly failure to understand the medium and the message of somatic symptoms for which expensive, unwarranted disability claims are filed and monetarily compensated. This failure is costly in dollars and human suffering. There can be no resolution of this painful and costly failure until there is adequate attention to the unconscious, dynamic factors to which I have alluded in this chapter. The health care dollar may increasingly go into the "medical" pocket, but that pocket will only get bigger unless the unconscious dynamic factors in medical complaints are addressed.

REFERENCES

1. Reed, L. S., Myers, E. S., and Scheidemandel, P. *Health insurance and psychiatric care: Utilization and cost.* Washington, DC: American Psychiatric Association, 1972.
2. Scheidemandel, P., Kanno, C., and Glasscotte, R. *Health insurance for mental illness.* Washington, DC: The Joint Information Service of the American Psychiatric Association and the National Association for Mental Health, 1968.
3. Silverman, S. *Psychologic cues in forecasting physical illness.* New York: Appleton-Century-Crofts, 1970.
4. Johnson, A. D. *The problem claim: A synopsis, an approach to early identification.* Washington, DC: The Department of Labor and Industries, 1977.
5. Stolorow, R. D., and Lachman, F. M. *Psychoanalysis of developmental arrests: Theory and treatment.* New York: International Universities Press, 1980.
6. Holmes, T. H., and Wolff, H. G. Life situations, emotions and backache. *Psychosom. Med.,* 14(1):18–33, 1952.
7. Freud, S. *Standard edition,* Vol. XXIV (pp. 340–341). London: Hogarth Press, 1974.

8. Ramzy, I., and Wallerstein, R. S. Pain, fear and anxiety: A study in their interrelations. *Psychoanal. Study Child*, 13:147–189, 1958.
9. Szasz, T. S. *Pain and pleasure: A study of bodily feelings*. London: Tavistock Publications Ltd., 1957.
10. Freud, S. Negation. In *Standard edition*, Vol. XIX (p. 235). London: Hogarth Press, 1974.
11. Kolb, L. C. Attachment behavior and pain complaints. *Psychosom. Med.*, 23(4): 413–425, 1982.
12. Ogden, T. H. On projective identification. *Int. J. Psychiatry*, 60:357–373, 1979.

22

Cost Effectiveness of Psychotherapy

Seth W. Silverman, M.D.

In the past century, practitioners of medicine relied on therapies that were largely anecdotal and unproven. Medical intervention was as likely destructive and ungrounded as helpful and rational. One hundred years later, the application of leeches has been replaced by implantation of the artificial heart as well as the ability to restore, transplant, or augment more parts of the body than society can afford to support. As a result of these and other new technologies, morbidity and mortality has been altered and life expectancy has increased dramatically. Subsequently, society devotes more of its resources to the care of individuals with chronic illness.

Coincident with the increased sophistication and availability of medicine has been a precipitous growth in expenditures for health sciences from both a relative and absolute viewpoint. In 1950, 4.4% of the gross national product (GNP), or 12.7 billion dollars, was devoted to health care; in 1970, 7.6% of the GNP, or 74.9 billion dollars, was attributed to medical costs; and in 1981 9.8% of the GNP, or 288.6 billion dollars, was spent. The field of mental health, specifically outpatient psychotherapy, has benefited disproportionately from this increase. Outlays for long-term care and outpatient psychotherapy treatment increased by 4% and 5%, respectively, and payment to psychiatrists increased from 13% to 18% of the mental health care pie (1).

Unlike other fields of medicine, psychiatry has been characterized as ineffective, costly, ungrounded, and fragmented. Why has psychotherapy engendered such derision? The answers are multiple and somehow inadequate. Psychotherapy, unlike other fields in medicine, utilizes few consultants, laboratory tests, ancillary personnel, and mechanical devices (2). These diagnostic aids tend to convince all concerned parties (including the payer) of the necessity and objectivity of a particular treatment modality.

Citing the lack of specific objective criteria for initiation and termination of treatment, third-party payers find it difficult to assess the worth of different psychotherapies. Insurance companies (including the government) are increasingly hesitant to allocate resources to a discipline that is so heterogeneous, internally divided, generally stigmatized, and unproven.

Has the field itself contributed to its own malignment and lack of security? Similar to other fields of medicine, psychiatry was rudimentary a century ago. However, leeches have been replaced by dramatic heart-lung transplants and PET scanners, while psychiatry's hypnosis has evolved into a less dramatic, more lengthy, and more costly technique known as psychoanalysis. At first glance it would appear that the field of psychiatry has regressed, while the rest of medicine has progressed.

Although the health care pie has gotten larger in recent years, there is reason to suspect that fiscal needs will supersede health care responsibilities, and a reproportioning of resources is inevitable. Contrasting articles appearing in medical journals in the same week may forecast how health care dollars are to be redistributed. On February 2, 1985, the *AMA Newsletter* reported that the Blue Cross/Blue Shield plan in Maryland would reimburse heart, lung, liver, and pancreas transplants without any additional increase in premiums (3), while on February 8, 1985, the Massachusetts Blue Shield insurance company told the *APA Psychiatric News* that it intended to scrutinize claims pertaining to three common outpatient psychiatric diagnoses. The Blues also planned an additional modification to their therapy policy which would reimburse only those expenditures for mental illnesses that resulted in physical impairment. This rather drastic measure was tabled (temporarily?) because of adverse public reaction (4).

DIFFICULTIES IN STUDYING PSYCHOTHERAPY

The basic nature of treatment with psychotherapy as a function of an interpersonal relationship makes attempts at objective measurement complex, lengthy, and problematic. Simply defining the treatment is a difficult task. For most purposes, psychotherapy can be considered to be the treatment of mental and emotional disorders based primarily on verbal and nonverbal communication between the patient and therapist (5). Accomplishing that simple task of defining the field, we have succeeded in narrowing down the number of schools of psychotherapy to be studied to be between 100 and 250 (2,5,6).

If we know what the tools are, it may be helpful to know for whom and for what reasons psychotherapy is used. The literature is unresolved with regard to which symptoms are indications for treatment. Most studies indicate that individuals who suffer from an acute disorder with anxiety and depressive and/or phobic characteristics are treatable by therapy. However, other illnesses are not so clearly addressed. Are there certain illnesses that are inadequately treated by talking alone? Was Parloff correct when he stated that "psychotherapy does not alone appear to be effective treatment for the symptoms of schizophrenia, manic-depressive psychosis, autism, alcoholism, or drug abuse. Further, psychotherapy has not yet been shown to be particularly effective in the treatment of severe obsessive compulsive behaviors" (2, p. 507).

The question as to which and whose treatment qualifies as psychotherapy has also been raised. Does the nurse clinician's presurgical visit qualify as a psychotherapy in contrast to the family practitioner's evening therapy hours? How does one account for and measure the increasing numbers of "therapists" whose educational and licensing requirements are so disparate? Assessing the impact of therapy is another unique difficulty. How is illness to be defined and where does an existential dilemma fit in the medical model?

Almost all psychotherapy trials would require a confidentiality modification. Therapeutic efficacy might be compromised to a larger extent than in other medical experiments because of the relative importance of trust in psychotherapy. Unlike other medical fields, diagnoses may not accurately reflect the severity or treatability of the illness. In addition, the relative and absolute skills of the therapist, including his orientation and personality, have rarely been measured or controlled.

What about the recidivism of different treatments? Some advocates have suggested a 10- to 20-year follow-up to determine whether a therapy is indeed actually effective. For example, an individual with chronic debilitating facial pain may obtain symptomatic relief with electric stimulation and analgesics. However, if this individual were treated in therapy where some of the precipitating unconscious factors were analyzed, he might experience sustained relief. Evaluation of both therapies on a short-term basis would demonstrate the supportive, analgesic, and symptomatic treatment obviously more effective. It is also more difficult to define and measure benefits, as subjective improvement may not correlate with long-term remission or financial reward (7,8).

Defining control groups is also complicated. Specifically, are individuals in therapy to be compared to (1) individuals who are not in therapy and have no wish to be, (2) patients who would like to be in therapy but are not, (3) patients who inevitably have different medical or social problems (9)?

Possible artifacts cited in some studies include observations that patients are studied when their psychiatric illnesses are peak and a change would be seen without treatment because of the natural course of illness. One might say that their improvements or lack of improvement may be a function of unique, unassayed, premorbid factors (especially motivation and chronicity) and not of the treatment itself.

Regardless of the reasons for not demonstrating efficacy, the era of accountability is here, and psychotherapists will receive less pie unless conclusive research is forthcoming, and as summarized by Martin Orne, "Modern psychotherapy antedates modern physics, biochemistry, molecular biology, behavioral genetics, and many other highly developed disciplines. We can no longer excuse lack of hard clinical and scientific data either by the newness of the field or by the complexities of its problems" (10, p. 30).

EXISTING PSYCHOTHERAPY RESEARCH

The unique complexities and urgencies of psychotherapy study have fostered a growth in research that is necessarily rudimentary, incomplete but formative. Cost-effective psychotherapy research originated 20 years ago utilizing medical expenditures as measurements of effectiveness. The therapies used were psychoanalytic psychotherapy and psychoanalysis. The study found the therapy group to use less inpatient medical services than the control group (11).

Meta-analysis of studies employing "psychologically informed intervention" on patients subjected to surgery (12) or myocardial infarctions demonstrated "educated" patients to have shorter hospital stays (13). Psychotherapy has also been shown on a dollar-for-dollar basis to be cost effective in net diminished utilization of health care services in the treatment of asthma, alcohol, and drug abuse (14,15). A retrospective analysis by Schlesinger et al. from the Blue Cross/Blue Shield Federal Employees Program analyzed data over a four-year period. Individuals who developed one of four chronic diseases were placed in one of two groups on the basis of whether they received outpatient therapy. Those individuals who used therapy 7 to 20 times (over a three-year period) used medical services less and achieved net health care savings (16).

In the 1984 Mumford study (17), 58 controlled psychotherapy studies were reanalyzed and compared to an analysis of health care benefit profiles in the Blue Cross/Blue Shield federal employees plan for 1974–1978. Both studies consistently demonstrated outpatient mental health care to be effective in decreasing costs for inpatient medical care. The results were greater in patients over age 55 but showed an inconsistent effect on outpatient medical care (17).

Studies that have attempted to measure subjective improvement without correlates to direct costs and savings are more problematic and less convincing.

A rash of papers has supported the view that no single school or therapeutic technique confirms or demonstrates superiority. Evidence cited to support this view includes consistent findings that at least two-thirds to four-fifths of individuals who are treated by psychotherapy improve, regardless of the school of therapy. A study done in 1977 analyzed 500 psychotherapy studies and found all psychotherapies to have a positive effect on some individuals receiving treatment. Seventy-five percent of those treated improved in relation to those receiving no treatment. In addition, patients whose primary symptoms included fear and/or anxiety, sustained an 83% remission (2).

How can we understand the apparent irrelevance of orientation with regard to outcome? The amount of therapist discomfort will probably be proportionate to the amount of time and sacrifice he has spent obtaining training. Critics have proposed that psychotherapy has no significant effect other than a general acceleration or condensation of growth in susceptible individuals. They contend that psychotherapy patients purchase a costly attitude although their original method of coping would have sufficed at a slower, more economical pace.

Could the uneven distribution of an effective, but as of yet unproven, technology account for the lack of credibility and homogeneity? Is it possible that the patient-therapist interaction is currently studied at the level of a syndrome, where multiple diagnostic entities (patients) and treatments (therapists) obscure differences in effectiveness?

In order to answer some of these questions, the National Institute of Mental Health (NIMH) began a collaborative multisite study whose function is to investigate three distinct treatment modalities for depression. The study originated in 1980 after three years of deliberation. The Treatment of Depression Collaborative Research Program (TDCRP) is the first multisite psychotherapy research project coordinated by the NIMH and has been widely acclaimed as a milestone in psychotherapy research. The TDCRP has attempted to standardize treatment protocols by using three therapies, cognitive-behavioral therapy (CBT), interpersonal therapy (IPT), and pharmacotherapy, for patients suffering from a major depression. The therapies were chosen because they met three basic criteria: (1) have specific applications for depressed outpatients, (2) could be taught in a standardized manner, and (3) have been proven effective for depression (18).

Both psychotherapies have preexisting teaching manuals and originate from nonoverlapping theoretical schools. CBT is derived from behavioral sciences, while IPT has psychodynamic underpinnings.

Therapists were chosen on their demonstrated ability (by videotape and interview) in one of the three treatment modalities and were trained over a 12- to 19-month period. In order to minimize the effect that different sites tend to have on drawing specialized patient populations, all sites are to test all methodologies. Diagnosis is phenomenological with specific exclusion criteria. The number of sessions is standardized, and all treatment sessions are audiotaped and videotaped. Outcome interviews at 6-, 12-, and 18-month-intervals are to be obtained with input from the patient, therapist, independent investigators, and others.

The study hopes to measure relative effectiveness of the three therapies, in addition to obtaining a better understanding of the determinates and specificity of change. The initial 18-month follow-up phase is scheduled for completion in 1986. The major spheres of change to be assessed are (1) general functioning and degree of disability, (2) depressive symptoms, and (3) specific effects of the unique therapy on its target symptoms. This information will be obtained by utilizing a battery of well-accepted tests for depression.

The NIMH TDCRP may serve as a template for future research. However, the specific and lengthy nature of this study makes application to other treatments promising but difficult.

IMPLICATIONS FOR PSYCHOTHERAPY

When Freud originally invented psychoanalysis, his treatment tool was used only by a select group of physicians for individuals suffering from disabling conversion symptoms. Improvement could be readily measured with amelioration of symptoms and a miraculous restoration of functioning. Psychiatry no longer limits itself to the treatment of individuals with conversion disorders, but has immersed itself in the controversies of character analysis and other disabling conditions. Broadening the indications for treatment as well as the group of individuals delivering the talking cure, has created an elephant that is currently ambiguous and ill-perceived and growing at a rate greater than the rest of the health care herd.

Psychotherapy research has suffered from using retrospective data and crude measurements of change such as altered medical utilization and net dollars saved. Measuring subjective improvement is a formative task. Epidemiological studies are flawed by not dissecting each therapeutic interaction into its antecedent and subsequent behaviors in an attempt to determine cause and effect. Little attention has been paid to the unique therapeutic coupling or the theoretical school employed.

CONCLUSION

Like other fields of medicine, psychiatry must address the issues of acceptance, accountability, and cost effectiveness. The widening scope and delivery of therapy and society's unusually intrusive influences on mental health care have impeded psychotherapy research. This occurs despite the fact that studies demonstrate conclusively that the great majority of patients who receive psychotherapy improve (2,19). The personality of the therapist and the patient-therapist fit appear to be important for growth and may be influenced by the school of training. Psychotherapy research needs to look at these factors and amplify the themes of the landmark NIMH TDCRP study now in progress. Our attempts to comprehend human (mal)adaption and its manipulation, in a controlled, objective, and, most important, reproducible manner, will necessarily result in the demonstration of a cost-effective treatment.

The criteria to determine who will treat which individuals, by what techniques, and for how much will be clearer when we can demonstrate what works and why. More stringent licensing and training requirements can then result in a more effective and rational field.

REFERENCES

1. *Economic fact book of psychiatry*. Washington, D.C.: American Psychiatric Press International, 1983.
2. Marshall, E. Psychotherapy works, but for whom? *Science*, 207:506–508, 1980.
3. *AMA Newsletter*, February 2, 1985.
4. *APA Psychiatric News*, February 8, 1985.
5. *A psychiatric glossary*. Washington, DC: American Psychiatric Association, 1975.
6. Klerman, G. L. The efficacy of psychotherapy as the basis for public policy. *Am. Psychol.*, 38:929–934, 1983.
7. Wolberg, L. R. Cost effectiveness in psychotherapy. *J. Am. Acad. Psychoanal.*, 9(1):1–5, 1981.
8. Marshall, E. Psychotherapy faces test of worth. *Science*, 207:35–36, 1980.
9. Kazdin, A. E., and Terence-Wilson, G. Criteria for evaluating psychotherapy. *Arch. Gen. Psychiatry*, 35:407–416, 1978.
10. Orne, M. Psychotherapy in contemporary America: Its development and con-

text. In D. X. Freedman and J. E. Dynud (Eds.), *American handbook of psychiatry*, 2nd edition, vol. 5 (p. 30). New York: Basic Books, 1975.

11. Duehrssen, A., and Jorswiek, E. An empirical and statistical inquiry into the therapeutic potential of psychoanalytic treatment. *Der Nervenarzt*, 36:166–169, 1965.

12. Mumford, E., Schlesinger, H. J., and Glass, G. V. The effects of psychological intervention on recovery from surgery and heart attacks: An analysis of the literature. *Am. J. Public Health*, 72:141–151, 1982.

13. Devin, E. L., and Cook, T. D. A meta-analytic analysis of effects of psycho-educational interventions on length of postsurgical hospital stay. *Nurs. Res.*, 32:267–274, 1983.

14. Jones, K., and Vischi, T. Impact of alcohol, drug abuse and mental health treatment on medical care utilization. A review of the research literature. *Med. Care*, 17(suppl.):ii–82, 1979.

15. Schlesinger, H. J., Mumford, E., and Glass, G. V. Mental health services and medical utilization. In G. Vandenbos (Ed.), *Psychotherapy: From practice to research to policy*. Beverly Hills, CA: Sage, 1980.

16. Schlesinger, H. J., Mumford, E., Glass, G. V., Patrick, C., and Sharfstein, S. Mental health treatment and medical care utilization in a fee-for-service system: Outpatient mental health treatment following the onset of a chronic disease. *Am. J. Public Health*, 73(4):422–429, 1983.

17. Mumford, E., Schlesinger, H. J., Glass, G. V., Patrick, C., and Cuerdon, T. A new look at evidence about reduced cost of medical utilization following mental health treatment. *Am. J. Psychiatry*, 141(10):1145–1158, 1984.

18. Elkin, I., Parloff, M. B., Hadley, S. W., and Autry, J. H. NIMH treatment of depression collaborative research program. *Arch. Gen. Psychiatry*, 42:305–316, 1985.

19. Karasu, T. B. Recent developments in individual psychotherapy. *Hosp. Commun. Psychiatry*, 35(1):29–39, 1984.

23

Preferred Provider Organizations and Psychiatric Treatment

Howard Gurevitz, M.D.

The American Health care system is undergoing a significant and rapid transformation. Current forces affecting the funding, service delivery, and, quite possibly, the quality of medical care are evident throughout the United States—at both national and state levels. These pressures are forcing physicians to face changes in their orientation toward their practice, patients, colleagues, hospitals, and purchasers of medical care in a manner more consistent with the traditional business world than has been the case in the profession of medicine heretofore. Meeting increased competitive challenges, forming and joining in organized systems of care, discounting rates, and a host of other features are facing physicians who have practiced mainly as fee-for-service providers compensated by usual, customary, and reasonable fees.

Pressure to change our system of health care, primarily to control costs, and to assure equity has been prominent in the United States since the 1940s. The national health insurance debate has repeatedly raged and abated. Medicare bankruptcy looms and the argument of "guns or butter" persists. The prediction of "corporate medicine" for the future appears to be coming to fruition—spurred by "pro-competition" federal and state policies (1). Yet, until relatively recently little has changed. Fee-for-service medicine at usual, customary, and reasonable rates has prevailed, although its future has been in constant jeopardy over the past 30 years.

Federal initiatives in health planning, professional standards review organizations (PSROs), and facilitating health maintenance organizations (HMOs) failed to slow the spiraling costs of health care. Voluntary efforts also failed as the percent of gross national produce on health expenditures rose from 4.4% in 1950 to 9.8% in 1980 (2). Business and industry found themselves facing unrelenting increases in fringe benefits and paid $1,200 to $2,400 per employee for health insurance in 1983, which comprises 50% to 75% of the total benefit package (3). The insurance industry also found itself paying a higher percent of health care cost, up from 34.5% in 1950 to 78% in 1980 with rate increases from 30% to 40% in 1981 (4).

THE PREFERRED PROVIDER ORGANIZATION

The arguments about what the fair share of the gross national product for health care should be or whether increased health care benefits improve health status are not the subject here, although they certainly must remain the focus of intense study as the United States undergoes rapid and drastic transformation in the social and public policy aspects of its health care system (5). My attention is directed at recent and rapid alterations in the relationships between the provider, purchaser, and consumer of health services, in what is hoped to be the answer to our national dilemma: equity, quality, and economy in health care. The current champion for this task is known as the preferred provider organization (PPO), and while my perspective is based largely on what is happening in California, the same scenario is underway in other states and nationally where legislation facilitating PPO development has been passed or is under consideration.

In June 1982 the California legislature, facing the prospect of a massive budget deficit, focused on the "runaway" costs of health care as a major target for reduction. AB-799 was passed; significant cuts were made in the Medicaid budget, and selective contracting for inpatient hospital services was authorized. The $200 million of cost savings to be achieved by this mechanism prompted the formation of a coalition of the business interests, the insurance companies, labor, and the elderly to point out that the cost shift for reduction in the cost of care for public patients would have to be borne by private patients. This led to the demand that private purchasers of health care have the same privilege of selective contracting with providers at "alternative rates" as was permitted in the public sector. Thus, AB-3480 was passed which permitted insurance companies and hospital service plans, or any other purchasers of service, to enter into contracts with physicians and hospitals for the care of their insured persons.

The model that is in most current vogue to carry out the intent of AB-3480 is the PPO. The concept of contracting for health care at below-market rates ("alternative rates") has historical precedents dating back to the early 1900s, and in fact, the California Physicians Service (Blue Shield) pioneered this type of benefit marketing in 1939 (6).

A PPO is defined as "an intermediary organization which enables payers to purchase health care services from selected providers, often at a discount, in return for an increased volume of patients for the providers" (7). Characteristics of a PPO include the following (8):

1. Selected and committed providers with treatment and cost patterns that support cost-effective care.
2. Negotiated payments that include either discounted rates or agreement to accept a schedule of maximum payments.
3. Utilization contracts to assure the need for, and appropriateness of, services which typically include prior authorization and concurrent review of inpatient services.
4. Consumer choice of provider, which encourages, through financial incentives, use of the PPO provider but permits use of other providers at greater consumer cost (i.e., increased copayments or deductibles).
5. Rapid-claims payment as an incentive to providers in anticipation of reducing paperwork and improving cash flow.
6. Incentives for each participant: the purchaser buys services at lower cost; the consumer pays less, or sometimes nothing, if a PPO provider is used; and the provider has an increased volume of referrals.

Differences between PPOs and HMOs occur in three areas. First, HMOs are required to offer comprehensive services and the financial responsibility of the subscriber is fixed. This is not true with PPOs. Second, in HMOs, risk is assumed since there is an agreement to provide all necessary services to a defined population for a fixed cost (capitation). This is true for HMOs, such as Kaiser, and those which are affiliated with an independent practice association (IPA) where a percentage of the fee-for-service payment is withheld as a reserve against cost overruns. And third, HMOs and PPOs differ in degree of freedom of choice of provider. One type of PPO, the exclusive provider organization (EPO), is similar to the typical HMO in that it is not responsible for payment of services except to those providers who have agreed and are selected to participate. Other PPOs will pay for services of nonparticipating physicians but require either a greater copayment or a deductible from the consumer.

The purpose of this chapter is to examine some of the problems which affect psychiatry and psychiatric practice as the forces which affect the general health care field bring about basic changes in the practice of medicine. The specifics for psychiatry need to be examined in terms of what is unique to our specialty and to psychiatric patients. Since the passage of legislation enabling selective contracting in California, over 200 applications for PPO status have been approved or are pending attesting to the strong competition in this area. But it is still too early to judge the results for medicine in general, or psychiatry in particular.

The Triage System

A PPO that incorporates a primary-care triage system will present significant problems for psychiatry. Capitated systems will intensify this problem. If a primary-care system is charged with the responsibility of controlling costs or if specialty referrals are a disincentive for profits to the organization, specialty services that do not seem absolutely emergent will be reduced. In the interests of cost saving this may appear reasonable and justifiable if (1) appropriate alternative care is provided and (2) the judgment about the lack of need for specialty care is correct. Unfortunately, both these conditions may be lacking in such a system and may, in fact, prove to be more costly (9).

Delays in providing appropriate care, temporizing about diagnosis, and lack of specificity of treatment may all contribute to regression and decompensation of patients. The failure to detect the present or potential seriousness of a mental disorder in the primary-care setting frequently leads to this outcome necessitating longer or more intense treatment.

The ideal system would ensure that the triage system would be as sensitive to mental problems as it would be to physical problems. At present this is not the case, and the example of unnecessary physical medicine treatment of the "worried well" attests to this fact. The solution to this problem would be to use the primary-care system with the capacity to determine whether and how psychiatric disorders are presented in that setting and the optimal means of dealing with them. This does not imply that every individual with a mental disorder should be treated by a psychiatrist, or even another mental health professional. It is only intended to point out that when psychological problems are implicated in either mental and/or physical disorders, psychiatric input/capacity at triage may prove to be the most cost-effective measure.

Psychiatric Services

An important issue to examine is the adequacy of psychiatric services in existing health benefit plans. Psychiatric services have not occupied an eviable position in the health care arena. About half of the charge/cost of psychiatric services is covered by insurance payments when compared to physical health services (2). Use of psychiatric services has been discouraged by social stigma. Stereotypes exist about the uninsurability of psychiatric care, the uncertainty about outcome, the difficulties in communication and confidentiality, the conflicting opinions of "experts" which frequently attract media attention, the myriad of "treatment" approaches and types of "therapists" who compete for a share of the available health dollar, etc. Psychiatry as a medical specialty is not comfortably ensconced in the house of medicine, nor is it unified with allied mental health professions.

At best, at least to begin with, we probably will continue to see a situation where psychiatric benefits within PPOs will be no better than what has been the case in traditional third-party benefits. However, since PPOs do not have to offer comprehensive services, there can be a significant attrition of psychiatric services. The profit motive may act so that these services are trivialized or are provided primarily by nonpsychiatric personnel in the interest of cost savings. The fate of the psychiatrist in the community mental health centers may be one of the key examples to avoid if high-quality mental health care is to be maintained for all patients.

As corporate attention becomes fixed on cost savings, it is obvious that increased attention will be given to inpatient care, which accounts for the largest share of the cost of psychiatric treatment. Outpatient benefits also will become subject to more restrictions, and justifications for long-term treatment will have to be subject to more frequent reviews of medical necessity.

The attitude and response of psychiatrists as their practices are affected by business methods fueled by competitive changes are an extremely important issue. Since psychiatrists deal with extremely sensitive problems in their patients' lives which historically have been neglected in health care plans, the prospect of competing with the increasingly procedurally oriented world of medicine is discouraging. The need to support a holistic view of the importance of psychiatric services and the needs of psychiatric patients and their families becomes a critical factor. The reimbursement system, prompted by definitions of medical necessity, will inevitably force psychiatrists to look toward medical models of disability and treatment that emphasize functions which psychiatrists perform as physicians. The recent advances in psychopharmacology and the biological understanding of some mental disorders certainly fit within the traditional medical model.

However, the role of the psychiatrist as a psychotherapist dealing with the interpersonal and intrapsychic aspects of mental illness may not be appreciated to the extent that is necessary. This sets off tensions between psychiatrists and engenders conflicts with nonpsychiatric mental health professionals who are competing for reimbursement for health care dollars, as psychotherapists. Psychiatrists are concerned about what the changes in the marketplace may dictate with respect to developing therapeutic relationships with their patients if systems within which they practice do not respect the subtleties and importance of a treatment alliance regardless of the treatment modality chosen. Of greater importance, however, is whether the reimbursement system will force a narrowing of practice of psychiatrists to only those patients who require hospitalization or who need somatic therapies. In view of this, we can anticipate that tensions between health professionals will increase as the pressure for independent reimbursement mounts.

Management of Costs

As competition increases, the options of cutting costs may increase. Apart from limiting benefits, entrepreneurs attracted to this new organizational model for health care may create false promises and raise expectations beyond hope of realization. This may be the case, since PPOs are regulated in a very ambitious manner in regard to scope of services, standards, and financial reserves. A decade earlier, California launched an ambitious venture in funding prepaid health programs, which led to numerous failures and defaults of many of these organizations. The same risks apply to the present model—the PPO.

The question of viability of PPOs needs to be examined as to their ability to fulfill the desire of their proponents—the management of costs. There is growing concern that the concept and the operation of a PPO will not be able to control costs and that organized practices requiring risk sharing on the part of providers will be needed in order to be cost effective.

Under the rubric of accountability a number of issues are clustered. One of them, justification of medical necessity, has become very familiar. The requirements for documentation to establish the need for treatment have become increasingly rigorous, especially for inpatient services. I believe this will continue and will eventually move toward a system of prior authorization and concurrent review for these services. While this may be seen as a problem, it could also be an opportunity to provide clearer data upon which our clinical judgments rest.

Peer Review

A more difficult problem is in the area of peer review and the conflicts engendered by practicing with someone looking over our shoulder. Psychiatrists' feelings and beliefs about confidentiality and their patients' con-

cerns about privacy will both be sorely tested by the inevitable requirements for creditable peer review. Most purchasers of services have made
it clear that any organized system of care they would support would have
to include a peer review system. Most, who have been aware of the American Psychiatric Association's (APA) efforts in CHAMPUS and other programs, have felt encouraged. Providers who would choose to be part of
a PPO would have to conform to review procedures for both inpatient and
outpatient services. Whatever system is devised must be sensitive to the
complexities and feelings of the patient and the provider—as well as to
the realities of the funding system. It is at this point that clinical sense and
fiscal resources must be balanced in a mutually equitable manner.

Liability

Since PPOs on a widespread basis are relatively new, questions regarding the liability relationship between a participating physician and the PPO
are not clear. Initially some PPO organizations endeavored to insert a hold-
harmless clause into provider contracts limiting or negating liability for
actions of the providers which may have been imposed by PPO restrictions on scope of benefits. While this seems to have been corrected, it still
is not clear as to what liability may ensue when a physician elects to participate in a PPO and abide by its criteria and standards.

The California Medical Association has cautioned that "physicians
should be aware that the risk of suit increases in this new environment"
and that PPOs and EPOs "significantly differ from traditional insurance
coverage" (10). It has been emphasized that risks increase owing to restrictions on standards of care, the impact of denial of care, potential liability
for patients' economic loss (by referral to a noncontracting physician
hospital or physician), and peer review liability.

An opportunity exists in the changing climate of funding of health services to improve the purchaser's view of the importance and value of
psychiatric services. Evidence has been accumulating over the last 30 years
as to the cost effectiveness of providing psychiatric services in lieu of, or
in addition to, physical health services. While most physicians may be
aware of the intimate mind-body interface, most purchasers of service are
not. Thus, optimum treatment for the ulcer patient may not include psychiatric care.

The APA and several of its component district branches have embarked
on ventures to contact major employers and insurance companies to increase their awareness of the potential positive benefits of psychiatric care
to improve employee performance and reduce health care costs. The out-

come of these efforts needs to be carefully evaluated with respect to its effect on health care benefits. The studies of medical offset costs related to the provision of psychiatric services to both the "worried well" and the "worried sick" populations have been impressive (11). Similarly, the reluctance of third-party carriers to reassess coverage of day treatment services or ambulatory benefits in lieu of hospital care needs to receive additional attention if cost containment is a serious goal. These concepts are not understood by purchasers of health care, which underlies the significant disparity between inpatient and outpatient coverage in most policies.

CONCLUSION

As we begin to explore the health care marketplace, the major impression is how little understanding there is of psychiatry and mental disorder. Our greatest task will be to correct this and establish psychiatry's role as a critical medical specialty in both managing cost of health care and assuring quality of treatment.

There is little differentiation in the minds of purchasers of service between psychiatrists and other mental health professionals as to their function and capabilities. Cynicism exists regarding diagnosis, treatment planning, and outcome.

We know more about mental disorder than is believed by those who make decisions about the scope of health benefits. We need to educate them about the importance of specificity of psychiatric diagnosis and treatment. The psychiatrist's role in the rational control of costs for both mental and physical disorders is crucial. Very convincing arguments can be made to demonstrate this, and they will have to be made by the psychiatry profession.

As pressures to move toward the preferential funding of organized systems of health care have mounted, providers of service have increasingly been exposed to the thinking and feelings that exist in business and industry. While we may be offended by having our professional services labeled "products" and the constant reiteration of "bottom-line" decision making, we cannot allow critical judgments about the value of psychiatric care to be made without our input. The stakes for our patients, for our profession, and for the entire health care system are too great to permit this. The case for the insurability of mental disorders is very persuasive (12). But the major task for psychiatry, as the system of health care evolves over the next several years, is to assure the support for good clinical practice as a major factor in achieving control of cost.

REFERENCES

1. Starr, P. *The social transformation of American medicine.* New York: Basic Books, 1982.
2. *Economic fact book for psychiatry.* Washington, DC: American Psychiatric Association, 1983.
3. *Why high?* Los Angeles: LA County Medical Association, 1983.
4. Murphy, K. C. Who's fueling the flames of rising health costs? *Private Practice,* May 1983.
5. Brook, R. H., Ware, J. E., Jr., Rogers, W. H., et al. Does free care improve adults' health? *N. Engl. J. Med.,* 309:1426, 1983.
6. Trauner, J. *Preferred provider organizations: The California experiment.* San Francisco: Institute for Health Policy Studies, 1983.
7. *Preferred provider organization contracting manual: Issues and strategies.* Los Angeles: Hospital Council of Southern California, 1983.
8. Ellwein, I., and Gregg, D. Interstudy researchers trace progress of PPO's. *FAH Rev.,* p. 20, July–August 1982.
9. Moore, S. H., Martin, D. P., and Richardson, W. Special report: Does the primary-care gatekeeper control costs of health care? *N. Engl. J. Med.,* 309:1400, 1983.
10. *Contracting and professional liability.* San Francisco: Contracting Alert, California Medical Association, Dec. 9, 1983.
11. Sharfstein, S., Muszynski, S., and Gattozzi, A. *Maintaining and improving psychiatric insurance coverage. An annotated bibliography.* Washington, DC: American Psychiatric Association, 1983.
12. Wells, K. B., Manning, W. G., Jr., Duan, N., et al. *Cost sharing and the demand for ambulatory mental health services.* Los Angeles: Rand, 1982.

24

Long-Term Psychotherapy and Psychoanalysis in a Changing Health Care Economy

John J. McGrath, M.D.

Our nation is currently undergoing a near revolution in both the methods of delivery of health services and the methods of payment for these services. Two major, interrelated factors have generated these extraordinary changes. The first has been the relentless rise in health care costs. Americans now spend over a billion dollars a day on health care, and the rate of increase has outstripped all other parts of our economy during both inflationary and recessionary periods. In addition, with the federal government and corporate employers paying over three-quarters of the bill, powerful coalitions have been formed capable of, and determined to, reduce their health care costs.

The second factor is that this significant sector of our economy, approaching 12% of our gross national product, had, until recently, remained outside of our economic system. Now, corporate America is moving rapidly to capitalize on what it sees as a virtually unparalleled opportunity. The cardinal signs of industrialization—centralization of capital and decision making; vertical integration, that is, the capability of offering all levels of care from primary to tertiary; increased control over human resources; and increased reliance on marketing and packaging techniques—are everywhere evident. Publicly owned hospital chains, far more powerful than their for-profit competitors, are becoming the dominant force in the medical marketplace. In this environment, as reimbursement methods change from fee for service on a cost-plus basis to a variety of fixed, prospectively priced schemes, decision making moves from physicians to corporate managers, and the tensions between quality of care and cost efficiency escalate. Diagnostic related groups (DRGs) currently apply only to inpatient Medicare services, and psychiatry is exempt from their provisions. However, it is necessary to be aware that a variety of other payment methods, relative value scales, capitation, and the entire alphabet of HMOs, PPOs, etc., are either actually in use or under serious study. Psychiatry, like the rest of medicine, is feeling the pressures caused by this upheaval in our economic landscape.

In order to help us forecast the effects of these charges on our specialty and particularly on the outpatient longer-term modalities, it is helpful to use the analogy of a pyramid of vulnerability. The base, or most stable, part of this pyramid is occupied by practices and procedures with the following characteristics: they are nonrecurring, cost predictable, more cost effective than their alternatives, and performed by an individual who can also perform a variety of similar procedures. A simple example would be an appendectomy done by a general surgeon. It is done only once, has a reliable cost-diagnosis predictability, is less expensive than the medical treatment of peritonitis, and is but one of a series of procedures a surgeon can perform. In contrast to this stable, safe practice, psychiatry is far up on the pyramid and precariously vulnerable. There are some special, quite important reasons for this which need to be understood.

Psychiatry enters this new era of competition already disadvantaged. Even in the bygone days of unquestioned cost plus reimbursement, psychiatric care and payment for that care was rationed in a variety of ways. Increased copayments or deductibles, arbitrary limitations on the number of inpatient days or outpatient visits, restricted lifetime maximums—these have long been standard features in psychiatric health insurance. In addition, stigmatization, prejudice, and the supposed existence of an alternative, tax-supported treatment system (that is, state hospitals and community mental health centers) have all been used to discriminate against both private and public reimbursement for mental illness.

Now, added to these historic problems are the specific difficulties brought about by the new ecology of corporate medicine.

Overall, psychiatric illnesses, and therefore costs, have a tendency to be recurring and not predictably time limited. The correlation between diagnosis and length of treatment is accurate only in the 15% range. That is to say, diagnosis alone does not allow one to construct actuarially meaningful predictions about costs and time in treatment; managerially, unpredictability is often a greater concern than high, but predictable, costs.

There is also continuing concern about the so-called "moral hazard." The belief persists that benefits for mental illness will be utilized to the extent they are made available, without regard to the medical necessity. Numerous studies proving the contrary and logic itself—since it is hardly a pleasant pastime to repeatedly visit a psychiatrist—have not shaken this myth.

The final factor to be mentioned is the new, but increasingly important, role of consumer demand in business-controlled medicine. Practices that were unnecessary, and usually considered unethical, in the era of direct payment to doctors are now commonplace. Marketing and the sophisticated use of "loss leaders," e.g., offering below-cost emergency room services to attract patients and thereby filling profitable hospital beds, are accepted tools of business and are now tools of the business of medicine. Customers—ultimately patients—are sold what they seek to buy. There is no clamor among the buyers of health care for mental health services. Ignorance, denial, and stigma each play a part in this. The end result, however, is that insurance that either excludes, or inappropriately limits, mental health services is salable because it is made to appear attractive through lower premiums.

Clearly, this is not an appealing picture of the future of psychiatry as a whole. Unfortunately, when we look at specific subspecialties within our profession, the picture is even more troubling. The unhappy distinction of occupying the pinnacle of our pyramid of vulnerability falls on the long-term, outpatient modalities.

Even the definition of what constitutes "long-term" is rapidly narrowing. Certainly traditional psychoanalysis must be included among the most threatened, as is exploratory psychotherapy with a customary frequency of twice weekly. Indeed, even weekly psychotherapy, implying insurance coverage of 50 visits per year, is a fading reality as 20 visits per year becomes a more common base.

In addition to the previously discussed factors which have put all of psychiatry at risk in the new economy of health care, there are some very special circumstances which threaten the long-term practices. A not necessarily all-inclusive list would include the following.

These modalities have a high cost per patient, producing a "target effect" among insurers, that is, the temptation to realize sizable savings by hitting a relatively small group. Then there is the seeming healthiness of the patient population. It is often difficult to explain the need for prolonged treatment when the patient is functioning in society. This factor also heightens the competition from other modalities, especially psychopharmacology, which can often be promoted as achieving the desired result in a more cost-effective manner. Nor is competition limited to other modalities, but is evident in the growing groups of other providers. These nonmedical providers are particularly appealing in a business environment that routinely looks for lower-priced personnel as a cost saving.

Psychotherapy is sufficiently far removed from the high technology and
physical invasiveness that characterize much of the rest of medical care
to make lesser trained personnel appear adequate in an uneducated consumer market.

Certainly, then, there is a formidable battery of negative forces mar-
shalled against long-term outpatient psychiatry. However, despair is not
a satisfactory endpoint, nor, fortunately, is it the only one. There are some
basic, perhaps simplistic, points of individual adaptation and organizational response that are worth considering.

It does not seem worthwhile to await the return of the past—little on
the current economic or political horizon supports such daydreaming. Nor
is it particularly useful, however appealing, to scapegoat the various levels
of organized medicine. The forces of change are far larger and more
powerful than medicine itself. What is useful in this arena is to join with
organized medicine as an informed, active presence.

On a personal level, the expansion of practice skills to offer a variety
of treatments (that is, products) and the realignment of what has traditionally been a solo practitioner market into larger multidisciplinary groups
should be seriously considered.

Expansion of our database, including a more precise epidemiology, and
better outcome studies, should be among our highest priorities. These are
the tools it will take to meaningfully market the value of our treatment
modalities to the new purchasers of health care and to the consumers of
our "products."

Our special training and our daily experiences with patients repeatedly convince us of the value of psychoanalysis and other long-term treatments. We must not abandon this belief, but neither can we expect it to
automatically endure in these times of great change. A clear assessment
of reality and a prepared, flexible adaptation to it are basic parts of our
daily "prescriptions." Now we must take this medicine ourselves.

Index

Abraham, Karl, 20, 21
Accountability, 118–119, 120, 249
Allen, A., 44, 179–180, 199
American Psychiatric Association (APA), 250
American Psychological Association, 48, 49, 113
Anal issues, money and, 18–22, 44
Anal stage, 18–21
Auster, S. L., 169
Autonomy
  fear of, 9–11
  formation of, 65
"Autonomy worshipper," 10
Avnet, H. H., 169

Baekeland, F., 132
Balch, P., et al., 133
Balsam, R. M. and A., 199–200
Baltimore-D.C. Psychoanalytic Society, 116
Bankruptcy, 70–75
Becker, E., 58, 59–60, 62, 63, 68
Berg, Adrian, 9
Billing, 86, 106, 152, 184–185. See also Fee(s)
Blanck, G. and R., 36, 37, 39, 44, 45
Blue Cross/Blue Shield, 113, 237
Borderline syndrome, 45–46, 160, 182
Borneman, E., 122
Brandt, L. W., 134
Brown, N. O., 58–59
Bruch, H., 38, 42
Buckley, P., 43
Buckley, P., et al., 105
Budman, S. H., et al., 165
Bureau of Labor, 49
Burnside, M. A., 48–53

Capitalism, 4, 21
Caplovitz, D., 70
Carlisle, A. E., 218–233

Cavenar, J. O., 37, 93, 160
CHAMPUS program, 250
Charles, E., 43
Chessick, R. D., 34, 38, 175–177, 199
Children, 24–25
  developmental models for, 5–6, 24
  treating, 160, 186
Chodoff, P., 111–120, 159
Cognitive dissonance theory, 133
Colby, K. M., 48
Community mental health centers, fee issues, 132–140
Confidentiality, 249
  and accountability, 118, 120
  third party payment and, 113–115, 170, 172
Console, W. A., 36, 37, 122
Conversion disorders, 241
Cost-effectiveness, 236–242
Costs, health care, 253–255
  management of, 249
Countertransference, 102, 103–104, 186, 203
  extending credit and, 213–214
  and fee-setting, 33–34, 39, 42, 43, 44, 98, 122, 123, 148, 150
  in HMO settings, 163–165
  negative, 74
  wealthy patients and, 55, 66–68
Credit, extending, 206–216

Davids, A., 37, 133, 138
Debt, 70. See also Bankruptcy
Denial, of wealth, 12–13
Depression, 14–15, 64, 240–241
  anaclitic, 63, 198
Derivative expressions (derivatives), 88–89, 90, 93
Developmental models, 5–8
Diagnosis, 135, 139–140, 146, 154–155, 214, 254
  third-party payment and, 114–115, 172–173

257

Diagnostic and Statistical Manual of
  Mental Disorders (DSM-II), 114, 115,
  135
Diagnostic-related groups (DRGs), 150,
  253–254
DiBella, G. A. W., 102–109, 184
Dickens, C., 70
Disability claims, 226, 228, 229–234
Divorce, debt and, 70
Dropouts, premature, 134–135, 136,
  138–140.
  See also Termination, premature
Duggan, T., 169
Duration of treatment, 160–161

Eissler, K. R., 121, 126–127, 128
Exposure, fears of, 172–173

Fantasies
  insurance coverage and, 171, 173
  "savior," 200
Father, 64
  guilt over surpassing, 12–13
Favreau, J., 122
Fear(s), 21
  of autonomy, 9–11
  of rejection, 13
  of risk, 13–14
  of wealth, 11–13
Federal Employees Health Benefits Program, 112, 119–120
Fee(s), 36–38, 79, 82–84, 88–90, 125, 135,
  197–200, 202, 224
  "adequate," 90–92, 99
  as administrative issue, 35
  "analyzing," 92–94
  in beginning practice, 175–187
  collecting, 106–107
  deferred, 91–92, 128–129, 189
  discussing, 105–106, 107–109, 124
  extending credit for, 206–216
  flexible, 33, 34, 38, 45, 46 (*see also*
    Sliding scale fees)
  insurance coverage for (*see* Insurance)
  low, 42, 92, 94–95, 105, 122, 133
  lowering, 105, 127, 128–130, 146, 154,
    186
  male/female therapists and, 48–53
  for missed sessions, 37, 39, 82–83,
    85–86, 88, 91, 146–147
  negotiating, 121–124
  no (*See* Free treatment)
  nonpayment of, 35, 39–43, 44, 45, 106,
    123, 156, 189–200, 203
  raising, 86, 106, 109, 128–130, 146

range of, 50–51
rigid, 33, 35, 37, 40, 45
setting, 33–35, 105, 107–108, 123,
  124–128, 178, 179, 180–181, 182, 199
sliding scale (*see* Sliding scale fees)
split, 83
symbolic meaning of, 123, 133
as transitional object, 44, 123
"usual," 125
wealthy patients and, 66
See also Money
Fee policy (-ies), 80–86, 104–109
  flexible, 33, 34, 38, 45, 46
  history of, 80–81
  rigid, 33, 35, 37, 40, 45, 46, 91, 197–198
  theory of, 82–84
  trainees and, 142–151
Fenichel, Otto, 21–22, 197
Ferenczi, Sandor, 19–20, 21, 197
Fiester, A., 132–133
Fingert, H. H., 42
Fox, Y. M., 180–181
Freedman, A., 128
Free treatment, 36–37, 42, 80, 92, 105,
  121–122
  Freud on, 17–18, 80, 121–122, 197
Freud, Sigmund, 18–19, 81, 241
  on fees, 17, 33, 36–37, 38, 80, 83, 88,
    90, 121–122, 180, 197
  on money, 17, 18–19, 44, 102, 121,
    227–228
Fromm-Reichmann, F., 33, 82–83, 199
Frustration, tolerance for, 44, 45
Fuqua, P. B., 17–22

Gambling, 14
Garfield, S. L., 132
Gedo, J., 44, 123, 198, 203
Gifts, 18, 20, 22, 183
Ginsburg, L. M. and S. A., 70–75
Glasser, M. A., 169
Goldberg, H., 10
Goldensohn, S. S., 158–166
Goldensohn, S. S., et al., 169
Gray, S. H., 170
Green, E. L., 169
Group therapy, 116
Guilt
  fees and, 37, 182, 183
  wealth and, 12–13
Gurevitz, H., 244–251
Gutheil, T. G., 175–187

Haak, N., 37, 39, 122, 197, 198, 203
Halpert, E., 97, 117, 169–174, 170–171

Health Insurance Plan of Greater New York (HIP), Mental Health Service, 158–166
Health maintenance organizations (HMOs), 152, 158–166, 244, 246
transference issues in, 159–163
Heroes, 59, 60
Hilles, L., 35, 45, 199
Hocart, A. M., 60
Hodges, A. G., 93
Hofling, C. K., 202–216
Hollingshead, A. B., 135
"Hospitalitis," 66

Identification, parental, 5–8
Identity
impaired, 65
therapist, 181–182
Immortality power, 61, 62, 63, 68
Impostors, 28–32
Imprisonment, psychological effect of, 70–71
"Inequality, origin of," 59
Insurance, 95–98, 111, 113, 120, 123, 155–156, 169–174, 225–227
national, 116
See also Third-party payment
Insurance forms, 169, 173
Intrusion, fear of, 172–173

Jacobs, D. H., 121–131
Jacobson, E., 70–71
Jones, Ernest, 19, 20
Judeo-Christian ethic, 4

Karasu, T. B., 43
Kennedy, J. F., 169
Kohut, H., 24, 60, 67, 68
Kramer, Y., 26
Krueger, D. W., 3–16, 24–32
Kubie, L. S., 37

Langs, R., 170
Length of session, 51, 52n.
Levin, A. M., 182
Liability, legal, 250–251
Lievano, J., 43, 122, 198–199
Lorand, S., 36, 37, 122
Love
money and, 9, 10, 183–185
therapy as, 199
Lundwall, I., 132

McGrath, J. J., 253–256
McRae, J. F., 132–140

Maternal deprivation, 63–64
Medical/nonmedical treatment models, 112–113, 248–249
Mehlman, R. D., 178
Menninger, K., 37, 38, 45, 138
Mentors, 6
Meyers, B. S., 34, 38, 43, 164
Mintz, N. L., 48
Misalliance, therapist-patient, 179, 186
Missed sessions, fees for, 37, 39, 82–83, 85–86, 88, 91, 146–147, 184, 202
Money, 10, 14–15, 21, 34, 48, 102–109, 224–234
and autonomy, 10–11
and feces, 18–20, 21, 22, 44
Freud's view of, 17–19, 44, 102, 121, 227–228
love and, 183–185
obsession with, 18
and pathological narcissism, 25–26, 32
as "propellant" to change, 80
psychoanalytic view of, 17–22
social psychology of, 58–61
as taboo, 48
wealthy patients and, 66
and work addiction, 26–28
See also Fee(s)
Morrison, L. J., 133–134
Motivation, patient, 37, 80, 117
Mowrer, O. H., 37
Mumford, E., 239

Narcissism, 21, 24–26
achievement and, 27–28, 32
fee setting and, 181
money and, 21, 60–61, 68, 117
pathological, 25–26, 32, 62–63
Nash, J. L., 37, 93, 160
National Institute of Mental Health (NIMH), 240–241, 242
Net worth, narcissism and, 24–26
Nonpayment, 35, 39–43, 44, 45, 106, 123, 156, 203
clinical management of, 189–200

Obligations, family, 93, 127
Olsson, P. A., 55–68
Orne, Martin, 239
Outcome, 89, 118–119

"Pain," physical, 226, 228–229, 230, 231, 233
Paolino, T. J., Jr., 34, 38
Parents
and child's sense of self, 24

Parents (*continued*)
  mirroring by, 24
Parental models, 5–7
Parloff, M. B., 238
Pasternack, S. A., 43, 103, 142–156, 179
Paternal deprivation, 64
Patient(s), 115
  acting out by, 126
  borderline, 45–46, 160, 182, 199
  as favorite child, 37, 92, 159, 198
  fees and, 37, 92, 117–118, 124–128, 145
  in HMO system, 159–165
  income of, 124, 146
  more disturbed, 44–45
  motivation of, 117
  nonpaying, 189–200 (*see also* Free treat-
    ment; Nonpayment)
  omnipotent fantasies of, 117–118
  poor, 18, 36–37, 161, 162–163, 197
  "sex symbol," 67
  wealthy, 55–68
Patient information brochure, 109
Peer review, 118–119, 249–250
Performance appraisals, 151
Pheterson, G. I., et al., 53
Phobia, success, 8–15
Pope, K. S., et al., 133, 139
Power
  "immortality," 61, 62, 63, 68
  money and, 59
Preferred provider organizations (PPOs),
    245–251. *See also* Health maintenance
    organizations
"Primary gain," 227, 230, 233–234
Private practice
  beginning, 175–187 (*see also* Therapists,
    beginning)
  purchasing a, 218–223
Professional standards review organiza-
    tions (PSROs), 244
Psychoanalysis, 17–22, 88–90, 92–98, 113
  "classical," 17n.
  fees and, 88–90, 92–98, 116–118, 121–
    124, 133, 202
  significance of money in, 17–22
Psychoanalytic technique, 17, 18
Psychotherapy research, 237–242
Psychotics, 136, 139
Puritan ethic, 4

Randolph, G. T., 182
Raney, J., 88–99
Rank, O., 58–59, 60, 68
Raths, O., 198
"Rat Man," 19

Redlich, F. C., 135
Reider, A. E., 189–200
Rejection, fear of, 13
Relax, inability to, 26
Resentment, therapist, 185–186
Resistance, 89, 98, 125
  free treatment and, 36, 170
  nonpayment as, 189
  third-party payment and, 117
Risk, fear of, 13–14
Rosenbaum, M., 202–216
Ross, M., 64
Ruben, M., 198
Rudestam, K., 132–133

"Savior" fantasy, 200
Scanlon, P., 160
Schafer, R., 71
Schlesinger, H. J., et al., 239
Schofield, W., 36, 52
Schonbar, R. A., 33–46, 181, 183, 184, 199
Schwartz, E. K., 183, 199
"Secondary gain," 17–18, 227, 230, 234
Secrecy, money and, 7
Self-esteem, 24, 163
  faulty, 25
  money and, 10, 14
  therapist, 181
  of women therapists, 52
  work compulsion and, 26–28
Semrad, Elvin, 200
Sense of self, developing, 24–25
Separation-individuation issues, 9, 24
Sexual identity problems, 93, 94
Sieverts, R., 70–71
Silverman, S. W., 226, 236–242
Sliding scale fees, 43, 83, 143–145
Social class
  fees and, 92
  transference issues and, 159–163
  See also Socioeconomic status
Socioeconomic status (SES), 133, 135,
    158–163
Sociopathy, 154–155
  of very wealthy, 63
Spending, compulsive, 10
Stone, M., 61, 63–64, 65, 66, 67, 185, 186
"Stress," 226
Success
  and depression, 14–15
  and "impostor" phenomenon, 28–32
  monetary, 5, 8, 14, 55–68 (*see also*
    Wealthy)
  narcissism and, 28
  work compulsion and, 27

Success phobia, 8–15
Super-rich. *See* Wealthy
Supervision
  administrative, 151–152
  discontent with, 153–154
  fee issues and, 130–131, 151–154
Symptomatic improvement, 89

Termination issues, 129
  in buying/selling a practice, 220–221
  premature, 130, 132–140
Therapist(s), 34, 181–182, 185–186, 238
  accountability of, 118–119
  beginning, 43, 50, 66, 105, 177–187
  collusion of, 73, 75, 172, 227
  envy of, 55, 67, 185
  fees and, 34, 42–43, 48–53, 79, 81–82,
    84–86, 104–109, 121–131, 177–187
  in HMO system, 163–165
  income of, 49
  male/female, 48–53
  narcissism and, 181
  as "prostitute," 183
  self-image of, 164–165, 181–182
  style of, 81–82, 84–86
  trainees, 142–147, 181 (*see also* Thera-
    pists, beginning)
  women, 49, 51, 52–53
"Therapyitis," 66
Third-party payments, 92, 93, 95–98, 111–
    120, 150, 155, 169–175, 225–227, 234
  confidentiality and, 113–115, 170, 172
  diagnosis and, 114–115, 172–173
  effect on treatment pattern, 115–116
  medical/nonmedical model and, 112–113
  by parents, 186
  reductions in, 225
  See also Health maintenance organiza-
    tions; Insurance
Time, money and, 20
Toilet training, 18, 21, 22
Tolstoy, L., 58, 60
Trainees, fees and, 142–147, 181. *See also*
    Therapists, beginning
Transference, 59–60, 67, 102, 103–104,
    190, 200, 203, 224

extending credit and, 213–214, 216
and fee setting, 33, 35, 38, 39, 123
in HMOs, 159–163
insurance and, 170
mirror, 31, 67
Transitional object, fee as, 44, 123
Treatment of Depression Collaborative Re-
    search Program (TDCRP), 240–241,
    242
Treatment setting, transference and,
    161–162
Treiger, P., 43, 103, 179
Triage system, 247
Tulipan, A. B., 79–87, 108

Unconscious
  collective "social," 60
  and insurance coverage, 169, 170, 173
  meaning of money in, 18–19, 20, 21–22,
    60–61, 68, 123
  physical symptoms and, 226

Veterans Administration, 37
"VIP," 55
Voiss, D. V., 224–234
Vulnerability, pyramid of, 254

Wahl, C., 65, 66, 67
Wealthy ("Super-rich"), 55–68
  narcissism, of, 62–63
  psychology of, 62–66
  psychotherapy with, 61–62, 65–68, 186
  sociopathy of, 63
Weiner, D., 198
Weintraub, W., 55
Winnicott, D., 198
Wolff, A., 183, 199
"Wolf Man," 74n., 80, 122
Women
  money issues and, 9
  as therapists, 48–53
Work compulsion, 6, 26–28
"Worried sick," the, 251
"Worried well," the, 247, 251